W9-CPF-074

REAL ESTATE
à la *Carte*

Selecting the Services You Need, Paying What They're Worth

JULIE GARTON-GOOD

A **Kaplan Professional** Company

This publication is designed to provide accurate and authoritative information in regard to the subject matter covered. It is sold with the understanding that the publisher is not engaged in rendering legal, accounting, or other professional service. If legal advice or other expert assistance is required, the services of a competent professional should be sought.

In accordance with federal law, ideas regarding fees and compensation models covered here are at random, solely for example purposes.

Publisher: Cynthia A. Zigmund
Acquisitions Editor: Mary B. Good
Managing Editor: Jack Kiburz
Project Editor: Trey Thoelcke
Interior Design: Lucy Jenkins
Cover Design: Design Solutions
Typesetting: Elizabeth Pitts

© 2001 by Julie Garton-Good

Published by Dearborn Trade, a Kaplan Professional Company

All rights reserved. The text of this publication, or any part thereof, may not be reproduced in any manner whatsoever without written permission from the publisher.

Printed in the United States of America

01 02 03 10 9 8 7 6 5 4 3 2 1

Library of Congress Cataloging-in-Publication Data

Garton-Good, Julie.
  Real estate à la carte / Julie Garton-Good.
    p. cm.
  ISBN 0-7931-4353-5 (pbk.)
  1. House buying—United States. 2. Residential real
estate—Purchasing—United States. I. Title.
  HD255 .G375 2001
  333.33′0973—dc21   00-012906

Dearborn Trade books are available at special quantity discounts to use as premiums and sales promotions, or for use in corporate training programs. For more information, please call the Special Sales Manager at 800-621-9621, ext. 4514, or write to Dearborn Financial Publishing, Inc., 155 N. Wacker Drive, Chicago, IL 60606-1719.

Dedication

To the millions of real estate consumers who have waited patiently for decades while the real estate industry grew up, wised up, and finally decided to pay attention to what the consumer wanted; and to the new breed of professionals, real estate consultants, who've made it happen!

Are You a Savvy, Reinvented Real Estate Consumer?

Take the quiz and find out!

1. Have you owned and sold three or more homes?

2. Have you ever been a for-sale-by-owner when selling a property?

3. When buying or selling real estate, have you ever wanted (and been capable) to do some of the work performed by professionals in order to save money?

4. As a seller, have you located a buyer yourself but still had to pay a real estate agent a percentage commission for the help you needed because that's the only way he or she worked?

5. Have you questioned why real estate fees penalize the consumer who sells an expensive home when it takes the same amount of time to sell a cheaper one?

6. Does it bother you that you pay the same amount of commission to an agent who sells your home quickly as you do to an agent that spends more time, energy, and money to market your home over a longer period of time?

7. Have you ever been hesitant to approach a real estate agent for information you needed because you were leery that he or she would try to sell you something in order to generate a commission?

If you answered yes to three or more of the questions, congratulations, you're a reinvented real estate consumer! The information in this book will help you become even more knowledgeable and empowered to obtain the real estate information and help you need, when you need it, paying only for what it's worth!

If you answered yes to less than three questions in the quiz, this book will be instrumental in teaching you how to save thousands selling, buying, and making cost-effective real estate decisions.

CONTENTS

Foreword   xi
Preface   xiii

1. The Consumer Is the Financial Winner in the New World of Real Estate Services   1

Percentage Commissions Deteriorate and Give Way to
New Models   1
Real Estate Consumers Express What They Want and Why They
Want It   4
An Industry's Evolution Provoked the Current Revolution   8
Physician Heal Thyself: Why the Traditional Real Estate Model
Shattered   12
The Future of Real Estate with Three Power Players   16
Real Estate Consultants: A New Breed of Real Estate
Professional   20
Real Estate Consultants Introduce a Variety of Compensation
Models   21
Fee-for-Services Real Estate: What It Is, What It Isn't   23
Use Consumer Road Maps for Navigating à la Carte Real
Estate   27
Tips for Maximizing Profits with Real Estate à la Carte   29
The Bottom Line: The Consumer Wins, No Matter What!   30

2. What to Pay for à la Carte Real Estate Services and How to Pay It   31

A la Carte Real Estate Is Flexible, More Controllable, and Cost-Effective   31

How Fee-for-Services Consultants Determine Their Fees   34

What's a Real Estate Task or Service Really Worth?   36

The Level of Service You Require Can Determine What You Pay   40

How to Determine If the Fee Structure Is Really Fair   42

Consumer-Designed, Consumer-Driven Compensation Models   45

Rebundling Services Could Bring Additional Cost Savings   54

Compensation Issues Can Appear Problematic for Buyers   55

Additional Compensation Models on the Horizon   55

Now that You Know the Options, Where Do You Begin?   56

3. The Seller's Fee-for-Services Road Map   57

The Seller's Road Map: Where to Go and What to Expect   57

Seller Checkpoint 1: Prepare the Property for Sale   60

Seller Checkpoint 2: Gather Property Information/Price the Property   66

Seller Checkpoint 3: Market the Property   76

Seller Checkpoint 4: Locate/Prequalify the Buyer   80

Seller Checkpoint 5: Draft the Sales Agreement/Negotiate with the Buyer   85

Seller Checkpoint 6: Troubleshoot the Sale/Close the Transaction   91

What the Numbers and Ratings Mean for Sellers   95

Where Do You Need Help in the Sales Process and How Do You Know?   97

4. The Buyer's Fee-for-Services Road Map   105

The Buyer's Road Map: Where to Go and What to Expect   105

Buyer Checkpoint 1: Design a Purchase Strategy   107

Buyer Checkpoint 2: Be Preapproved for a Mortgage   112

Buyer Checkpoint 3: Choose the Neighborhood and the IfProperty   121

Buyer Checkpoint 4: Check Property Information and Pricing   127

Buyer Checkpoint 5: Draft the Purchase Agreement/Negotiate with the Seller   134

Buyer Checkpoint 6: Troubleshoot Your Purchase/Close the Transaction   138

What the Numbers and Ratings Mean for Buyers   142

Where Do You Need Help in the Sales Process and How Do You Know?   145

5. Seller's Applications for Fee-for-Services Real Estate   153

Are You Really Prepared to Handle the Sale of Your Own Home?   153

The Assistance You Need Is Either Level One or Level Two   156

The Meat in the Middle May Be Your Greatest Hurdle   158

The Help You Need at Each Seller Checkpoint   166

Five Rules of Thumb for Seller Fee-for-Services   173

What to Do If You're Short on Time   174

What to Do If You're Short on Money   174

What to Do If You're Short on Patience and/or Know-How   174

Obtaining Fee-for-Services as a Risk Reduction Tool   175

Fee-for-Services Can Serve as the FSBO Lifeline   176

6. Buyer's Applications of Fee-for-Services Real Estate   177

How Consultants Can Assist Even the Most Savvy Buyer   177

The Assistance You Need Falls into Two Major Categories   178

Buyers Must Be Aware of the Meat in the Middle   180

Myriad Ways You Can Use Fee-for-Services Assistance as a Buyer   187

Five Rules of Thumb for Buyer Fee-for-Services   192

What to Do If You're Short on Time   192

What to Do If You're Short on Money   193

What to Do If You're Short on Patience and/or Know-How   193

7. Unique Real Estate à la Carte Applications to Save You Money   195

Where to Go, How to Know, and What to Expect on Your Side Trips   195

Real Estate Problems a Consultant Can Help You Solve   198

The Top Ten Most Common Ways a Real Estate Consultant Can
   Assist You   204
Cautions in Finding Answers to Special Real Estate
   Problems   218
Test Your Ability with a Miniquiz   219

8. Locating and Contracting with Real Estate Fee-for-Services Providers   221

The Consultant Begins with Assessing Your Real Estate
   Needs   222
Working with Real Estate Consultants with Advanced
   Designations   227
How Real Estate Consulting Differs from Real Estate Selling   228
How to Locate and Evaluate a Real Estate Consultant   233
Professional Documentation Provided by the Real Estate
   Consultant   235
Contracting with the Real Estate Consultant for the Services
   You Need   236
Determine the Role the Real Estate Consultant Will Play in
   Helping You Reach Your Objectives   240
What If You Desire to Sever the Agreement with the
   Consultant?   241
What about Approaching a Real Estate Agent You've Worked
   with Previously to Assist You?   242
Red Flags When Interviewing a Real Estate Consultant   242
When Could Hiring a Real Estate Attorney Be Preferable over
   Using a Real Estate Consultant?   244

9. Deciding What Help You Need If You're Stuck Midstream   245

If You Find You Need Help Midstream   245
Steps to Take in Tackling a Real Estate Problem   249
If You're Still Stuck   250

Resources   251
Index   263

The Internet and consumer empowerment is fundamentally changing the real estate industry by enabling consumers to assume greater responsibility and control over transactions. As of October 2000, 41 million online consumers had already used the Internet to find real estate–related information, an increase of 18 million since February 2000. In the next two years, 29 percent (18 million) plan to buy or sell a home, with over a third (36 percent) having past experience researching real estate information online.

To meet consumer demand, over 500 new firms have entered the online real estate market since 1996, hoping to use technology to make buying, selling, and financing a home faster, easier, and less expensive. New choices like fee-for-services programs, live auctions, and real estate agents bidding for your business are just a few of the innovations.

Based on consumer surveys, empowered online homebuyers and sellers also demand change in the traditional agent compensation structure. In fact, the nontraditional segment of the online homebuying and selling markets (e.g., for-sale-by-owners and fee-for-services related transactions) could represent as much as 75 percent of total sales by 2005. Already, according to a recent professional survey, 30 percent of agents discount more than 50 percent of their commissions. Trends like these will constantly challenge real estate professionals to reinvent themselves into more "high-tech, high-touch" cost-effective team players, working *with* homebuyers and sellers.

Real Estate à la Carte: Selecting the Services You Need, Paying What They're Worth is the first published comprehensive review of fee-for-services alternatives and is a great resource for consumers and industry professionals alike. The new approaches detailed will ultimately help you maximize your satisfaction with the process and contribute to a more profitable ownership experience.

Nick Karris, Senior Real Estate Analyst
Gomez Advisors, Inc. <gomez.com>
The eCommerce Authority
Boston, Massachusetts

If you're like many Americans, you enjoy walking into a cafeteria and being instantly bombarded by the vast array of choices. Depending on how hungry you are and how much cash you have in your pocket, you can choose a bundled meal (like today's special) or go with individual, à la carte selections like a sandwich and dessert. Whatever you choose, you'll pay only for what you take. And even though you swear you'll never eat another bite, hunger pains will be back again in six to eight hours!

Making decisions as a real estate consumer is very much like visiting a cafeteria. There are so many selections of services to choose from, some bundled in a full-meal package, others available as à la carte selections. For some, the few coins in our pocket dictate that we forgo dessert and, instead, focus only on the meat of the meal, which I liken to hiring a consultant to negotiate a home purchase or sale. For others, the lack of available time takes priority over cost, mandating that we call to order a prepackaged meal that's delivered to us, which I liken to accessing full listing real estate services through a brokerage. Even though we decide not to eat the lima beans, we've paid for them just the same.

As little as one year ago, options like these were not readily available to the real estate consumer. As a seller, you either listed your home with a real estate brokerage or you sold the house yourself. As a buyer, you hired a buyer's agent to assist you or you navigated the purchase on your own. But the Web, independent service providers (many of them online aggregators), and real estate consultants changed all that. Today's reinvented world of real estate allows a consumer to access individual services needed and pay only what they're worth.

Let *Real Estate à la Carte: Selecting the Services You Need, Paying What They're Worth* serve as your menu and expeditious road map into the exciting and cost-effective world of unbundled real estate.

For sellers, we'll cover:

- The six steps of the seller's real estate transaction (what to do, when to do it, and why)
- Quizzes to determine where you need help
- Innovative ways to pay for the services you need (It's not about percentage commissions anymore!)
- How to evaluate a real estate consultant and other service providers
- How to contract with professionals for the services you need and pay only what they're worth

For buyers, we'll cover:

- The six steps in the buyer's real estate transaction (what to do, when to do it, and why)
- Quizzes to determine where you need help
- Various ways you can compensate a professional for the assistance you need (and perhaps receive a rebate!)
- The critical meat in the middle of the transaction that's vital to keep your purchase together until closing
- How real estate consultants can interface with the seller and actually save you money.

And for all homeowners, we'll cover:

- The top ways a real estate consultant can save you money (many you may not have considered, like protesting your property taxes)
- Equity management tips to maximize your equity and reduce the costs of owning real estate
- Myriad no-cost/low-cost online services to keep you plugged in, tuned in, and savvy as a reinvented real estate consumer.

Whether you're a for-sale-by-owner going it alone to maximize your equity, or a buyer seeking counsel on framing a successful offer, this book is for you. And even if you've decided that you're satiated by your real estate experiences and will never be hungry for them again, don't be too sure. It's surprising how needs like disputing a property line or deciding whether to improve your current home or move will find you reaching for this book to locate the help you need at the price you feel it's worth.

So grab your tray, select what you're hungry for, and enjoy the journey into the consumer-driven, cost-effective new world of real estate à la carte!

> Frugally yours,
> Julie Garton-Good
> The Frugal HomeOwner®
> <www.juliegarton-good.com>

The Consumer Is the Financial Winner in the New World of Real Estate Services

The modern consumer's knowledge about the real estate process is more like a checkerboard than a blank slate. Homebuyers and sellers need to be able to buy services that fill in the gaps in their own knowledge. Fee-for-services will benefit many consumers. The irony is that it also will allow real estate professionals to be paid for their expertise.

Frank Cook, Publisher
Real Estate Intelligence Report

Percentage Commissions Deteriorate and Give Way to New Models

Percentage Real Estate Commissions Can't Always Be Justified

You meet with your attorney to discuss filing for divorce after 20 years of marriage. As the conversation concludes, you ask the attorney the $64,000 question, "How much will you charge me?"

His response, "My fee is equal to 6 percent of your personal and joint/marital assets."

Flabbergasted, you storm out of the office, muttering, "You're crazy! No one would pay an attorney that much or in that way. It's totally unjustified."

Yet, for the past century, real estate brokers have been compensated exactly in that manner. Millions of sellers annually pay brokers hefty percentage commissions based on the selling price of their home. And the math is staggering. In 2000, approximately 5.1 million single-family homes (new and resale) were sold, down from approximately 6 million the year before. Roughly 18 percent (or 918,000) of those homes were sold by-owner with no commissions paid with another 5 percent (255,000) exempt from commissions as builder sales or owner/built homes. If 6-percent commissions were paid on the balance of 3,927,000 homes sold at the 2000 median national sales price of $139,900, the real estate brokerage industry pocketed more than 32 billion dollars in commissions—many times the size of the budget of some third-world countries.

How Much Can You Save by Fighting Percentage Commissions?

You can do your own math when it comes to figuring out to what slice of the real estate commission pie you've contributed or will contribute. In fact, have you considered the total amount in commissions you're likely to pay in your lifetime—$3,000, $13,000, or as much as $30,000 or more? On the average, you'll purchase and sell four or more homes. At the 2000 median sales price of $139,900, that equates to more than $33,500 in commissions during your lifetime! For many Americans, that's equal to one or more years of gross annual (pretax) income. In your pocket, this additional hard-earned, American-dream equity could send your child to college, supplement an aging parent's Social Security income, or pad your retirement nest egg.

What if you had that commission money of $33,500 to invest at a meager 6 percent annual return? Over 30 years, it would grow and compound to more than $192,400. Pencil to paper, saving real estate commissions can mount to serious money in your pocket.

Then there's the compounding factor of the commissions paid. It's true to say that every time you purchase a house, you pay and often finance the commission. For example, let's say that you own three homes over a period of 30 years, selling every 10 years. You purchase the first for $50,000, the second for $100,000, the third for $200,000, and eventually sell one last time for $288,000. Assuming minimum 10 percent down payments on each purchase and financing the balance at an average 8 percent interest, as a buyer you would pay $76,231 in principal and interest over 30 years to finance the 6 percent commissions. Added to the additional 6 percent commissions you paid as a seller at each closing ($35,200), this totals more than $111,000 in out-of-pocket costs over 30 years. Without taking into consideration the time-value of money, the 6 percent has compounded into a whopping 19 percent. It makes as little sense as financing $3,000 worth of household appliances over 30 years!

The Traditional Percentage Real Estate Model Unravels

You may be thinking, "Wow, I'd love to save that much money by selling my house on my own without paying a real estate agent; but if I find I need help, won't I be required to pay a percentage commission?"

Ten years ago, the answer was probably yes (due to the inflexibility of the real estate brokerage business), but today, the answer is a resounding no! In fact, as seen in the divorce example, paying a percentage commission makes little sense. And given the unraveling and unbundling of the real estate transaction due to you, the savvy consumer empowered by the Internet, you can access the real estate services you need, when you need them, and pay only for the help you receive.

Unbundling the Real Estate Transaction Precipitates Fee-for-Services

Welcome to the unbundled world of real estate services. No longer will you be locked in the tedious and often nonproductive process of the one-size-fits-all sellers' and buyers' real estate models. If you only need help negotiating with a buyer, it's available. If a buyer needs an unbiased third-party analysis to compare whether renting or buying a house makes the most financial sense, she can find it. This revolutionary and empowering consumer approach is called fee-for-services, à la carte real estate, or unbundling. Much like eating at a cafeteria where you pass by myriad culinary choices, unbundling breaks the real estate sellers' and buyers' menus into digestible, affordable minimeals. A dieter can eat the lime Jell-O and bypass the cherry cheesecake. A for-sale-by-owner can rent a for-sale sign from a real estate broker or sign company for $20 and save thousands of dollars in commissions!

Real Estate Consumers Express What They Want and Why They Want It

You (and the Internet) Shifted the Paradigm; Seven New Consumer Realities

As a real estate brokerage owner, real estate educator/author, and syndicated columnist whose career has spanned nearly three decades, I prided myself on predicting (with some accuracy) what you want from the real estate industry and why you want it—then came the paradigm shift of the past five years.

Pulled by the Web and its free-flowing glut of real estate information, you, the real estate consumer, reinvented and transformed yourself into a new and innovative breed. You want property information immediately, mortgage preapproval online (and soon real estate closings online), and you gravitate to the most expedient, cost-effective sources available (human or otherwise) to obtain them.

I became aware of this radical shift in needs while gathering information for a previous book, *The Frugal HomeOwner®'s Guide to Buying, Selling, and Improving Your Home,* published by Dearborn in 1999. Although I interface with tens of thousands of people each year through platform speaking and writing, I'd never had the luxury of one-on-one debriefing through focus groups. I asked real estate consumers like you what they liked and disliked about the real estate sales and purchase process. Over the span of five years, I asked questions, took notes, and dialogued with several hundred people from one coast to the other. I asked sellers to describe the components of an ideal sale; conversely, I asked buyers what bugged them most about the transaction process and how they would streamline it. The input and results were startling, particularly in the polarity between their ideas and traditional real estate industry practices. I'll refer to the findings as the Frugal Home-Owner®'s Consumer Assessment Study. The results clearly showed that the buying and selling models used in real estate (as well as the services available from professionals) bare little resemblance to what you want as a techno-savvy homeowner. The findings comprise seven major realizations, four of which deal with money.

Consumer Reality 1. You will pay for personalized real estate services, but you dislike paying a predetermined percentage of your home's equity, sometimes not even achieving the results you wanted in the way you wanted them.

Consumer Reality 2. If a real estate agent sells a property quickly, he should be paid less, not more. Much in the way a doctor's quick diagnosis of a hot appendix should result in less cost due to fewer hospital and doctor visits, selling a property quickly frees the real estate agent to explore additional income-generating activities with other prospects. You don't like being penalized by paying a full fee when you contribute to an expedient sale requiring less time, money, and effort from the agent.

Consumer Reality 3. Some want to be team players with real estate professionals and perform various tasks in the selling and buying process. Likewise, you expect to be financially rewarded for doing so. Much like a listing agent would cooperate and fee-split a percentage commission with the agent who introduces a buyer to the property, you expect the same reward when performing tasks on your own in the buying and selling process. As one outspoken consumer shared with me, "If agents are willing to share fees with agents they're in competition with, why not with me as a seller who's paying both of their fees?" A profound, insightful, and logical question.

Consumer Reality 4. You want what you want, when you want it, and will gravitate (with few exceptions) to the most cost-effective source to obtain it. You object to being slotted in a one-size-fits-all approach to selling or buying that strips you of control in the transaction. You want the flexibility to choose only the services you need and pay what they're worth (the major driving force behind the burgeoning number of for-sale-by-owners who access and embrace online services).

Consumer Reality 5. You are leery of taking real estate agents' advice at face value because you believe they're only trying to sell you something. Because real estate agents typically only get paid when something is sold, you discount much of the advice (even the sound and sage variety given by competent agents), believing that it's yet another ploy to make a sale.

Consumer Reality 6. You place the highest value on visible, tangible real estate services. That which is hidden and not differentiated is discounted. When I asked sellers in my study which segments of the agent's skills/services were deemed most valuable, 85 percent rated the comparative market analysis (CMA) used to determine the market value range of the property as the most vital tool. This far overshadowed the obvious people-related strengths of negotiating and counseling required to put the transaction together and keep it together until closing. Your message is loud and clear that unless a task is differentiated and visible in the sales and purchase process, its value is discounted and you are unlikely to pay for it.

Consumer Reality 7. You care more about results than about service. I found this a real eye-opener because the real estate industry views service to consumers as the primary value-creating bastion (even though it's the most costly business activity in a real estate brokerage). In fact, when I asked members of a seller's focus group, "How was the service you received from the real estate agent who listed your home for sale, even though the house didn't sell?" most were at a loss to even define service!

The best example was a poignant response from one woman when I asked her about the service she received. It epitomizes how far off the pulse of the consumer the real estate brokerage business truly is. Because Mrs. Ramirez's initial response to the question was a blank look, I posed it again.

"Mrs. Ramirez, when your property was listed with the agent, what type of service did you receive?"

This time her response was an honest, "I guess I don't know what service is."

So I elaborated, "Service is how well the agent kept in touch with you, let you know what was going on, sent you copies of the advertisements he ran, sent letters that let you know how many showings there had been—in other words, he paper-trailed you with what was happening during the listing period."

"Oh, so that's what you call service!" she said sarcastically. "You know, over six months I got a whole garbage can full of service from that agent. What I didn't get was results! I didn't get my house sold."

Her response hit me like a cosmic two-by-four—too much service and not enough results have contributed to the chasm between what you want and what the real estate professionals deliver. Professionals are so busy providing you with service that it's getting in the way of focusing on tangible results!

The wake-up call for the real estate profession from these seven realities is that you, the patient, lived; but the doctor (the traditional real estate industry professional) lapsed into a coma. And unless a rapid recovery resuscitates him into a more malleable, consumer-focused professional, his next job may be in an entry-level position, making small change from the same clientele that just months before paid him thousands.

An Industry's Evolution Provoked the Current Revolution

Meager Beginnings

In order to pinpoint how you can best save money in this new revolution, it's important to know a bit about the history that provoked it. Several significant milestones over the past 100 years directly impacted the evolution and subsequent revolution happening today.

Folklore has it that the earliest method of selling and transferring real estate actually included a mechanical exchange of a clod of dirt from seller to buyer (a far departure from the labor- and paper-intensive transaction process of today).

Selling real estate in the late 1800s took on more of a coffee klatch environment than a business one. You might assume that early real estate brokerages sprang up near banks, but the true location was in or near the barbershop. Inside the door from where the candy cane barber pole stood was a hotbed of business flurry, everything from who cheated whom in a recent card game to which property owners might need to liquidate their land holdings to settle a debt. And because most men visited the barbershop on a monthly basis, it was a steady, ongoing source of real estate information and leads.

America's gold rush and land booms of the late 1800s brought real estate sales into its own with heavy demand and the need for an orderly process to divide land and record its ownership. This brought about a need for at least one person in the town to catalog available property and keep track of possible buyers. Voila, the real estate broker was born! Because of the necessity to maintain a central, public source for land ownership, real estate transfers were recorded in a central governmental source (usually a county auditor or recorder's office). This first milestone (making land records public information) is indirectly responsible for the evolution of easily accessible property information and listings online.

But the initial problem for the broker was not information, but compensation. As a gatherer and chronologist of information, it was unlikely that anyone would compensate him merely for these efforts. He had to find a way to build his cost of doing business into the sale.

The Birth of the Percentage Commission

Early real estate brokers realized that until they sold something, no one would pay them for their attempts. And until a seller listed his property with a broker and it (hopefully) eventually sold, the seller feigned being cash poor, unable to compensate the broker. That's why for the past century, real estate agents have been compensated based on a percentage of the sales price. Once the sale is closed, the broker is paid. This contingency fee or success fee became the standard compensation model, especially in the residential real estate sales community. Interestingly enough, initially only the selling broker received compensation. No commission was shared with the listing broker (the one who actually gathered the property information and marketed to find a buyer) because listings were seen as a necessary evil—you had to have listings to get sales! Although one might contend that the buyer pays compensation to the broker within the sales price, this milestone is responsible for dictating that the seller be responsible for paying the commission from his sales proceeds. This practice did little to create broker value in the eyes of the buyer.

Co-op Listings and Fee-Splitting Comes of Age

As the number of real estate brokers grew, so, too, did the desire to share information about property available for sale—informally at first (exchanging information during morning coffee at the local diner), but later growing into the formal system we today term the multiple listing service or MLS. While pocket listings (those not shared with co-operating brokers—brokers who brought buyers to purchase the property) and open listings (those in which the seller gives numerous brokers the listing, agreeing to pay the commission to the one who secures the buyer) still exist, a majority of today's marketplace is comprised of exclusively listed properties. This allows one broker to control the listing, yet share the information with potentially thousands of agents and millions of consumers. And with the advent of the Web, MLS information today is freely accessible by the public through megalisting sites like <www.realtor.com>, <www.homeseekers.com>, and <www .homeadvisor.com>. This milestone, the agent's loss of control over information, radically changes the way you work with the real estate professional. You no longer need the agent in order to access information. You now need the professional for interpretation, negotiation, and advocacy on your behalf.

The Broker Loses His Stock-in-Trade with Little to Replace It (So Far)

The open sharing of property information provides you with empowerment and flexibility. Simultaneously, well-capitalized online dot-com start-up companies offer you alternatives to traditional real estate channels, providing everything from talking yard signs to mortgage loans. In an effort to beat Web resources at their own game and develop better connectivity to you, real estate agents embrace technology, connect their modems, and launch cyber sales campaigns. But without establishing another stock-in-trade to showcase their value, some futurists predict that real estate professional legions may eventually shrink by 50 percent.

*T*he reason behind this mess is the way traditional real estate agents have been employed, as contract laborers in most cases. The entry level is low, with only a few weeks of training needed to hang a license and start competing with veterans. The sink-or-swim method employed by brokers who want to hold as many licensees as possible in the hope that the fledgling agent will sell one or two houses before flaming out is a ridiculous way to do business. Why not build an industry of professionals, instead of constantly putting out fires caused by inexperienced or desperate agents?

> Blanche Evans, Editor
> *Realty Times*
> Author, *Homesurfing.net,* Dearborn

Lack of Education Yet Another Stumbling Block

It's tough to demand respect as an industry and tout being a professional when entry-level education requirements to obtain a real estate license in most states are only a fraction of the hours demanded of barbers and cosmetologists! And while your hair can grow back, it's doubtful that the cash in your wallet will (at least not in the near future). Brokerages moan about the revolving door act of continually having to recruit and train new agents. What they fail to realize is that they're the very ones who lower the education bar every time they lobby against state legislature increasing education requirements to real estate licensees. It's the agent's lack of preparedness that causes the majority of attrition in the industry and the traditional broker has long reaped what he's sown.

Time Frames for Listing and Selling Property Are Accelerated

Before technology, it took real estate agents days, even weeks, to gather data, take pictures, and list a property for sale. This was followed by additional weeks of extensive marketing (generally print-based). Before technology, it was unusual to receive a call (other than one prompted by seeing a for-sale sign in a yard) in the first week or so after listing the property because the labor-intensive process took time to disseminate information to agents and prospective buyers.

While print marketing is still viable today, time frames for distributing information are slashed and information about the property is often launched online (complete with digital photography) often before your signature is dry on the listing contract. This milestone, as referenced previously in Consumer Reality 2, reflects that when things happen quickly, services are perceived to be worth less in terms of what you'll pay for them. This led to discounts on commissions and, in some markets, commission wars between brokers.

But unlike the pretechnology system where agents used an insider formula (meaning they had the tools and the control) to market a property, you now have access to the tools and often have the expertise to mount your own successful marketing campaign alone (even launching your own domain online to showcase your property). Your experience in previous homeselling experiences, coupled with state-of-the-art marketing tools, make you a formidable threat to real estate agents.

Physician Heal Thyself: Why the Traditional Real Estate Model Shattered

Business Model Has Low Profitability and Lack of Control

The eroding and potential demise of the traditional real estate sales industry has not come about solely due to reinventing yourself and access to Web-driven services. Much of the blame for the threatened industry lies in the low-profit, low-control business model, the real estate brokerage. In fact, it's estimated that in 1999, pretax profit for median-sized brokerages in the United States was a pathetic 3 percent. Although somewhat difficult to believe, despite billions of dollars generated annually in real estate commissions, most brokerages have little profit and even less control of product—two components necessary for success and longevity in any type of business.

Think about it. You don't see entrepreneurs of note like Bill Gates or Mary Kay Ash starting up businesses using the real estate brokerage model where the broker/agent has little control over the product being sold (i.e., the house), spends money up front with the hope of eventually being reimbursed for the cash outlay and efforts, and finds one day that the client decides to take the product (the listing) off the market only to later sell it directly to a buyer first introduced by the broker (with no compensation to the brokerage, of course).

When I try to explain the brokerage business model to businesspeople in other industries, it's apparent how absurd and flawed it is. While visiting Australia, I found myself describing to an Aussie broker how American real estate brokerages work. The chap looked at me in disbelief and asked, "Are all real estate brokers rich in your country? Otherwise, how can they afford to do business without taking any money up front, yet shell money out on a seller's behalf with no guarantee of reimbursement?" In Australia, real estate goes to auction first; if it doesn't bring a successful bid, brokers are then forced to list the property. But in both instances, a nonrefundable marketing fee is taken up front to cover the cost of doing business.

Fast-Paced Market Further Fractures the Brokerage Model

Even though it won't be totally evident until the market cools, the booming real estate market of the past decade has had a potentially negative impact on the brokerage business model—so much to do, so little time, with profitability taking a back seat in favor of expansion, especially where technology is concerned. But when the dust settles from the flurry, some brokers may realize that working for another company, in another industry (especially one providing health benefits, a pension, and a matching retirement account) would have been more remunerative.

Why Is the Broken Listing/Selling Model Still Around?

You may be thinking, "If the current listing/selling model is so irreparably broken, why is real estate still sold this way?" Several responses come to mind:

- In a buoyant market boasting high employment, you are eager to purchase property as quickly as you can, using any process that generates results. The process used is questioned only if it's seen as detrimental to achieving results.
- Strong sellers' markets make attracting buyers effortless. The process used to market the home through a brokerage would only be questioned if it wasn't working, not because it is.
- With real estate appreciation at record heights, it's often deemed more important to get the sale completed, paying a percentage commission to a broker in lieu of wasting precious time to sell the property as a for-sale-by-owner.
- It's not common knowledge that you can openly negotiate fees with real estate brokers; and/or you may have been told that if you did list for less than X percent commission, the property won't be shown as readily by other brokers who could make more selling a competing property.
- Brokers willing to offer consumer-friendly fee arrangements and unbundled, à la carte, fee-for-services have found resistance from other professionals. At the very least, the enterprising broker will find herself defending slanderous remarks from peers used as ammunition to compete for listings with sellers and sales with buyers.
- Although the Web is an empowering and potentially cost-saving tool for selling your house, you may not be comfortable enough with its use, choosing instead to stick with traditional listing and selling methods, even if they cost more.

What Will Drive the Coffin Nail in the Current Business Model?

You only have to reflect on industries like travel and stock brokerage to see the collision course for the traditional real estate model. Events that could precipitate its demise include:

- The shift from a seller's market to a buyer's market. Desperate sellers often resort to selling the property on their own, often after having it listed with a real estate brokerage for a period of time. And if power in the transaction shifts to the buyer, equity currently paying a broker's percentage commission could become the difference between profit and loss for some sellers.
- An increase in the amount of foreclosed properties. Lenders who take properties back in foreclosure are least likely to list properties with real estate brokers. And if lenders become federally approved to sell real estate, the lender will be in open competition with real estate brokers. Any guess as to the winner in that battle?
- A marked increase in interest rates. When interest rates rise, fewer buyers are able to qualify for financing required to purchase homes, resulting in fewer home sales. Fewer homes selling cause sellers to panic, believing that they can better attract buyers by lowering their price (typically done by trimming costs of sale, particularly the commission).
- Lawsuits settled that point to restraint of trade issues in price-fixing brokerage commissions. Several large lawsuits are currently pending, with others under appeal on this volatile topic. Much like the early court cases involving discrimination in housing, if courts of law can prove that price fixing is a reality in the marketplace, brokers could be forced (virtually overnight) to employ a different method of being compensated for their services.
- Your increased Web empowerment! The explosion of for-sale-by-owner properties online (and the buyers they

attract) is striking the deathblow to percentage commissions and pounding the final coffin nail in the archaic brokerage model. Just as the Web has revolutionized the way we shop, work, and spend our leisure time, it's harnessing that power to shift the real estate paradigm in your favor.

The Future of Real Estate with Three Power Players

Three Characteristics You'll Look for in a Real Estate Services Provider

Many innovative business models are competing for your attention in this new world of real estate services. Some specialize and deliver only one puzzle piece while others will promise to handle your every real estate need for life! Online auctions have the potential to list your house one minute and have an offer the next. Don't worry about driving across town to the title company for your closing. It will occur in cyberspace via an electronic transaction platform like that found at <www.iproperty.com> where verification of your identity is confirmed by your electronic signature, fingerprint, or a snapshot of your retina—real estate à la the Jetsons!

In order to make the cut as a new real estate model, you require a real estate service provider (person or company) to deliver you with three important criteria: flexibility, greater control, and less cost than before. Without these components, a provider won't survive your scrutiny, but unlike the previous real estate model, 21st century real estate providers will suffer an expedient, not a languishing, death!

After the Shakeout, Three Entities Prevail

As many surveys indicate (including the 1999 Arthur D. Little, Inc., survey commissioned by the National Association of REALTORS®), three primary entities will play the new game of real estate: for-sale-by-owners, aggregators, and fee-for-services consultants.

Power Group 1: For-Sale-by-Owners Will Dominate the Market

Depending on the source and date of the statistics, for-sale-by-owners (FSBOs) are expected to grow to approximately 40 percent of the available property market in the next several years. This means that for every 100 properties for sale in the marketplace, 40 of them will be FSBOs. While it's doubtful that this increase will be uniform across all real estate markets in the United States, the sheer volume will more than double the current number of FSBOs found in even the hottest seller markets. No longer will FSBOs be merely an ancillary market segment that real estate agents could choose to work with from time to time. By sheer numbers, for-sale-by-owners will be a force to be reckoned with as the largest market segment.

The increase in FSBOs is due in large part to the demographic bulge of baby boomers. Boomers want to maximize home sale profits to purchase a vacation retreat, and/or free up cash for retirement. As we continue to live longer, we're more likely to tap into our equity for both luxuries and necessities. In reality, a baby boomer in the future is more likely to lose a house to the inability to pay escalating real estate property taxes than to mortgage foreclosure. Additionally, boomers will be called on to assist their parents in covering supplemental costs of health care and the similar property taxes and housing expenses they may struggle to pay.

But it's obvious that whatever age group you fit, you're committed to maximizing your equity as a for-sale-by-owner from here on out. At a recent consumer seminar on real estate equity management, I asked participants if they planned to use an agent when they sold their current home. Fewer than 25 percent said they would consider it. Most felt that because they had sold several homes before, had the Web to assist them, believed it was worth the time it takes to sell it themselves and save the commission, and didn't believe being a FSBO required a degree in rocket science, they were more motivated and fairly confident they would be successful on their own. More reinforcement of how inadequate the traditional real estate professional was in convincing consumers that paying thousands of dollars in a percentage commission was worth it.

Dot-com real estate companies are rapidly taking over the once-sacred roles of a larger group of real estate people. They are moving across the World Wide Web at the speed of thought and moving into one regional market after another. Soon the dot-coms will begin to merge into a few large national firms somewhat like the large national and international real estate franchises did in their day of the past. The dot-coms are offering exactly what consumers want in a variety of ways and fee-for-services is the norm with one-stop shopping, value-added concierge, and a multitude of choices directed at the techno-able and savvy consumer who demands more, better, faster, and cheaper.

> Team Toolbox
> Realestatetoolbox.com
> Principals, Tom Pickering, Sherry Peters, and J. David Shinn

Power Group 2: Aggregators Will Strive to Meet the Needs of the Real Estate Consumer

By definition, an aggregator is an entity that brings together various products and/or services in order to meet a need or solve a problem. The most prevalent aggregators today are the online aggregators, gravitating by the thousands to the large, potentially lucrative playing field of dot-com real estate. And, in turn, real estate consumers are gravitating to them as well. Via these megasites, you can access everything from home buying/selling information, to talking brochure boxes and lockboxes. The power of the aggregator will grow in leaps and bounds by 2010. So much so that surveys cite that current (and yet to be launched) online aggregators could provide as much as 20 percent of the real estate services we require. As with the potential 40 percent market share estimated for

FSBOs, the potential 20 percent market share of aggregators will shave numbers off the original market stakeholder—any real estate brokerages left standing. Given the numbers in the other two primary players' groups, what role will remaining real estate agents play in the revamped world?

Power Group 3: Real Estate Agents Will Reinvent Themselves into Fee-for-Services Consultants

Doing the math, if 40 percent of the future's real estate market share will be attributed to you as for-sale-by-owners with a 20 percent share for aggregators, that leaves 40 percent potentially available for real estate agents and brokers. The good news is that the hard-pressure salesperson, who treated you like her monthly mortgage and car payment, will vanish. Survivors left to assist you will be results-oriented real estate consultants.

After going out on a very slippery limb with this real estate consultant prognostication more than four years ago, I'd love to take credit for this prediction, but, unfortunately, I arrived at this theory by researching the more obvious conflicts and pressures of the marketplace (based on talking to you, the consumer) rather than the glow of my crystal ball. When large numbers of for-sale-by-owners coupled with increasing numbers of online giants take control of the marketplace, it's obvious that the people-side services contributed by real estate professionals must change to better address your needs. But as you have voiced, it's not a little, but a massive change that's required. If you need help, you want to work with someone as a team player who focuses on results and is capable of interpreting information to help you make an informed, cost-effective real estate decision.

Brokers/Owners of Firms (and Staff) Orchestrate the Puzzle Pieces–Mostly through Cyberspace

The principal broker/owner of a firm and the brokerage support staff will help you orchestrate your purchase or sales transaction, oversee and monitor any consulting services provided to you, and make sure that the individual consultant you're working with is meeting your needs and time frames. The real estate brokerage will specialize in all phases of the process (much like a general oversees his troops).

While some brokerages with fixed business facilities will remain, automating the transaction will no longer require brokers to occupy the expansive brick-and-mortar offices of the past. The good news for consumers is that you'll have access to transaction information online 24/7/365 and won't need to spend time driving to a fixed facility to meet with an agent or close a purchase or sale.

Real Estate Consultants:
A New Breed of Real Estate Professional

The Consultant Will Focus Solely on Your Needs

Conversely, the individual consultant working with you will solely focus on your needs and the results you're seeking, leaving troubleshooting and related tasks to the brokerage. Unlike the past, the consultant won't be involved in menial, time-consuming tasks like running papers to title companies and removing for-sale signs. She'll be proactive, not reactive, providing you with finely tuned, high-level skills like negotiating on your behalf with local planning and zoning officials, contesting your property tax assessment with the county, or helping you design a sound real estate investment strategy. Gone will be the salesmanship pressures you felt when working with commissioned-based agents. The consultant will be your definitive source of unbiased information on this level playing field and you will be calling the shots!

Consultants Will Specialize

Many real estate consultants will specialize in product-focused niches (like helping you design your new home), while others will focus on demographically segmented needs (like working with a senior citizen to make a home handicap accessible). You will have your choice of well-qualified consultants, many of whom have spent decades in a previous career related to their specialty.

For example, you could use a certified appraiser to consult with you on ways that remodeling your home would add the most value at resale. Or consult with a home inspector prior to tackling that upgrade in your electrical system. The options are virtually endless!

Consulting Applies to All Dimensions of Real Estate Needs

As you can see, real estate consulting often has nothing to do with buying or selling anything. That's why using consulting services is not only likely to get you quickly to your end result, but help you build faith in the real estate profession, dispelling those in-it-just-for-the-commission feelings. By compensating consultants based on results and removing the inherent pressure of salesmanship, it's a win-win for you and professionals alike.

Real Estate Consultants Introduce a Variety of Compensation Models

Methods of Compensating Consultants Are Limited Only by Your Imagination!

Just as limitless as the many ways you can benefit by using a consultant, so, too, are the payment options available to compensate him. As we'll cover in depth in Chapter 2, consultants (typically through their parent employing firm) can be paid an hourly rate, flat fee, percentage (this time, you decide the percent to pay!), or even a meager flat fee plus a bonus based on how much money the consultant is able to save you. For example, if the consultant, through her expertise, is able to determine by dissecting the seller's records that a house you're interested in purchasing is actually worth $10,000 less than the listed price, you win on the price and the consultant is rewarded with 10 percent of your savings as a bonus!

For real estate consumers, one-size-no-longer-fits-all![SM]

Julie Garton-Good, DREI, C-CREC

Break Free of One-Size-Fits-All—and Save!

Have you ever ordered a one-size-fits-all piece of clothing sight unseen, only to find that you're the exception to the claim? It's even more distressing to uncover, usually at the least opportune time, that the fit you need in real estate services isn't offered, is outside of the norm, or is just too expensive. Your need could take the shape of a professional to help you decide how to get your home in market-ready condition. Or your need could be a bit more daunting, finding someone (besides your overpriced lawyer) to negotiate with your mortgage lender to allow you to catch up the four payments you're behind on.

If you're empowered and ready to save money, it's time to scrap the ill-fitting stuff you don't need (or want to pay for) and try on a tailor-made, yet affordable ensemble of custom-designed, unbundled real estate services. Your basic pattern for success will be a combination of online services coupled with help (when needed) from a real estate consultant. You'll pay only for what you use and select what you need, when you need it, from the broad selection of à la carte real estate services available at low or no cost. You'll be in control of the transaction from beginning to end, results-focused to obtain the right fit in the predetermined time frame. Let the unbundling begin!

Fee-for-Services Real Estate: What It Is, What It Isn't

Caution: Don't Confuse Unbundling with Fee Discounting

As seen in Figure 1.1, unbundling is dividing real estate services into separate parts, resulting in greater flexibility, more potential control, and at possibly less cost than bundled real estate services historically available. Once unbundled, each service or task you access is assigned its own value with the intent that using components separately will result in less overall net cost and greater flexibility than bundled services.

We've always had the latitude (but perhaps not the guts) to barter with a real estate agent for a lower percentage fee (called fee discounting), but that's markedly different from unbundling. In fee discounting, you ask for the entire bundle of services, but you pay less for them. In unbundling, you pay what you determine a fair price for each service used from the bundle. This often is decided by negotiating with the consultant or service provider with whom you're working.

As you begin to access unbundled real estate services, be aware that many real estate professionals from the old school of one-size-fits-all may confuse fee discounting with unbundling. Here's an example you might use for clarification. It uses one of my favorite unbundled foods, pie.

You manage a local bakery that specializes in pies. Each day, you price fresh pies to sell in two ways: as an entire pie (bundled) and by the slice (unbundled, à la carte), charging one-sixth of the whole-pie price for each piece.

If a whole pie doesn't sell by the second day, it's considered stale. Because it's now in competition with fresh pies, a marketing edge is required. The previous day's price is discounted

Figure 1.1   Service Blocks

When Bundled:
You can't differentiate between real estate services;
Perceived value is diminished.

C M A

Counseling

Negotiating

(fee discounting), even though it took the same amount of time, cost, and effort to make as the full-price, fresh pie. In fact, the day-old pie might have more costs attributed to it, like plastic wrap for keeping it refrigerated over night.

For more than a century, real estate brokers discounted fees (usually not without some heavy-duty negotiating!). Today, unbundling real estate services gives you and your service provider or consultant a cost-effective and fair way to access what you need, yet pay what it's worth (with no stale, wasted, or discounted services left over).

Tailor-Made, Individually Priced, Results-Oriented Menus

Figure 1.2 shows various types of unbundled/fee-for-services applications available to you as well as how fees can be structured with a real estate consultant or other service provider. As

Figure 1.2   Price Blocks

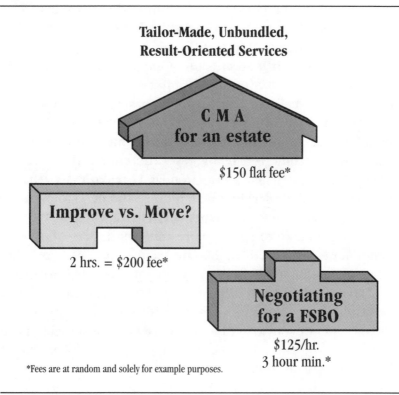

Tailor-Made, Unbundled,
Result-Oriented Services

C M A
for an estate

$150 flat fee*

Improve vs. Move?

2 hrs. = $200 fee*

Negotiating
for a FSBO

$125/hr.
3 hour min.*

*Fees are at random and solely for example purposes.

we'll explore in depth in Chapter 2, hourly fees, flat fees, and percentage fees with a cap are just some of the many payment structures available. Some consultants (often dictated by the real estate licensing laws in their state) use nonrefundable retainer fees, others use refundable retainers, and yet others receive payment only upon completion of the work.

When contracting to receive services, it's vital that you first determine (as specifically as possible) the end results you're seeking before you even begin the process of screening and negotiating with consultants (let alone jump at the lowest bid!). Until your goal is in view, it will be impossible to determine what constitutes fair compensation for what you need to achieve.

For example, the consultant quotes you a flat fee of X dollars to negotiate with the buyer you find and bring the sale to a successful close. His quote is drastically lower than what three other consultants quoted you. Is this cause for concern? Perhaps. The adage "if it sounds too good to be true, it probably is" might apply here. Just as you interviewed traditional commission-based real estate agents in the past to determine which one you felt most comfortable working with and could best get the job done, the initial interview drill is much the same with real estate consultants. The biggest difference is that a competent consultant will give you an itemized breakdown of the cost of his time, outside services he'll require and need to pay for (if applicable), as well as a timeline showing approximately how long it should take to reach the results you desire. All of these components are based on the end results you desire and how they can best be accomplished. By obtaining this information from all consultants interviewed, you'll have an idea of whether a consultant is charging a competitive fee, has capped additional costs (so you won't be penalized), and is logical in time frames and the game plan proposed. Chapter 8 details how to find, negotiate, and work with consultants.

A la Carte/Fee-for-Services Cover Every Real Estate Need

The flexibility of unbundled services is obvious if you're selling a house and believe there are only a few areas with which you need help (like closing the sale). But what about purchasing a home? Can you work with a real estate consultant as a buyer? Absolutely.

Let's say that you find a for-sale-by-owner property that you love, but are concerned that if you don't negotiate strongly and expediently with the seller, another buyer will snatch it up!

The solution? Hire a real estate consultant by the hour to negotiate with the seller, draft the purchase contract, and then complete any other tasks you're concerned about in order to get the sale closed. If the consultant assisted you on an hourly basis from that point to closing, you could expect to pay for probably no more than 5 to 15 hours' worth of the consultant's time—a small investment for winning the house you want and quickly and effortlessly closing the sale.

A growing area of concern for homeowners is what to improve in their house and how. This is another area where a consultant can be worth her weight in gold!

You have decided that instead of selling (because you love the neighborhood and the school system) you'll stay put in your current home and make some improvements. But how can you tell which ones will recoup your investment if you do eventually sell? A real estate consultant can give you an idea of the selling prices of properties with similar amenities as well as what type of finished product (terrazzo tiles or parquet) would be most acceptable to a potential buyer.

As you can see, there are myriad ways a real estate consultant or service provider can help you solve even your toughest real estate problem. We'll cover a broad selection of them in Chapter 7.

Use Consumer Road Maps for Navigating à la Carte Real Estate

Road Maps for Sellers, Buyers, and Real Estate Side Trips

I own a house in Idaho, perched 600 feet above the Clearwater River. Two hundred years ago, Lewis and Clark navigated that river in search of the body of water we know today to be the Pacific Ocean. It must have been exciting, yet incredibly scary, waking up each day not knowing what they would encounter around the next bend. The Corps of Discovery expedition had no maps or legal descriptions to guide them and woefully underestimated the time the trip would take. They paid dearly at times, with sickness, exhaustion, and death.

I'm sure you're wondering what in the world the Lewis and Clark journey has to do with locating unbundled real estate services? Besides the fact that they were traveling over real estate a majority of the time, Lewis and Clark used simple, often rudimentary, tools by which to chart their course, the foremost being a compass. As long as the compass needle registered west on their outbound trip, and east on their return, they had the confidence to keep going.

While your journey into unbundled real estate services certainly won't be as treacherous (or hopefully as long) as the Corps of Discovery, you have similar compasses or road maps to guide you.

If the services you need point to selling a house (either on your own or in tandem with a real estate consultant or services provider), choose the seller's road map. Conversely, if buying is in your future, use the buyer's road map as your guide. Or if your real estate needs fit neither seller nor buyer categories, use the side trip road maps found in Chapter 6.

As we'll cover in depth in Chapters 3 and 4, respectively, the seller's and buyer's road maps each have six distinct checkpoints to keep you on track. Spending time analyzing the route you'll take and what to anticipate along the way will save you time, resources, and missteps in the future.

Comparing the Seller's and Buyer's Road Maps

Unbundled, the real estate transaction is a logical series of six major components or checkpoints for sellers and six for buyers (but unfortunately, not the same six!). Some of the segments are a few hours in duration, while others last weeks or even months, but the end result is ideally the same—closing a successful sale or purchase with the least hassle and the greatest reward.

The seller's road map contains the following six checkpoints:

1. Prepare/stage the property for sale
2. Gather property information/price the property

3. Market the property
4. Locate/prequalify a buyer
5. Draft the sales agreement/negotiate with the buyer
6. Troubleshoot the sale/close the transaction

The buyer's road map contains the following six check-points:

1. Design a purchase strategy
2. Be preapproved for a mortgage
3. Choose the neighborhood and the property
4. Check property information and pricing
5. Draft the purchase agreement/negotiate with the seller
6. Troubleshoot the purchase/close the transaction

In comparing and contrasting seller and buyer components, many are reactions or counteractions to the other party, with only two items similar (numbers 5 and 6). These components of negotiating and closing the transaction are not solely specific to real estate but are intrinsic to many types of large-expense consumer purchases (like automobiles, life insurance policies, and stock investments). If you understand a bit about each of these transaction phases, it will help you determine how much of the transaction you can/should do on your own as well as what services you need to obtain from a real estate professional.

Tips for Maximizing Profits with Real Estate à la Carte

Using Consultants and Technology Equals Maximum Profit to You

Just as this chapter started by enumerating your savings in the new world of real estate (all potential $32,000 of it), so will the chapter end. After all, money is the alpha and omega when it comes to solving your real estate problems and maximizing your profit. Using unbundled, fee-for-service providers (online and off) in tandem with real estate consultants gives you the inexpensive, automated tools you need coupled with the personalized, real-world expertise of a knowledgeable person! Real estate services that can be handled cheaper and more expeditiously using technology and automated services are at your disposal. Yet, when you need analysis, input, and scrutiny from an unbiased professional to aid in your decision-making process, the real estate consultant is the answer.

The Bottom Line:
The Consumer Wins, No Matter What!

After 100 years of evolution and revolution in an industry where you, the end-user, had very little input (often none) regarding what you needed, when you needed it, and how much and when you wanted to pay for it, you are the undisputed victor in the battle. To you go two empowering prizes for your real estate future:

1. *The power of high tech.* Any real estate services that can be duplicated by technology will save you incredible amounts of time, effort, and money.
2. *The power of high touch.* When technology won't solve your problem, rely on the real estate consultant to take you back in time a century ago when hometown barber as broker addressed the specialized, individual needs of his clientele—bringing your journey full circle.

What to Pay for à la Carte Real Estate Services and How to Pay It

Cutting-edge real estate professionals are using technology and new approaches like a "Menu of Services and Fees" and/or the "One-Stop Real Estate Shop" concept to meet pent-up consumer demand for smarter, faster, and less expensive ways to buy or sell a house or other real estate.

The fact is that the Internet can save real estate professionals a lot of time and money. More and more of these professionals are passing some of that savings on to the consumer. . .

Jay Rogers
Buyer's agent/real estate consultant

A la Carte Real Estate Is Flexible, More Controllable, and Cost-Effective

There's More than One Way to Save Money Using Fee-for-Services

A la carte real estate services allow you, the real estate consumer, to access the help you need when you need it and pay what it's worth. As a savvy seller you may want to rent a yard sign and lockbox, but tackle the balance of the sale on your own. Or perhaps you're an unassisted buyer who finds a for-sale-by-owner property and wants to contract for a real estate consultant's help in negotiating and closing the purchase. Consumers are voting with their wallets, paying flat fees, hourly fees, and a variety of combinations in between! Perhaps most interesting is that consumers like you are doing two things the residential real estate industry professional predicted you'd never do: pay retainers to consultants and service providers to secure the real estate services you need, and participate in the risk/reward aspects of the transaction as they relate to the amount of fees you pay and the terms under which you pay them.

It's Critical to Differentiate between Fee Discounting and Unbundling

As covered in Chapter 1, there's a vast difference between discounted real estate fees and unbundled fee-for-services. And until you understand the difference, you could be destined to either overpay and/or not receive the end result you need.

Discounting is paying less, but still receiving all of the services in a bundle to complete a certain task like selling a home. Unbundled fee-for-services is choosing what you need, as you need it, and paying only for the services you receive. At first glance you may wonder why a consumer wouldn't want to have it all, especially when he can pay less for it. Unfortunately, there are potential pitfalls in working with discount brokers that can actually cause consumers to lose, not save, money.

Cautions Involved in Working with Discounted Commission Companies and Similar Service Providers

Commission price wars between full-service brokerages have infiltrated real estate markets across the country. In an effort to garner a larger swath of a market, attract attention, and annihilate the competition, many brokerages are slashing fees by 25 percent or more and becoming discount brokers. While touting that they provide full service to consumers, many often have little idea of the effect reducing commissions will have on their ability to stay in business and deliver results-oriented service to consumers. Subsequently, they may trim the quantity or quality of services you receive, causing you to fall short of your objective and end result. These cutbacks may not be apparent to you as the consumer because the brokerage and agents keep singing the full-service refrain; however, the discount broker who is not staying on top of what it costs to stay in business could take your listing today and be out of business tomorrow! A sage, professional broker, responding to an agent who queried when he'd be slashing commissions like discount brokers in their marketplace, responded: "Never. It makes no sense to compete with someone who's trying to go out of business!"

Second, the discount real estate brokerage business is based on volume, not quality. The more consumers a discount broker can attract, the lower her pricing structure can move and still allow her to stay in business. Discount brokerage is a little like taking your car to an auto mechanic solely because he quotes the shortest time frame and cheapest costs. How can he do it? With volume. But to accomplish volume, he often sacrifices quality and best results. Should he find another component of the car needing repair, he may choose to overlook it due to his tight time schedule and the need to repair more cars. Or he might approach you to pay additional money to solve the problem. Either way you've lost confidence in the mechanic and his business. Over time, he will realize that his focus on volume instead of quality and best results has destroyed the hope of repeat customers as well as the prospect of many new ones. Defending legal actions against the company erodes what little is left of his bottom line and he's forced to close his doors.

In addition to discount brokerages, price wars between real estate brokerages are also precipitated by the onslaught of dot-com companies providing a wide array of both discounted and unbundled services, many at bargain-basement prices. Online companies like <www.homebytes.com>, <www.cyberhomes.com>, and <www.ziprealty.com> are drawing consumers online by providing cost-effective alternatives in cyberspace, available 24/7 with unique online and telephone response systems to make the consumer feel connected, informed, and important.

In the final differentiation between discount brokerages and unbundled fee-for-services companies and fee-for-services providers, it's important to understand how each varies in application. The discount brokerage assumes that you need the whole menu of services and are willing to transfer control to the broker/agent to attain it. More importantly, fee discounters assume that you have only one need—to reach the one result they hope to attain for you (i.e., a sale) and that a cheaper price quoted is more important than results. In contrast, the fee-for-services company or consultant assumes that you are capable of performing and orchestrating various parts of the transaction, that you want to exercise primary control in what transpires, and that you want tailor-made, needs-based results with someone or something responsible for guiding you there.

The bottom line is that the first step in determining what to pay for a real estate task or service is to have a working knowledge of the difference between discounted services and unbundled fee-for-services. If you fail to understand the distinction between the two, you may find yourself short of the assistance and services necessary to reach your real estate goal even if it is going to cost you less. In other words, be careful not to sacrifice results at the altar of cost savings.

How Fee-for-Services Consultants Determine Their Fees

In order to determine what to pay for a real estate service, it's helpful to understand how consultants determine their fee structures. Before a consultant can set her fees, she needs to determine:

1. The type and level of the skill required. Will the task be performed entirely by the consultant or will other team players (like unlicensed assistants or researchers) be

involved? This could also include administrative or clerical assistance, cost of supplies, technology required, etc.

2. The cost factor (often in per-hour terms) for each assisting in the task
3. The approximate amount of time it would take each party to complete the task
4. Any other external services, consultants, or costs involved (like surveys, appraisal fees, etc.) to complete the job. While many consultants quote external services separately outside of their fees, those services need to be addressed in itemizing costs for the overall project.

Here's one model consultants use for determining the hourly value of their time on an annual basis: The gross amount of income required (including federal and state taxes) divided by the number of hours the consultant desires to work during the year multiplied by three equals the approximate rate for one hour of the consultant's time. This last step takes into consideration that expenses and overhead must be paid from the gross as well as compensating for downtime and other uncontrollable factors that occur in business.

Using this model, a consultant needing to make $75,000 before taxes who works 1,800 hours per year would need to charge $125 per hour for her services.

$$\$75,000 \div 1,800 = \$41.66 \times 3 = \$124.98$$
(rounded up to $125 per hour)

This formula is not only used for determining fees for consultants, but for other professional and technical workers such as architects, plumbers, and attorneys.

What's a Real Estate Task or Service Really Worth?

Identifying Four Components Can Help

But how can you determine what's fair to pay for an individual service because the traditional real estate model of the past compensated service providers by paying them a percentage of the sales price to cover all services—whether or not you required or used them?

The good news is that you can determine the value of a task or service by evaluating several factors including the:

- Level of expertise the task requires
- Length of time it takes to complete the task
- Number of components to the task (i.e., a variety of professionals involved in various specialty segments of the task)
- Availability of the service in the marketplace; in other words, the impact supply and demand plays on the service or task you require

The bad news is that these components may carry different weights based on your individual situation. Remember that because one size no longer fits all when it comes to real estate needs, pricing structures will fluctuate based on the individual task as well as your ability to negotiate a win-win pricing structure with your service provider.

The National Association of Real Estate Consultants™ Makes Consumers Aware of Options

Founded in 1999 in an effort to spread the word about accessing cost-effective unbundled services from real estate consultants, the National Association of Real Estate Consultants (NAREC) designed a fair consumer pricing brochure (a copy of which is found in Figure 2.1). Incorporated into NAREC's code of ethics, the brochure is used exclusively by Consumer-Certified Real Estate Consultant™ (C-CREC) designees and distrib-

Figure 2.1 Fair Consumer Pricing

"Seven Guidelines for Fair Consumer Pricing"
from
The National Association of Real Estate Consultants™
(NAREC)

As a Consumer-Certified Real Estate Consultant™ (C-CREC™) designee, the consultant assisting you must adhere to the Code of Ethics of the National Association of Real Estate Consultants™. The following "Fair Consumer Pricing Guidelines" are a vital part of that Code and can help you determine approximately what a service or task is worth to you as a real estate consumer.

Seven Guidelines to Help Determine the Fees You Pay

While each C-CREC™ determines his or her own pricing structure based on a variety of factors, there are seven general rules of thumb to help you determine approximately what a service or task should cost you. They are:

1. Expect to compensate the professional as you would others in equal standing in similarly related professions. For example, a real estate consultant with ten years of experience should receive an hourly fee in line with what a real estate attorney with the same level of expertise would charge. A real estate appraiser doing fee-for-services work could garner fees similar to those of a CPA. While there are exceptions, this rule of thumb should prove helpful in gauging costs.
2. Determine whether the service you need is a level one skill (informational) or level two skill (interpretative) since it can impact the fee you pay. For example, interpretative skills where advocacy, negotiating, and representation are required from the consultant could be priced higher to compensate for a higher degree of skill employed. Conversely, level one fees of an information-gathering or administrative nature may carry lesser-priced fees.

Figure 2.1 Fair Consumer Pricing (Continued)

3. Don't be "penny-wise and pound-foolish" as Ben Franklin admonished us. It's dangerous to gravitate to the lowest-priced service just because it's cheapest. Instead, focus on the services that will provide the results you're looking for, i.e., quick sale, highest net proceeds, lowest closing costs, etc. Consider any added value a consultant or company can provide as compared to the more cost-effective competition. A bargain-basement fee may entice you to do business with a company only later to find that their focus is volume, not meeting your individual needs.

4. Don't let the sum of the parts exceed the whole! In other words, don't defeat the financial savings of unbundled à la carte services only to later find that you've paid too much in individual fees and still haven't reached your desired end result. For example, as a seller you decide to pay "x" for a comparative market analysis (CMA), "y" to rent signage, and "z" to compensate the consultant for ten hours' worth of negotiating. Unless you initially tally up all of the services/tasks you need and their corresponding costs in advance, you won't be able to choose the most cost-effective fee structure to satisfy your needs.

5. Be aware of the myriad ways a real estate consultant can be compensa ing on the business model he/she uses). You might negotiate a reduced percentage fee, a flat fee, or an hourly fee with a cap. Or perhaps you could negotiate a rebate of the fee back to you for services not required to close your sale. The lesson is that even though reaching minor success in a purchase or sale by paying à la carte fees is enticing and seemingly cost-effective, being unrealistic about the depth of help you need could churn minor fees into an albatross more costly than the heftiest commission in the marketplace.

　　If you realize midstream that you need additional services that you haven't contracted to receive, renegotiate the fee structure with the real estate consultant. For example, you may find that moving to a different compensation model can save you money by capping the hourly fees you're paying and still reward the consultant with a contingency fee when results are complete.

Figure 2.1   Fair Consumer Pricing (Continued)

6. Understand the difference between and the application of contingent and noncontingent fees. A contingent fee is one received for a task that is likely to happen, but not guaranteed. For example, you place your house on the market with a full-service real estate broker and agree to pay a contingent fee if the house sells. While it's hopeful that the house will sell at the terms and conditions you specify, a sale (the results) is not guaranteed. If a sale does occur, you would pay the broker his percentage commission out of your proceeds at closing. With the traditional contingent fee model of the past, the real estate broker and his agents bore the majority of risk and costs up front in the hope that a house would sell. Because of this, many consumers felt little power or need to negotiate lower fees with brokers. Until the property sold (if ever) it would cost the consumer nothing.

   By contrast, a noncontingent fee compensates work where an outcome is more assured. For example, you hire a consultant to prepare a comparative market analysis (CMA) on a house you want to purchase. He performs the work and you pay his fee. Even though you may not like the market range of the property as indicated by the CMA, an outcome (the approximate market value) is determined. Understanding the difference between contingent and noncontingent fees can lend creativity to what you pay and how you compensate a professional or service provider.

7. Realize the impact paying a retainer fee has on your business relationship with the C-CREC™. Just as you want to move quickly to the cost-effective results you desire, so too does the consultant. It's often in your best interest to exemplify your willingness and motivation by placing a retainer with the consultant before launching the relationship. It shows your good faith and allows the consultant to prioritize his business efforts by working only with consumers who are motivated and results-oriented. Your C-CREC™ designee will explain his retainer policy during your initial interview.

   The Consumer-Certified Real Estate Consultant™ assisting you will be more than happy to discuss various pricing models and fee structures available through his consulting practice.

Copyright ©2000, National Association of Real Estate Consultants™
CNA™ and C-CREC™ are trademarks of the National Association of Real Estate Consultants™.

uted to each consumer during their initial meeting with the consultant. The focus of the brochure is to help the consumer determine fair compensation for unbundled real estate services, describe various ways real estate consultants can be compensated, and show the consumer the power of retainers in moving quickly to results-oriented outcome. NAREC hopes that sharing information with consumers about fair pricing guidelines for real estate services will level the playing field between consultant and consumer as well as help control unscrupulous would-be consultants from price gouging as is sometimes the case when new approaches and services are introduced to the public. Chapter 8 covers additional ways NAREC effectively works to bring consumers and real estate consultants together. Additionally, you can find contact information for the organization in the Resources section at the end of this book.

The Level of Service You Require Can Determine What You Pay

Understanding the Difference between Level One and Level Two Services Can Save You Money!

The real estate consultant is unique among real estate licensees in that he understands there are two distinct service levels required by consumers: level one assistance and level two assistance. Level one help is often information gathering in nature or administrative based and provides you with the facts and support you need to make an informed real estate decision. It can best be described as informational. For example, pulling the information together to help you decide whether to improve your current home or move to another is one type of level one assistance. After receiving level one help, you weigh the pros and cons and come to your own conclusions.

A higher, more representation-based assistance is found with level two help. At level two, the consultant advocates for you and represents your interests much like an attorney would do for a client. Level two assistance requires a higher level of expertise and personal skills, often those of negotiating and interpreting information on your behalf. Level two service is best described as interpretative. After gathering information for you (a level one task), the real estate consultant might need to represent you in a client capacity in order to bring the project to a successful close (in the sale of your home, for example). As we'll see in various seller examples in Chapter 5 and buyer applications in Chapter 6, both levels of service are found in troubleshooting all types of real estate problems.

Questions to Ask the Consultant Concerning Level One and Level Two Services

There are several ways understanding the difference between level one and level two services can help you save money.

First, it's good to ask the consultant what portion of the fee, if any, is attributed to level two services. If it's a high percentage, you may want to consider doing some of the information gathering on your own and have the consultant check it to help lower the fee.

Second, you may want to work with a consultant who has another person (like a clerical assistant or a personal assistant) performing level one skills. By compensating another person at a lower level one rate, you may be able to lower the overall fees you pay.

While there are no set formats or absolutes for pricing real estate services, seven guidelines follow to assist you in determining what's fair.

How to Determine If the Fee Structure Is Really Fair

Let Seven Rules of Thumb Be Your Guide

There are seven rules of thumb to help you determine approximately what a service or task should cost you in fee-for-services real estate:

1. As seen previously, the level of service, level one or level two, can impact the fees you pay. For example, level two fees that require advocacy, negotiating, and representation from the consultant could be priced higher to compensate for a higher degree of skill and more liability on the consultant's behalf.
2. Expect to compensate the professional as you would others in equal standing in similarly related professions. For example, a real estate consultant would garner fees similar to those of a certified real estate appraiser or a CPA. In much the same way you'd pay a plumber or electrician for work provided to upgrade your house, likewise the real estate consultant would be compensated. While there are exceptions, this rule of thumb should prove helpful in gauging costs. Don't forget that you can apply annual income numbers to the three-step consultant's hourly fee approach seen previously to determine if what you're asked to pay seems fair.
3. Don't be penny-wise and pound-foolish as Ben Franklin said. It's dangerous to gravitate to the lowest-priced service just because it's cheapest. Instead, focus on the services that will provide the results you're looking for (i.e., quick sale, highest net proceeds, etc.). Consider any added value a consultant or company can provide as compared to the more cost-effective competition. As seen previously with discount real estate brokerages, a bargain-basement fee may entice you to do business with a

company only later to find that its focus is on volume, not meeting your individual needs.

4. Don't let the sum of the parts exceed the whole! In other words, don't defeat the financial savings of unbundled à la carte services only to later find that you've paid too much in individual fees and still haven't reached your desired end result. For example, as a seller you decide to pay X for a comparative market analysis (CMA), Y to rent signage, and Z to compensate the consultant for ten hours' worth of negotiating. Unless you initially tally up all of the services/tasks you need and their corresponding costs in advance, you won't be able to determine whether or not the unbundled package is cheaper than the whole "bundle," paid for via commission.

5. If you realize midstream that you need additional services that you haven't contracted to receive, renegotiate with the real estate consultant. You may be able to change to a different compensation model, limit the hourly fees in lieu of paying a contingency fee when the results are complete, etc. This can happen when you're too optimistic about the tasks you can perform on your own. For example, as a buyer, you contract with a consultant to provide up to five hours of work at $100 per hour for negotiating and paperwork with the for-sale-by-owner. It's successful, you're buoyant, ready to tackle the rest of the purchase. If you score well in the miniquizzes you'll find in Chapter 4, that's great. But if you score poorly or marginally at best, it could be more realistic to bite the bullet right now and negotiate with the consultant to take the sale all the way to a successful closing. As we cover in Chapters 5 and 6, the meat in the middle of the sale from the time negotiating occurs until the sale is closed is most critical to the success of the transaction.

If you find you need additional services from the consultant, there are a variety of ways you can compensate him for them. You might negotiate a reduced percentage fee, a flat fee, or an hourly fee with a cap. Or perhaps you could negotiate a rebate of the fee for services not required to close your sale (which we'll cover later in this chapter). See how fun it can be to access services and save money using various types of fees and pricing structures? The lesson is that even though reaching minor success in a purchase by paying à la carte fees is cost-effective and enticing, being unrealistic about the depth of help you need could churn minor fees into an albatross more costly than a hefty percentage commission.

6. Use the median cost projections for each checkpoint of the transaction to gauge what a service is worth. The six major phases or checkpoints that apply to sellers and buyers in real estate transactions are detailed in Chapters 3 and 4 and provide you with median cost projections if you were to complete each task yourself. While the median cost covers the average expense of completing the task (including $25 per hour compensation for your time), that amount is based on being capable, willing, and able to contribute the time it takes to complete the job. If this is not within the realm of possibility for you, compensating a consultant at two or more times the stated amount would be well in line with other professional fees you'd expect to pay.

7. Know the difference between contingent and noncontingent fees. A contingent fee is one received for a likely result, but not guaranteed. For example, you place your house on the market with a full-service real estate broker and agree to pay a contingent fee if the house sells. While it's hopeful that the house will sell at the terms and conditions you specify, a sale (the result) is not guaranteed. If a sale does occur, you would pay the broker his percentage commission out of your proceeds at closing. With the contingent fee model of the past, the real estate broker and his agents bore the majority of risk and costs up front in the hope that a house would sell. Because of this, many consumers felt little power or need to negotiate lower percentage fees with brokers in the past. Until

the property sold (if ever), it would cost the consumer nothing.

By contrast, a noncontingent fee compensates for work where an outcome is assured. For example, you hire a consultant to prepare a comparative market analysis (CMA) on a house you want to purchase. He performs the work and you pay his fee. Even though you may not like the market range of the property as indicated by the CMA, an outcome (a value) is determined. As you'll see in the fee structure information that follows, you can use a retainer with either contingent or noncontingent fee arrangements. Understanding the difference between contingent and noncontingent fees can lend creativity to what you pay and how you compensate a professional or service provider.

I am finding a growing number of buyers asking for reduced fees in exchange for them going out and finding the properties they want to see, then calling me when they are ready to view the inside of the property. This is actually the way most of my buyers work, but more are now asking for a fee reduction because they are doing this part of my job for me.

> Chris Newell, ABR, CRES, RMM
> Real estate consultant
> Milton, Ontario, Canada

Consumer-Designed, Consumer-Driven Compensation Models

One Size No Longer Fits All

What type of payment options could you negotiate in a fee-for-services arrangement? And what are some ways you could most efficiently negotiate to partner with the consultant in order to reduce the amount of fees you pay?

Only your imagination and what you can aptly negotiate with the service provider or consultant restrict you. Consumers are designing thought-provoking, unique ways to compensate fee-for-services professionals. And, conversely, professionals compensated by these new income models are reporting that, for the first time, they're being compensated in direct proportion to their expertise and the services they provide. Here are just a few of the many innovative approaches:

Percentage fee. You might think that the percentage commission would vanish when the traditional real estate model did, but it didn't. What remains, however, bears no resemblance to the typical traditional or range-of-market fees you could see when glancing at multiple listing service (MLS) listings. You can negotiate a percentage fee determined by the amount of participation by the consultant as well as what stage(s) of the transaction the consultant assists you in.

For example, if you hire a consultant midstream in the transaction you could consider that approximately 10 to 15 hours of work would remain. The fee percentage you'd pay would be equal to hourly compensation for a maximum of 15 hours. Let's say that your sales price was $100,000 and that the consultant's fee was $100 per hour. For 15 hours of his time, it would equal $1,500, or 1.5 percent of your sales price. The logical question is what difference does it make paying the consultant a flat or hourly fee compared to a percentage of the sales price? Perhaps not much. However, should you be forced to lower your price prior to closing (to cover work repairs, etc.), the consultant would share in the loss by receiving less in the percentage commission. If you desire to work with a professional who is in the midst of converting from traditional percentage sales to real estate consulting, she might initially feel more comfortable with this approach than another.

Could the consultant hesitate in working solely on a percentage fee and being paid at closing? Perhaps, because it goes back to the contingent-fee position of traditional real estate with fees being lost entirely should the transaction not close, not to mention the potential income lost from other projects she could have been working on during the time she spent with you. Providing an ample, nonrefundable retainer to the consultant and/

or agreeing to pay her hourly for X number of hours should the sale not close, could be ways to offset this concern.

Percentage fees can be used in tandem with flat fees as well. For example, if you're a seller who wants to control the majority of your marketing activities, like showing the house, you might save money by listing your house with a fee-for-services broker who charges only a modest flat fee to place your home in the multiple listing service (MLS). You also reserve the right to pay no additional fee if you sell the property on your own. If a buyer is found through a licensee in the MLS, then you'd agree to pay an additional fee (flat or percentage) to that agent. This approach combines exposing your property through the MLS with the ability to save money by doing your own marketing and perhaps locating a buyer for additional cost savings.

Percentage fees are often the way real estate service providers (particularly on the Web) are compensated. Many allow you to sign on to the service, which includes listing your property and choosing a professional to assist you, for a low fee or for no fee. Once the service is complete, you then pay a percentage of the sales price, or a predetermined flat fee. Check the Resources section at the end of this book for service providers in the various real estate categories in which you're interested.

Hourly fees. Hourly fees may be the way you feel most comfortable compensating your fee-for-services professional. This is particularly true if you're

- accustomed to paying professional fees for other service providers like attorneys or CPAs, or
- you are a professional yourself who charges professional fees, and/or
- you are a die-hard FSBO that balks at the thought of paying a percentage commission or other fee you feel is unjustified. Set against paying a percentage or flat fee commission, you might embrace having greater control over the sales process plus more feedback in working with a real

estate consultant on an hourly basis and progress through the sale in bite-size increments.

Hourly fees work well for buyers who are unassisted or otherwise need specialty information and help as well as for current homeowners. As you'll see in Chapter 6, many times a buyer needs input from an impartial third party who is not trying to sell contracting, landscaping, or other types of home-improvement services.

The two biggest questions about hourly fees are:

1. How can I make sure that the consultant puts in the amount of time I contract for?
2. How can I prevent against hourly fees adding up to or exceeding other commission types available?

Most consultants will be happy to log and annotate how each hour of their time was spent reaching results for you. Moreover, most have already estimated the approximate amount of time it takes to achieve median results for many real estate situations. They are happy to tell you about the tasks involved, the sequence, and the approximate amount of time each takes.

In order to keep hourly fees in check, I suggest that you protect yourself by capping the total number of hours you'll pay (i.e., up to a maximum of X dollars). If the fee does approach the cap and more time is required, negotiate initially with the consultant for the option to convert to a more cost-effective fee structure. Depending on the circumstances and time frame remaining, this could involve converting to a percentage fee or providing an additional contingency bonus once the results are reached.

Flat fee. This provides a safety net for you as the real estate consumer because you'll know the maximum amount you'll pay for a task or service. However, it does little to reward you for any work you contribute in assisting the consultant; and there is the potential that you could overpay the consultant if the task is completed quickly.

Let's say that the consultant quotes you a flat fee of $800 to protest the assessed value of your property to potentially lower your property taxes with the county. He states that he will report back during the next business day to let you know how things are proceeding.

He is glad to report the next day that he's successfully whittled $10,000 off the assessed value, producing a $500 drop in your property taxes. You're glad that he was successful, but a bit upset because you overpaid for his services because he spent so little time obtaining the results.

That's why a more cost-effective alternative could be the hourly fee with a flat-fee cap (as seen previously with hourly compensation). Additionally, you might want to consider the fair and cost-effective variation that follows.

*M*y advice would be to create your own scope of services, identifying what you need help on at each step in the homebuying/selling process. Tell the real estate professional that you will pay an appropriate hourly fee, say $100 per hour for professional time and $50 per hour for administrative tasks. Ask to see a time sheet and to inform you each time $500 is reached in new billings. Here's the key: make sure it's clear that you want the difference between the professional's total billing at the end of the contract and the respective listing or selling fee rebated to you. For example, as a buyer, let's say you only need 25 hours' help which equals $2,500 in professional fees. Against a selling agent's cooperating commission of $6,000, you'd receive a credit/rebate for $3,500 (if legal in your state).

Bill Wendel
Consumer advocate

Flat fee plus possible hourly fees and rebates. This is a unique combination of a flat fee that's whittled down by a predetermined hourly fee whenever the consumer assists the professional in performing the task. Conversely, the professional receives additional hourly compensation (up to a cap) for work provided that exceeds a predetermined amount of hours.

For example, you could assist with something minor like holding an open house or showing the property for a fee reduction, or provide a more major contribution like successfully negotiating price and terms with an unassisted buyer. The consultant isn't strapped performing activities that the consumer is capable of doing (emphasis on *capable*). Conversely, the consumer saves money and becomes a team player with the professional.

Obviously, the downside of this type of rewards system is the possible administration involved. It's important to assign a value for each task the consumer could be compensated for as well as that cap of additional fees (capped on an hourly or flat fee basis) attributable to the consultant. For the balance, it's best to work on the honor system using language in the fee-for-services agreement that defines what type of activities the rebate will and won't cover. As you'll see in the following section, rebates span a wide number of real estate fee activities for buyers and specialty real estate services.

Paying the lowest of several fee choices. For example, let's say that it's tough to determine exactly how long a consulting project may take to reach your objectives. Why not agree to pay the lowest of an hourly fee, flat fee, or percentage? The consultant is compensated for the amount of time/effort spent, and you're not overpaying!

Fixed costs versus variable costs. This approach works well if you need to access several types of service, some with fixed costs, others with variable. The consultant may charge you his fixed cost (his fee) and ask that you pay additionally for variable costs, like advertising used. As with all types of fee structures, it's best to have a detailed agreement regarding when payment is due as well as caps, even for the variable expenses.

Rebated fees. Rebates help create a win-win relationship for consumer and consultant. Although most commonly used with sellers, a buyer can receive a rebate for services not used (often creating a credit to the buyer at closing). In most cases, percentage fees or capped flat or capped hourly fees are initially quoted by the consultant. Any rebate would be a credit against any fee balance owed upon completion of the project.

Rebates are incentives for the consumer to contribute what he is capable of and willing to do and creates a team approach with the consultant. Likewise, consultants win in rebating fees because they are free to move on to other projects. Perhaps the biggest selling point that persuades a consultant to work in rebated fees is the repeat and referral business that it generates. Once a consumer has had the positive experience of being compensated for his efforts, he sings the praises of the consultant and the money he saved to others. Building business is effortless for the consultant who realizes that results require a team effort, one that should reward the consumer.

Any type of fee (percentage, flat, hourly, or combination) can have a rebating provision. The only caution lies in knowing the rules and regulations that govern real estate licensure and sales because some states prohibit rebates to consumers because they're deemed to be a type of fee-splitting arrangement with nonlicensed persons. In some states this is remedied by semantics where the rebate is called a "credit" to the consumer. In other words, not income received from commissions, but monies that were not necessary to close the transaction. The Resources section at the back of this book lists the contacts for the real estate licensing divisions in each state.

Whether you're receiving a rebate or a credit, most are determined by services not required or used and/or time frames.

For example, it's a hot market and you feel your house will sell quickly even though you want to list with a company that would have the potential to perform all of the selling tasks for you. So you negotiate that should the house sell in the first two weeks on the market, you'll be rebated 50 percent of the listing fee at closing. The company wins because its advertising has been minimized. You win because you've saved thousands of dollars!

Here are some other rebate variations to consider.

Hourly fee with percentage commission rebate for seller. A seller pays X dollars per hour to list his home with all or part of the listing commission side rebated. This is a good model for a seller who wants to participate by holding his own open houses, showing the property, and prescreening buyers. Alternatively, each task that's completed by the consultant is compensated when it's performed (billed by the consultant in agreed-upon intervals). This is also good for sellers who want to test the market with a certain price or terms because they're paying as they go and are committed to obtain feedback and answers especially if the price is too high or the terms unrealistic.

Hourly fee with percentage commission rebate for buyer. The buyer pays X dollars per hour with all or part of the selling side of the percentage commission rebated. Because a larger percentage of buyers work with percentage commission-based agents (because the seller usually pays the entire fee), this is a great way for the buyer to, in essence, bring less cash to closing or possibly even receive a check when purchasing the house! This approach works well when a buyer is prepared to purchase and well motivated to bring about a quick closing.

Teamwork/shared risk approach (retainer, hourly, and rebate). This unique approach allows consumers to share in the risk/reward of a selling or purchase transaction because they pay for services used during the process, but stand to win handsomely with rebated fees at closing.

The consumer pays a retainer to the consultant upon completion of a needs assessment and/or marketing plan to indicate her willingness to joint venture in the applicable purchase or sale. Depending on the real estate licensing laws of a state, the retainer could also be in compensation for the needs assessment performed (potentially sidestepping any state rules prohibiting the use of retainer fees). The balance of the fee is collected upon closing the sale (based on negotiating an hourly or flat fee charged for the actual number of hours expended by the brokerage/consultant, capped at a certain number). Any hours over the cap (if applicable) are to be approved by the consumer and billed at X dollars per hour. All or part of any percentage commission or other fee offered in the sale is rebated to the consumer. By spending several hundred dollars in hourly fees, the well-prepared, savvy consumer could stand to recoup thousands of dollars in rebates.

Retainer fees. In Chapter 8, we address retainer fees in depth. Not only do they help motivate the consultant to prioritize your project and move quickly to results, they also help motivate you to buy in to the process and become a stronger team player with the consultant.

The biggest concerns over retainers are several states' laws prohibiting consumers from paying them. Likewise, some states won't allow consumers to participate in rebated fees. While these laws were once put in place to protect consumers, they do nothing but tie our hands in this real estate climate. Greater flexibility needs to evolve in order to obtain and pay for the real estate services we need. As I'm known to remark, what the consumer wants, the consumer gets. Until this decade, real estate consumers didn't realize that they could increase the quality of a business relationship by using retainers. Or stand to save thousands through rebated commissions and fees. But now that consumers are willing to share the risk of real estate transactions, they should be able to participate in the financial rewards as well. If you live in one of the states where rebates and/or retainers are prohibited by law, listed in the Resources section at the back of this book, consider writing to your legislator and governor to repeal the law. You and countless others have nothing to lose and everything to gain.

Rebundling Services Could Bring Additional Cost Savings

Combinations to Provide What You Need, Paying What It's Worth

The various fee structures mentioned in this chapter pertained primarily to unbundled, à la carte services. But it's possible that once unbundled, you can group several services you need into a new bundle to save additional time and money.

For example, let's say that you're working with a real estate consultant who's assisting you in closing a purchase with a for-sale-by-owner. He's charging you a flat fee of $1,000. Before that transaction is closed, you find an investment property to purchase that's listed with a real estate broker who's offering a $2,500 flat fee to the selling agent. You negotiate with the consultant to lower his $1,000 fee to $500 because he will net $3,000 by helping you with both purchases.

Caution: Make Sure Rebundled Services Are in Your Best Interest

While you may be able to glean additional cost savings if individual services are rebundled, make sure that it's in your best interest to do so. In order to compete with other full-service brokerage companies, you might find a company rebundling services to lure you into a full-service, percentage fee commission. This is done under the guise of showing you that because you'd pay more with individual, unbundled real estate services, you might as well rebundle them and obtain full service. If this approach gets you results faster and more economically, that's great. Just make sure it's not a ploy to hook you into a longer-term, more expensive solution.

Compensation Issues Can Appear Problematic for Buyers

Clauses in Agreements Can Help

Because the traditional commission structure has always been viewed as a debit from the seller's proceeds, the real estate and lending industry struggles even today to allow buyers to pay various fees to obtain the professional assistance they need. The mortgage industry (particularly the secondary market where mortgages are sold to investors) can be a particular roadblock because they oppose financing fees into the loan package. When up against this roadblock, here's a clause I've found effective when placed in the purchase and sales agreement and thus authorized by the buyer and seller:

> All parties agree that included in the price being offered shall be a fee equal to _____ (i.e., *X* percent of the sales price) to be paid to the Buyer's Agent/Broker's Name at time of closing from the proceeds of the transaction provided by the Buyer and or lender, or other payment source of _____, and that the Buyer's Agent/Broker is receiving no compensation whatsoever from the listing brokerage.

As with any clause placed in a real estate agreement, it's wise to have legal counsel review it to make sure it fits your situation and objectives.

Additional Compensation Models on the Horizon

From Free Listings to Fees Paid to Consumers!

The sky is truly the limit when it comes to innovative approaches to structuring the services you need into affordable packages! One brokerage in Illinois is charging no fee for taking property listings. Instead, the seller pays $99 per hour for only the services needed and provided by the listing company. Additionally, the seller would pay selling compensation to the company that sells the property. The broker of this company bases his no listing fee on the fact that because he offers title insurance, mortgage loans, homeowners insurance, and other ancillary services through subsidiary companies, he's losing nothing by agreeing to take the listing for free.

A Canadian real estate brokerage recently announced it would pay consumers $500 for each listing. The company's rationale was that it was willing to pay to attract quality listings and would financially benefit by receiving a portion of the selling side of the transaction. If the past six months are any indication, a lot more marketing and unbundled services models will sprout in the months to come.

Now that You Know the Options, Where Do You Begin?

I hope this overview of the most common ways to structure payment plans for fee-for-services has sparked your gray matter. In application chapters for sellers, buyers, and specialty real estate applications, we'll provide more specific examples of how you can win big with various fee combinations.

However, as a rule of thumb, here's a compensation tip to keep in mind: Most long-term real estate tasks (duration of more than 30 daysv are most cost-effective if based on flat fees with caps, negotiated percentage commissions with rebates, or any combination thereof. Short- to moderate-term real estate tasks (less than 30 days) are most cost-effective if based on hourly fees, flat fees with caps, rebates, or any combination. In other words, the shorter the task, the more narrow the fee parameter (such as hourly). The longer and/or more risky the perceived task and/or where you have less control over the end result, you stand to benefit to a greater financial degree with fee caps, rebates, and risk-reward formulas.

I hope you're convinced that your imagination and your ability to aptly negotiate with the real estate consultant or service provider are the only restrictions to financial gain when it comes to à la carte, fee-for-services real estate!

3

The Seller's Fee-for-Services Road Map

*M*ahatma *Gandhi was once quoted, "I must hurry to catch up to my followers." Today it's the real estate industry that is hurrying to catch up to its consumers. For so long, real estate practitioners supported themselves on the percentage fees paid by the few sellers whose properties sell. The industry learned to justify those percentage fees by explaining that it performed all these services of which the seller was not aware, but "trust me" those services will cause your house to sell for more money.*

Today sellers are questioning those fees and asking what services could possibly cost that much. One attorney said, "I'd like to charge those kinds of fees. I just paid $15,000 and my house was only on the market for 24 hours!"

Marie Spodek, GRI, DREI
National real estate educator
Author of *Consumer Red Flags*,
Real Estate Education Company

The Seller's Road Map: Where to Go and What to Expect

The Six Seller's Checkpoints

You may be tempted to plant the for-sale sign in your yard, run an ad in the local penny-pincher newspaper and officially announce yourself to the world as a for-sale-by-owner (FSBO, pronounced "fizbo"). But unless you take the time to understand what happens during the sale, you may find yourself floundering as an unsuccessful FSBO, out of time, out of marketing money, without a sale in sight.

You'll remember from Chapter 1 that the seller's road map contains six distinct checkpoints to assist and guide you through the process.

1. Prepare/stage the property for sale
2. Gather property information/price the property
3. Market the property
4. Locate/prequalify the buyer
5. Draft the sales agreement/negotiate with the buyer
6. Troubleshoot the sale/close the transaction

Just as missing checkpoints in a road rally or race will cost you penalties or disqualification, skipping over checkpoints as a seller can be even more disastrous in the loss of thousands of dollars in equity, a sale that falls, or a lawsuit against you by a disgruntled buyer. And, as detailed in the section that follows, you can choose your own à la carte menu to navigate through each checkpoint. True to the new world of unbundled real estate services, one size no longer fits all and you get to choose what's most comfortable for you!

Use the Estimated Time Frames, Costs, Ratings, and Barometers as Guides

Using the barometers. Throughout this chapter, barometer graphics indicate the level or degree of participation. Minimum participation is shown by the 25 percent barometer, average participation by the 50 percent barometer, and above-average participation is represented by the 75 percent barometer for each phase/checkpoint in the sale. That way, if you decide to do only the minimum amount of activities specified (and they are the bare-bones minimum), you'd have an idea of what to expect (or not expect).

Checking time estimates. 🖊 It's important to note that the time estimates (symbolized by the clock face) are averages. These estimates are gathered from my experience and the experiences of 100 real estate consultants polled as part of my "Frugal HomeOwner®'s Consumer Assessment Survey." But as you'll see at the conclusion of each checkpoint, when sellers were asked to estimate the amount of time it would take for each component of the sale, their estimates were approximately 35 percent low! This points to the fact that while the seller's focus is on getting the house sold, the consultant or other real estate service provider often orchestrates the behind-the-scenes puzzle pieces of which the seller is often unaware.

It's also important to realize that time frames will vary based on several other important factors. These include the physical size of the property (e.g., square footage, lot size) and the type of problem you're tackling (from small problems like cleaning/sorting a closet to in-depth ones involving the structure, the plumbing, or the electrical system).

Additionally, you'll need to gauge time based on the degree of challenge you face in a particular situation. Patching a leaky roof takes several hours; but replacing an entire roof in the heat of summer seems to take an eternity!

Last, but certainly not least, you'll need to gauge the climate of the real estate market before it's possible to determine how long each checkpoint may take to accomplish. Activities in a seller's market could be radically accelerated, while the amount of time could double for the same activity in a buyer's market (as we'll cover in seller's checkpoint 3 on marketing the property).

Using cost estimates. 💲 Rough cost estimates (to achieve average results) are listed for each checkpoint (with the dollar sign symbol) to help you determine the approximate cost of your time and materials/supplies required. Using $25 per hour for each hour of time you'd spend on a task, it's two to six times less than what a professional would charge you to perform many jobs, especially those of a technical or highly specialized nature.

Pay attention to the checkpoint rating. [image] Because each component in the sale can, to some degree, make or break it, we've assigned each checkpoint a numerical rating (10 being the highest, 1 the lowest) to indicate the potential impact this checkpoint has on a successful sale. The number represents how likely this phase of the transaction is to interfere with achieving your goals of best price, timely sale, and the fewest number of headaches.

Seller Checkpoint 1: Prepare the Property for Sale

Depending on the condition of the real estate you own, preparing the property for sale (also called staging the property) may be the easiest piece of the selling puzzle or the most laborious. In good shape, a property might take only several hours to prepare for showing to prospective buyers. In dire condition, it could prove more financially viable to raze the house and sell only the bare lot or take a major price cut to spare the hundreds of hours and thousands of dollars to prepare the house for the market.

Curb appeal is vital. It's amazing how curb appeal (or the lack thereof) can impact prospective buyers. In a worst-case scenario, buyers may not want to venture inside a house that appears unkempt and is lackluster from the curb.

The good news is that much of the cleanup and yard work required to enhance curb appeal is relatively easy and inexpensive to do.

To best determine how to prioritize what needs to be done, walk across the street and view your property as a prospective buyer would. What do you see? Hedges and trees that need trimming? A screen door in need of repair? A positive first impression of the house is critical to attracting viable buyers, as well as the price, terms, and timely closing you're after.

Inside the house, clean is king! In prioritizing how best to prepare the inside of the house for sale, make cleaning a top priority. Prospective buyers will overlook many things, but a dirty house is not one of them. Their thinking is that if the seller doesn't even clean the house, what else (that they can't see) is wrong with it (like major problems including electrical or plumbing).

Begin with the kitchen and bathroom(s). When cleaning (and painting) start with the kitchen and bathroom(s) first where cleanliness is top priority to buyers. Making the porcelain gleam and the floors shine will do more to impress buyers than most any other type of sprucing up you can do. If time permits, clean the living room thoroughly as well. If buyers are very interested in your house, you can tell because they'll stay in your living room for an extended period of time. Make sure walls are spot-washed, your front door (inside and out) is free of fingerprints, and your living room flooring is vacuumed, mopped, or shampooed. The last thing you want is the prospective buyer's baby dragging his blanket across a grime-laden floor!

25%

Minimum requirements to prepare the property for sale (estimated time: 6 to 10 hours)

Outside:
- Remove debris
- Mow the lawn
- Clear a path to the front door (remove clutter from walkway)
- Scrub front door (inside and out)

Inside:
- Remove debris and clutter (newspapers, recycling, etc.)

- Remove any expensive or priceless items from view (jewelry, coin collections, etc.). Box these up and remove from the house, if possible
- Clear an easy walking pathway through the house
- Thoroughly clean the kitchen and dining area
- Thoroughly clean the bathroom
- Clean living room flooring and spot-clean walls
- Lightly clean the balance of the house
- Replace all burned out lightbulbs
- Repair major nonworking or unsafe components (like electrical wiring, furnace fan, etc.) or be prepared to compensate a buyer with lower price or other more favorable terms

Outcome seller could expect using minimum requirements:
- Radically fewer-than-normal showings (buyers may drive by but then not want to come in)
- Longer-than-median time on the market than similar homes (time could potentially double)
- Drastically lower-than-fair-market sales price and more costs to seller (could equate to the amount of time in hours and cost of supplies, materials, etc., required by a buyer to get the property in similar shape to other houses they've seen)

50% ⬤▬▬▬▬▭

Average requirements to prepare the property for sale (estimated time: 10 to 20 hours)

Outside:
- Remove debris
- Mow the lawn and trim hedges and trees, especially near walkways and front door
- Clean and/or repaint front door; replace torn screens on door and screens on windows in front
- Clean front step area

- Repair all unsightly and unsafe exterior components (like roof, fascia, siding), or otherwise be prepared to reflect buyer compensation by price or terms you're offering

Inside:
- Remove all debris (newspapers, recycling, etc.)
- Remove any expensive or priceless items from view (jewelry, coin collections, etc.). Box them up and remove from the house, if possible
- Deep-clean bathroom
- Deep-clean kitchen
- Deep-clean living room flooring and spot-clean walls
- Replace nonworking lightbulbs and fixtures
- If paint is worn or unsightly, repaint rooms in the following order of priority: kitchen, bathroom, living room, hallways, stairways, other rooms
- Repair major nonworking or unsafe components (like electrical wiring, furnace fan, etc.) or be prepared to compensate a buyer with lower price or other favorable terms
- Repair appliances (or be willing to reimburse buyer for cost of repair)
- Repair damaged surfaces (like countertops, flooring, paneling, etc.) or be prepared to compensate buyer with a lower price or other more favorable terms. When repairing, tackle areas in the following order: kitchen, bathroom, living room, hallways, stairways, other rooms (in priority of use frequency)

Outcome seller could expect using average requirements:
- Sale within the median marketing time
- Some possible negotiation/softening on price (depending on the market and the item for which compensation is sought)
- Buyer requests seller make or pay for work repairs

75% ⬤━━━━━━━

Above-average requirements to prepare the property for sale (estimated time: 20+ hours)

Outside:
- Remove debris
- Mow the lawn and trim hedges and trees; clean out any unsightly/distracting flower beds (plant brightly colored new ones at the front of the house, weather permitting)
- Repair any cracks in walkway, paving in driveway
- Paint trim and any other unsightly or worn paint (especially at front of house and on all eaves)
- Clean and/or repaint front door; replace torn screens on windows and doors; replace any broken glass in windows
- Clean and repaint front step area
- Wash exterior windows; if exterior house surface appears dirty or has heavy cobwebs, etc., have it power-washed
- Repair unsightly and unsafe exterior components (like roof, fascia, siding, etc.)
- Repair or replace worn exterior components (like roof, siding, fencing, etc.) if it can be done cost-effectively given the price you're asking and how quickly you want the house to sell

Inside:
- Remove debris (like newspapers, recycling, etc.)
- Remove any expensive or priceless items from view (jewelry, coin collections, etc.). Box them up and remove from the house, if possible
- To best focus the buyer on the house (rather than on your possessions), remove approximately 60 percent of items from dressers and mantles (especially family photos and knickknacks)
- Deep-clean bathroom
- Deep-clean kitchen
- Deep-clean living room flooring and spot-clean walls

- Clean balance of house, focusing on areas where dirt is most visible (hallways, stairways, rooms receiving heaviest use)
- Replace nonworking lightbulbs and fixtures
- If paint is worn or unsightly, repaint rooms in the following order of priority: kitchen, bathroom, living room, hallways, other rooms
- Repair major nonworking or unsafe components (like electrical wiring, furnace fan, broken windows, etc.). A repair required on an otherwise-acceptable property may be used by the buyer as a negotiating tool to deeply discount the price or to make other contract demands
- Repair all appliances
- Do cosmetic and repair work on countertops, floors, and walls, tackling them in the following order: kitchen, bathroom, living room, hallways, stairways, other rooms
- Replace dated materials (wallpaper, flooring, countertops) if they would be distracting or unappealing to the buyer or require that the buyer be compensated at a greater cost than that of your replacement (use the same room priority as above)

Outcome seller could expect using above-average requirements:

- Quick sale (earlier than the median sales time in the marketplace)
- Having to show the home fewer times than required on the average
- More potentially motivated buyers, which could garner more offers to choose from and/or drive up your sales price
- Market-value sales price
- More favorable terms of sale (fewer contingencies, etc.)

Potential impact preparing the property for sale has on a best price, timely sale, and few hassles: 6

 Cost for average results: Between $800 and $1,000+, depending on repairs to be made

 Average amount of time for average results: 20 hours
Average amount of time sellers estimated this component would take: 16 hours

Seller Checkpoint 2:
Gather Property Information/Price the Property

If time is at a premium, this is one checkpoint in which doing a thorough job is in your best interest. Not only does it contain the highest possibility for errors, it bears the highest liability for you with buyers, meaning a greater potential for being sued!

Information about the property. Unlike putting a dab of shine and polish on the house for curb appeal, the information gathered about the property and determining the market value of the property must be done methodically and thoroughly. That's why you'll find more minimum requirements in this category than in any others. As a guide, it's best to obtain a copy of a real estate agent's listing agreement to gather information (or use the property fact sheet found in Figure 3.1). It will help you be thorough and the completed form can serve as a prospective buyer's information sheet.

The legal description (what you are selling). Besides a street address, you'll need the legal description for the property. This can be found on your annual property tax assessment notice, on a previous title report for the property, or by

Figure 3.1 Property Fact Sheet

MECHANICAL SYSTEMS

HEATING

Age, condition, and operation of main system _____

_____

Thermostat(s) _____

_____

Room-by-room heating _____

_____

COOLING

Age, condition, and operation of main system _____

_____

Thermostat(s) _____

_____

Room-by-room cooling _____

_____

ELECTRICAL

Adequacy of service _____

_____

Light switches _____
Doorbells _____
Exterior lighting _____

PLUMBING

Overall _____
Water heater _____

WASTE (SEW ERS OR SEPTIC)

Flush toilets _____
Consult owners on condition ____
_____

Obtain service record _____

APPLIANCES

Range _____
Oven (all controls) _____

_____

Dishwasher (run full cycle) ____

_____

Refrigerator/Freezer _____

_____

Compactor_____
Disposal _____
Washing machine _____
Dryer _____
Other _____

_____

INTERIOR SPACES

WALLS, CEILINGS, AND FLOORS

Overall condition _____
Water stains _____
Cracks _____
Settlement _____
Decay _____

BASEMENT AND CRAWL SPACES

Walls _____

_____

Floor _____

_____

Water penetration _____

_____

KITCHEN

Cabinets _____
Countertop _____
Floor _____

_____

Figure 3.1   Property Fact Sheet (Continued)

BATHROOMS	EXTERIOR CONDITIONS
Toilets (tank and operation) _____	Roof _____
_____	Floor _____
_____	Windows/Doors _____
Floor (around tub, shower, and toi-	_____
let) _____	Steps and stairs_____
_____	_____
_____	Decks/Porches
Shower (check controls) _____	_____
_____	_____
Tub (check controls) _____	Pools and accessories_____
_____	_____
Tile _____	Sprinkler _____
GARAGE	Landscaping _____
Doors_____	_____
Floor _____	Drainage _____
Walls _____	_____
	_____

calling your county assessor/recorder's office or a title insurance company in your county.

Square footage of the house. A recent homebuyer survey reports that 71 percent of buyers state that receiving the most house for their money is very important when they purchase. That's why one of the first questions a prospect may ask is, "What's the square footage of the house?" In most real estate markets, the square footage is calculated by measuring the outside dimensions of the house (width × length = total square feet), but be careful not to include any footage that's not actually living space (like the garage or an attic too short to stand in). Take care in calculating split-level and multilevel square footage because the configuration (and size) of each floor could vary. Drawing a floor plan on paper helps you visualize and calculate square footage if your home is unique in design.

Floor plan and room configuration. Buyers always want to know the number of bedrooms and baths, whether the house has a family room/den and office, and the type and size of garage (if any). Often, as with elderly buyers, the location of a room (like a main-floor bedroom) is important. Be sure to make prospective buyers aware (at initial contact) of any room or feature that's larger or more unique than found in most homes. For example, if your master bedroom is a spacious 40 feet by 30 feet with its own separate deck, hot tub, and reading alcove, be sure to emphasize it (especially to baby boomers who rate a master bedroom suite high on their list of priorities).

Other improvements (storage sheds, hot tubs, fencing, etc.). You might not have purchased the house solely because of the handyman workshop, but if it's an added-value feature, make sure to highlight it on your information sheet.

Pricing the property. It's vital to remember that the price you can get from a ready, willing, and able buyer has nothing to do with what you paid for the house, what you still owe the lender on your mortgage, or how much you've spent on improving it. Market value is determined by what properties with similar amenities in neighborhoods similar to yours have sold for recently (usually within the last six months).

To calculate an estimate of what your property is worth, you need to complete a comparative market analysis or CMA (see the example in Figure 3.2). A CMA rates how your property stacks up against other properties similar to yours that sold recently. As you can see by the form, the market value of your home is determined by adding or subtracting the value of amenities from the sale prices of comparable properties. If your home has an amenity not found in the comparable sale, you'd subtract the value of the amenity from what that house sold for (because it lacked the feature your house has).

You can obtain a CMA in several ways. Information is available from real estate agents who take listings and participate in the local multiple listing service (MLS). The agent may not

Figure 3.2 Comparative Market Analysis

EWM
Esslinger • Wooten • Maxwell
Realtors®
Competitive Market Analysis

Associate ______________________

Office Phone ______________ After Hours Phone ______________

Date ______________

Comp #	Address	19___ Assessed Value	Bedrooms/ Baths/ Garage	Year Built	Lot Size	Date of Sale	Listing Price	Sale Price	Adjusted Square Foot Area	Price Per Square Foot	Features Adjustment + or -
	Subject Property										
						X	X	X		X	
	Recently Sold										
	Currently for Sale										

Only you can set the price for your property, but to aid you in your decision, we have researched the current real estate market and offer the above information for your review.
This is intended to be an estimate of value and not intended to create an Agency relationship.

Suggested Price Range $ ______________ **to $** ______________

charge you for this information or for preparing a CMA for you, but his motive is to convince you to list your house with him. That's why it can be more objective to hire an unbiased real estate consultant to prepare a CMA for you.

You can pay a real estate consultant to prepare a comparative market analysis for you, though in a handful of states, real estate licensing law prevents a licensee from taking a fee to prepare a CMA. Depending on the level of computerization used, it should take most consultants between one and two hours to prepare a fairly thorough CMA, plus the time it takes in visiting the property and consulting with you on the findings.

Estimates of market value can also be obtained online. Some service providers, like <www.experian.com> and <www.cs wonline.com>, charge between $15 and $30 to give you comparable sales information for your neighborhood. If going this route, be careful to note both the sales dates as well as the date the information was last updated. Without the most current sales information in a very active market, you could be shorting yourself out of thousands by pricing the house too low.

25%

Minimum requirements to gather property information and price the property
(estimated time: 10 to 12 hours)

- Obtain legal description and property tax information from courthouse or title company
- Measure square footage of house
- Complete property fact and amenities sheet or flier; add a picture of the house to the sheet/flier and make copies to distribute to prospective buyers
- Obtain a property disclosure form (if your state is one that requires sellers to complete and give it to prospective buyers). The form can be obtained from a real estate licensee or from the real estate licensing division in your state. The

locations for each state's licensing division can be found in the Resources section of this book.

- Compile information about your current homeowners insurance (premiums paid, exceptions to coverage, etc.). In parts of the country where insurance is tough to obtain (like Florida and California), it's often easier and more cost-effective if the buyer uses the same carrier.
- Price the property. Prepare a comparative market analysis from one or more of the sources listed at the beginning of this section.

Outcome seller could expect using minimum requirements:
- In a best-case scenario, the buyer won't find an error or omission in your information; or the one she finds won't be significant enough to mount a lawsuit against you
- Setting the price too high will slow down the marketing time or prevent the house from selling at all
- Setting the price too low sends off red flags to buyers, making them wonder why it's being offered so low
- Gathering insufficient or no information about your mortgage payoff and/or liens against your property that must be paid off at closing can result in less or no proceeds to you at closing

50% ⬛⬛⬛⬛⬜⬜

Average requirements to gather property information and price the property
(estimated time: 12 to 20 hours)

- Obtain legal description and property tax information (from courthouse or title company)
- Measure square footage of house
- Complete property fact and amenities sheet or flier; add a picture of the house to the sheet/flier and make copies to distribute to prospective buyers

- Obtain a property disclosure form (if your state is one that requires sellers to complete and give it to prospective buyers). The form can be obtained from a real estate licensee or from the real estate licensing division in your state. The locations for each state's licensing division can be found in the Resources section at the back of this book.
- Obtain payoff information about your mortgage from the lender. A toll-free number should be on your payment coupon or other documents from the lender. The lender may charge you $15 to $20 to obtain this information. Ask if the loan is assumable by another borrower, and if so, under what conditions.
- Check public records to determine if any liens or other legal actions are posted against the property (such as mechanic's liens for unpaid improvements or federal tax liens). A title company is a good source for this information.
- Compile information about your current homeowners insurance (premiums paid, exceptions to coverage, etc.). In parts of the country where insurance is tough to obtain (like Florida and California), it's often easier and more cost-effective if the buyer uses the same carrier.
- Price the property. Prepare a comparative market analysis from one or more of the sources listed in the introduction to this section.

Outcome seller could expect using average requirements:
- Sale within the median marketing time
- Some possible negotiations/softening on price if information gathered by seller proves to be inaccurate
- Searching for missing or additional information after the sale is in progress which could cause roadblocks in the sale and delay closing

75% ━━━━━━━━━━

Above-average requirements to gather property information and price the property
(estimated time: 20+ hours)

- Obtain legal description and property tax information (from courthouse or title company)
- Measure square footage of house
- Complete property fact and amenities sheet or flier; add a picture of the house to the sheet/flier and make copies to distribute to prospective buyers
- Obtain a property disclosure form (if your state is one that requires sellers to complete and give it to prospective buyers). The form can be obtained from a real estate licensee or from the real estate licensing division in your state. The locations for each state's licensing division can be found in the Resources section of this book.
- Obtain payoff information about your mortgage from the lender. A toll-free number should be on your payment coupon or other documents from the lender. The lender may charge you $15 to $20 to obtain this information. Ask if the loan is assumable by another borrower; and if so, under what conditions.
- Check public records to determine if any liens or other legal actions are posted against the property (such as mechanic's liens for unpaid improvements or federal tax liens). A title company is a good source for this information.
- Compile information about your current homeowners insurance (premiums paid, exceptions to coverage, etc.). In parts of the country where insurance is tough to obtain (like Florida and California), it's often easier and more cost-effective if the buyer uses the same carrier.
- Obtain a copy of the conditions, covenants, and restrictions (if applicable) for the property. A title company is a good source for this information.

- Obtain a copy of the plat map or subdivision map for your property. Boundary lines or property measurements in question may require the property to be surveyed.
- If rural property, find information about any water rights or shares of water district stock that would transfer with the property (especially important if the property is farmed or animals are raised)
- Locate operating manuals and warranties (if applicable) for heating system, improvements like pools and hot tubs, and appliances
- Price the property. Prepare a comparative market analysis from one or more of the sources listed in the introduction to this section and put the property on the market at a price no higher than what the market value indicates.

Outcome seller could expect using above-average requirements:
- Timely closing
- Average amount of closing costs to seller (because outside assistance with attorneys or other professionals is reduced)
- Greater than normal risk reduction against potential law suits over property information and disclosure

Potential impact this component has on best price, timely sale, and few hassles: 9

Cost for average results: Between $500 and $1,000+, depending on activities/assistance required (i.e., property survey, legal assistance to remove property liens, and how well you price the property)

Average amount of time for average results: 20 hours
Average amount of time sellers estimated this component would take: 14 hours

Seller Checkpoint 3: Market the Property

If you've done a good job pricing the property and gathering information about it, the marketing checkpoint should be far less tedious, and more fun, than the first two. Marketing includes determining your target (who is most likely to purchase the property), locating and placing a yard sign, and writing advertising/promotional pieces and placing them in the proper media locations to attract potential buyers.

There are, however, several important factors that can impact even the slickest marketing campaigns, such as the current type of real estate market and the economic climate at the time.

Is it a buyer's or a seller's market? It's vital that you know whether a buyer's or a seller's market prevails before you launch your marketing campaign. The features of a buyer's market include a glut of property on the market, lots of eager sellers, and fewer potential (or qualified) buyers. A seller's market (which has prevailed in most markets in our country for the past few years) includes a shortage of property on the market, lots of eager buyers, and fewer potential sellers. This means that sellers could potentially ask a higher price than they could in a buyer's market, with homes not on the market increasing in value as well.

A seller in a buyer's market may have to whittle down his price and entice buyers with incentives, like helping to pay their closing costs. A seller in a seller's market may be inundated with offers early in the marketing process, creating a potential problem (albeit one a seller would love to have) in deciding which one to take.

To determine the type of market you're currently facing, look back over the comparable properties used to determine the market value of the house. Did they appear to sell quickly and at or near list price? If so, it's probably a seller's market. But if selling times exceeded the median for your market area and buyers purchased homes at far less than the list price, it's probably a buyer's market.

The impact of the economic climate. Another important consideration when marketing your home is the status (positive or negative) of your local economy. If employers are creating new middle-income or better jobs and consumers are spending money, you're more likely to have a fair share of prospective buyers. If the local economy is stalled with only minimum-wage jobs available, your marketing time may take longer and/ or you may need to do some niche or specialty marketing to attract buyer/prospects who relocate from other areas.

The local economy definitely impacts the number of potential buyers you'll have based on the type of property you're selling. For example, if you're trying to sell a high-end home during a rocky economy, it may cost you more to mount out-of-area ads to attract the few buyers who could afford your home.

Consumers can save a tremendous amount in listing commissions by using an online option for selling a home. The Internet has allowed homesellers to take more control of the transaction through the use of Web-based tools and MLS exposure, therefore leveling the playing field with the traditional agent.

> David Clark, President and CEO
> Homebytes.com.

Determine your target market. Once you've determined the type of market and the condition of the local economy, it's time to determine who's most likely interested in your home. Because you can hit a target more precisely with a rifle than you can with a shotgun, having a detailed buyer profile of the type of prospect you're shooting for is vital.

You need to decide:

- Who would be most likely to purchase the house, an individual or a large family?

- What amount of annual income is necessary for the buyer to qualify for a mortgage? (We'll cover this in-depth in Seller Checkpoint 4.)
- Is the buyer likely to be currently living in the area or more likely relocating to the area?
- What type of buyer would the amenities of the house and the neighborhood appeal to?
- Based on the answers to the previous questions, what type of advertising campaign would best attract prospective buyers?

Look first to the Web for help. When it comes to marketing, it's exciting to be a seller today. The Internet has a plethora of no cost/low costs ways to market your home—everything from renting a yard sign to listing your house for free on dozens of Web sites. If you begin your marketing campaign online using the sites listed in the Resources section of this book, you're likely to save time and money, and more readily attract the type of buyer you're looking for.

25% ⬛▬▬▬▬

Minimum requirements to market the property
(estimated time: 4 to 6 hours)

- Profile the type of buyer you're looking for
- Make sure your property fact sheet/flier highlights the type of amenities this buyer looks for
- Place yard signage
- Place an ad in at least one publication that would target your profiled buyer

Outcome seller could expect using minimum requirements:
- A sales time longer than the market median
- Few qualified buyers, more browsers
- Discount of sales price due to attracting fewer buyers

50%

Average requirements to market the property
(estimated time: 6 to 15 hours)

- Profile the type of buyer you're looking for
- Make sure your property fact sheet/flier highlights the type of amenities this buyer looks for
- Place yard signage
- Place an ad in at least one publication that would target your profiled buyer
- Deliver your property fact sheet/flier to the occupants of the properties across the street, to both sides, and behind your property because purchasers are often recruited by other homeowners in the area
- Use the Resources section at the end of this book to locate no-cost marketing tools to assist you (online and off)

Outcome seller could expect using average requirements:
- A sale in the median time for the market
- Selling price close to market value
- Some concessions to buyer because fewer-than-normal multiple offers occur

75%

Above-average requirements to market the property
(estimated time: 15+ hours)

- Profile the type of buyer you're looking for
- Make sure your property fact sheet/flier highlights the type of amenities this buyer looks for
- Place yard signage
- Place an ad in at least one publication that would target your profiled buyer
- Deliver your property fact sheet/flier to the occupants of the properties across the street, to both sides, and behind

your property because purchasers are often recruited by other homeowners in the area
- Use the Resources section at the end of this book to locate no-cost marketing tools to assist you (online and off)
- Place your property information in one or more of the FSBO sites online (they may charge for this service)

Outcome seller could expect using above-average requirements:
- Quicker sales time than median for market (equating to less cost for marketing)
- Sales price at market value or higher
- More buyers than usual, creating multiple offers from which to choose
- Backup offers taken should initial buyer wash out

 Potential impact this component has on best price, timely sale, and few hassles: 5

 Cost for average results: $500+, depending on the amount of marketing expenses required

 Average amount of time for average results: 15 hours
Average amount of time sellers estimated this component would take: 6 hours

---

Seller Checkpoint 4: Locate/Prequalify the Buyer

Your marketing plan is under way and it's attracting prospective buyers. Your job is to make sure they're qualified to purchase your property (financially and motivationally), being careful not to do so in a manner that could irritate or alienate them. The good news is that there are myriad approaches and tools available to you to make sure you spend time working only with qualified buyers.

Information you need to obtain about the prospect. The phone rings and a prospect announces that she'd like to see your house in one hour. What should you do? Common sense dictates that you first gather some information about the buyer and her circumstances before agreeing to the appointment. You need to keep in mind that although you're anxious to show the house, until you pose several questions you have no idea if this person is a serious buyer or someone merely wanting to case your house for a future burglary. A viable buyer will understand that being cautious when working with a stranger is acceptable in today's society.

While it's not important to gather all of the following information, obtaining as many answers as you can is in your best interest. Ask the prospect:

- *What's your name and phone number?* You can promise not to contact her again if you find she's not interested in the house. But obtaining a name and number should be a minimum requirement before allowing anyone to enter your home.
- *Have you been preapproved for a loan?* Just as a conscientious real estate consultant would never start showing homes to buyers before knowing what they could afford, make sure the prospect knows that it's common practice for buyers to be preapproved for a loan before shopping for a house. Preapproved means that barring any change in the buyer's financial picture, the lender has qualified her for *X* amount of mortgage at a maximum interest rate of *Y.* If she has been preapproved, the lender can give her a letter of preapproval that you can ask to see.
- *How long have you been looking for a home?* This can help you gauge how motivated she is as well as any time frames she needs to meet. The prospect might say that she's relocating to town for her job and has only six weeks

to do it. That indicates both a strong motivation and a quick time frame to purchase. Conversely, someone who's been looking for four years and doesn't want to move until school is out next spring might not have the motivation it takes to give you a competitive offer or be able to close in your time frame.

- *What's most important to you in a house?* This is a great way to determine her hot buttons and showcase how your house can fulfill her needs. During the showing, be sure to reemphasize the information she shared with you in the initial conversation.

Showing the property to prospects. Just as you employed caution in prescreening prospective buyers, use the same caution when showing the house. The following are suggestions that can move the showing along in a timely and safe manner:

- *Never show the house without first prescreening the buyer and setting an appointment.* If a prospect sees your sign and walks up to the door, ask him the prescreening questions before he enters the house. The several minutes it takes should not be a problem if he's serious about viewing the house.
- *Never show the house alone.* Make sure someone else is home even if she doesn't accompany you on the showing. Alone in the house, an unscrupulous buyer team could ask you to show one of them the backyard, while the other ransacks the bedroom for jewelry or other valuables.
- *Ask what the buyer likes and dislikes about the home as you escort him through the house.* Does it suit his needs? If so, take off your seller's hat and put on your salesman's! It's not merely enough to show the house, you must ABC (always be closing) the buyer on minor points in order to reach the major one—his commitment to purchase. As we'll see in greater depth in Checkpoint 5, ask questions like, "If I could answer all of your questions about the property and we could decide tentatively on terms of a

sale, is there any reason we couldn't write up a purchase contract today?" Asking prospects what they dislike about the house also gives you input on what you might need to repair or change to attract exactly the right buyer for the property.

- *Seek the proper information in order to answer a prospect's question.* Don't unnecessarily extend your liability by guessing at a fact or figure. Instead, tell the prospect you'll provide the information later. It's a good opportunity to restate how your house could suit the prospect's needs.
- *Follow up with interested prospects.* If someone is interested but not prepared to commit today, be sure to obtain his permission to follow up with him in the next day or two. It gives you a way to eliminate prospects who aren't interested (and didn't want to say so to your face) or reinforce benefits of the house to those who are potentially interested.

25%

Minimum requirements to locate/prequalify the buyer (estimated time: 4 to 6 hours)

- Show the property to buyers (even though no one else is home with you)
- Ask questions to close the buyer

Outcome seller could expect using minimum requirements:
- A sale taking longer than the median time for the market
- More prospects but fewer potential buyers to choose from (because you did not follow up with buyers)
- More showings equating to more of your time spent pre-screening and showing the house
- Higher marketing costs because the process will take longer

- Higher likelihood of negative outcome (property stolen from the house—or worse) due to showing the property without someone else in the house

50%

Average requirements to locate/prequalify the buyer
(estimated time: 6 to 10 hours)
[Note: Performing average-requirement activities could actually save time over those of the minimum because you'll work with more qualified buyers who have already been prequalified, which should cut time off your activities.]

- Prescreen all buyers before allowing them to view the house
- Show the property to prescreened buyers only when another person is home
- Ask buyers what they like and dislike about the home
- Ask closing questions to obtain an offer from a buyer

Outcome seller could expect using average requirements:
- Sale in median time for market
- Moderate number of showings
- Loss of possible buyers when questions not answered in a follow-up contact to prospects

75%

Above-average requirements to locate/prequalify the buyer
(estimated time: 10+ hours)

- Prescreen all buyers before allowing them to view the house
- Show the property to prescreened buyers only when another person is home
- Ask buyers what they like and dislike about the home
- Follow up with the prospect on questions he had

- Ask closing questions to obtain offers from multiple buyers to select the best one
- Follow up with interested prospects one day after they view the house

Outcome seller could expect using above-average requirements:
- Sale in less time than median for market
- Ability to choose the best offer from several buyers
- Least personal time spent prescreening prospects and showing the property
- Less marketing costs due to quicker sale

 Potential impact this component has on best price, timely sale, and few hassles: 5

 Cost for average results: $300+

 Average amount of time for average results: 10 hours
Average amount of time sellers estimated this component would take: 8 hours

---

Seller Checkpoint 5: Draft the Sales Agreement/ Negotiate with the Buyer

It finally happened. You got an offer. Now the fun really begins! While you may be tempted to jump at the first buyer to throw earnest money at you, don't. Sure, it might turn out to be your only offer, or it could be the first of many.

This checkpoint will help you gauge how many (if any) potential offers you might expect and how to evaluate offers you receive, all in the shortest time frame with the best results.

Should you take the offer? Absent psychic powers, you need to evaluate how many additional offers you could expect (and how long it could take) or whether the offer you're considering is perfect to accept as is and/or with changes you'd propose. There is a lot of information to sort out and decisions to make in an environment fraught with time pressures.

Here are the five steps to take when evaluating if the offer is suitable to accept:

1. Does it accomplish your major objectives? For example, if netting the most cash was your priority, does it accomplish this? Or if you wanted the quickest sale, can this buyer meet that requirement?
2. How long has the property been on the market? If today's the first day the sign hit the yard and the offer doesn't quite meet your objectives, counter back to the buyer with the changes you desire. He can only say no. And it's likely that if you have one offer the first day, more may follow. If no more offers come, you could return to the prospect making the original offer and see if he's still interested. Perhaps after contemplating your terms, he may decide to accept them.
3. How many showings and strong prospects have you had? If the property's been on the market a long time and this is the first offer you've had, you may need to bend a bit in meeting your objectives and take the offer.
4. Does the offer contain any contingencies that could not be removed in a timely manner? The last thing you want to do in the early stages of marketing the house is tie yourself up by taking an offer that doesn't have a strong possibility of closing in a timely fashion. If you do take the offer, it's wise to include a right of first refusal, allowing you to keep the property on the market and notifying the buyer if another acceptable offer comes in. The buyer then has X amount of time (predetermined between you and the buyer) to remove the contingency or forfeit the sale (with earnest money being refunded).

5. Before you accept an offer, be sure to complete a net sheet that estimates approximately what you'll be paying for closing costs, the amount required to pay off any outstanding mortgage(s), and any other costs anticipated (e.g., agreeing to pay discount points for the buyer). A sample net sheet is found in Figure 3.3.

*N*egotiating *a real estate transaction is the single most misunderstood step in the homeselling process. It's an area where consumers frequently lose money, and/or opportunity, by not hiring a professional to assist them. Pricing a home correctly and negotiating a transaction effectively are the two areas where consumers receive the greatest return on their investment when they receive advice from a competent real estate professional.*

Roger Turcotte, DREI, C-CREC
National real estate educator and negotiations specialist

Negotiating strategies to assist you. As with any sale or purchase, negotiating with the buyer must be focused on win-win results. That's why the following tips will help you anticipate what to do and how to do it.

When negotiating with the buyer, remember:

- You may want to win all the marbles, but that's unlikely to happen. Decide before negotiations begin what you want to win and what you're willing to lose.
- Never have just one last issue to negotiate because someone will win and someone will lose (and it might just be you!).
- Try to determine the buyer's hot buttons and make concessions on some or all of them. Contrary to popular belief, the buyer's biggest focus may not be getting the property for the cheapest price.
- Always place yourself emotionally in the buyer's shoes before responding to an offer (especially one you feel is insulting such as a ridiculously low offered price). When emotions replace pragmatism, you're likely to lose more than you gain.

Figure 3.3 Sample Net Sheet

Prepared for: _____ Address: _____

Prepared by: _____ Estimated Closing Date: _____

Selling price $ _____

Approximate Indebtedness

    First loan   @ _____% $ _____

    Second loan   @ _____% $ _____

    Other   @ _____% $ _____

Gross Equity $ _____

Seller's Estimated Costs

    Brokerage fee $ _____

    Title insurance policy (sale price) $ _____

    Long-term escrow set-up fee $ _____

    Escrow closing fee $ _____

    Mortgage discount $ _____

    Contract preparation $ _____

    Attorney fees $ _____

    Appraisal fee $ _____

    Interest to closing $ _____

    Property tax proration $ _____

    Payoff penalty $ _____

    Recording fees $ _____

    Reconveyance fee $ _____

    Required repairs $ _____

    City inspection $ _____

    Local Improvement District (LIDs) assessment $ _____

    Misc. $ _____

                                                            $ _____

    _____

If Income Property

    Prorated rents $ _____

    Security or cleaning deposits $ _____

Less Total Estimated Costs $ _____

Subtotal $ _____

Estimated credits

    Reserve account $ _____

                                                            $ _____

    _____

Plus Total Credits $ _____

Estimated Seller's Proceeds $ _____

Less Loan Carried by Seller $ _____

Estimated Net Cash Proceeds $ _____

Seller _____ Date _____

- The initial offer from a buyer sets the stage for what's to come. For example, if a buyer asks for everything in his first offer, you can expect him to be less than realistic when you deny a majority of his demands. Even though you're tempted to be just as demanding in return, it's doubtful that doing so will help you reach any reasonable end result with this prospect. Try going the extra mile and meeting him on more than 50 percent of his requests (if they don't damage your primary objectives). Hopefully, he'll see that you're being more than fair in making concessions and be willing to make some of his own to you.

25% ⬤━━━━━━━━

Minimum requirements for negotiating with the buyer (estimated time: 2 to 4 hours)

- Accepting the first offer that comes in (with little or no negotiating)

Outcome seller could expect using minimum requirements:
- A sale that takes longer than normal to close (if at all)
- Lower net proceeds than expected
- Negative impacts to seller (personal property sacrificed, etc.) because seller failed to weigh the pros and cons of the offer
- More costs of sale (because little/no negotiating occurred with buyer)
- Buyer could ask seller to make additional concessions prior to closing (because seller didn't put up negotiating resistance before)

50%

Average requirements for negotiating with the buyer
(estimated time: 4 to 8 hours)

- Evaluating multiple offers (pros and cons) as they come in; making counteroffers on some, rejecting others
- Determining your net proceeds prior to any offer being accepted
- Caving in to buyer concessions that aren't in your best interest (in order to get the negotiating process over with)

Outcome seller could expect using average requirements:
- Closing sale in average period of time
- Some shortfall in net proceeds due to concessions made to appease buyer
- An average number of glitches to troubleshoot prior to closing

75%

Above-average requirements for negotiating with the buyer
(estimated time: 8+ hours)

- Evaluating multiple offers (pros and cons) as they come in; making counteroffers on some, rejecting others
- Making concessions to buyer only on items that don't impact achieving your primary end result/focus (e.g., highest net proceeds, quickest closing time, etc.)
- Determining your net proceeds prior to accepting any offer
- Taking backup offers should the buyer in first position fail to close the purchase
- Asking buyer to clarify with the lender as soon as possible any loan costs you'll be responsible for paying at closing

Outcome seller could expect using above-average requirements:

- Quicker-than-average closing
- Higher net proceeds
- Fewer closing costs
- Safety net with backup buyers

 Potential impact this component has on best price, timely sale, and few hassles: 9

 Cost for average results: $1,200+ (based on leaving at least $1,000 on the table due to negotiating without a third party)

 Average amount of time for average results: 8 hours
Average amount of time sellers estimated this component would take: 4 hours

---

Seller Checkpoint 6:
Troubleshoot the Sale/Close the Transaction

The good news is that you're rounding the bend on closing the sale. The caution is that this particular bend is responsible for many a fatal crash on the transaction highway! Falter here and you stand to lose it all—the time, the buyer, and the sales proceeds. And as a sneak preview to how important this checkpoint is, it's the only one out of the six to garner a 10 rating! So open strong lines of communication with the buyer and other parties to the sale. The finish line is just around the corner!

Respond quickly to remedy problems. Troubleshooting the sale (especially holding it together) requires you to respond quickly to remedy problems and promptly meet the time frames you're given. For example, it's important to coordinate activities with players to the transaction (like the appraiser, the home inspector, etc.), remembering that until they complete their respective tasks, the closing won't occur.

Constantly monitor the progress of the sale. When it relates to a real estate closing that's pending, silence is not necessarily good news! Don't assume that the buyer's financing is going smoothly because she hasn't called with information to the contrary. Or that the home inspector didn't find work repairs you'll need to handle before closing. You must be proactive, checking in with all parties to the transaction on a regular basis, especially the buyer. (In fact, doing so can tip you off that the buyer is having a deadly attack of buyer's remorse that could cause her to jump ship. Detected early, it might save the sale.)

Paper-trail the property walk-through before closing. Prior to closing, it's imperative that you accompany the buyer back through the property for a final walk-through. It's necessary for the buyer to see that, in fact, nothing has changed since last visiting/inspecting the house. It's also necessary for you to document (in writing) that the buyer accepts the property in its condition (as documented on the form). If she later claims that she didn't notice the sloping floor in the bathroom or the warped door in the laundry room, but they're itemized on the walk-through inspection report, you're in the clear.

Review your closing documents prior to signing. Unlike buyers who have one business day before closing (as prescribed by federal law) to review their closing documents, there is no such law protecting sellers. It's up to you to ask the closing agent (in advance) to extend the same courtesy to you that is extended to the buyer. If you have any questions about a closing cost or how one was determined/prorated, it gives you a chance to get the answer. This is especially important if you have agreed to pay some of the buyer's closing costs or discount points. The purchase agreement could be vaguely worded or interpreted erroneously by the buyer's lender regarding the amount for which you're responsible. By catching the error prior to the closing date, you can easily correct it. After the fact, you lose leverage and the problem is less likely to be remedied.

25%

Minimum requirements to troubleshoot the sale/ close the transaction
(estimated time: 4 to 6 hours)

- Respond to requests from buyer and any other parties involved in the transaction (appraiser, home inspector, etc.)
- Show up to sign the closing documents
- Hand off keys to buyer after you vacate the property

Outcome seller could expect using minimum requirements:
- Taking longer than average to close the sale
- Many more glitches to troubleshoot than normal
- More personal time spent troubleshooting sale
- Potentially lower net proceeds because more concessions may be required by seller

50%

Average requirements to troubleshoot the sale/ close the transaction
(estimated time: 6 to 10 hours)

- Make sure loan application, appraisal, and home inspection are completed in a timely manner
- Keep in touch periodically with all parties to the transaction
- Have the buyer complete the walk-through inspection prior to closing

- Hand off keys to property, garage door opener, etc., to buyer after you vacate the property

Outcome seller could expect using average requirements:
- Closing in a median period of time
- Potentially lower net proceeds because buyer may require additional incentive concessions to continue in the purchase if the closing drags on

75%

Above-average requirements to troubleshoot the sale/close the transaction
(estimated time: 10+ hours)

- Make sure loan application, appraisal, and home inspection are completed in a timely manner
- Keep in touch on a weekly basis with other parties to the transaction
- Have the buyer complete the final walk-through inspection in advance of closing; have buyer sign a statement agreeing that the house is in the same condition as when last viewed
- Ask to review your closing documents one day prior to closing; take extra time to ask all questions
- Ask to review your net proceeds' calculations one day prior to closing; take extra time to question any charges/prorations you don't thoroughly understand
- Prepare important documents (e.g., warranties, etc.) and other items (e.g., door keys, garage door opener, etc.) to hand off to buyer at closing (or upon your final move from property)
- Show up to sign closing documents; use this as last opportunity to ask questions before signing documents

Outcome seller could expect using above-average requirements:

- Closing in shorter time than market median
- Highest net proceeds
- Least possible roadblocks
- Able to follow through on your moving plans in a timely fashion with least headaches

---

 Potential impact this component has on best price, timely sale, and few hassles: 10

 Cost for average results: $250 to as much as the market value of the property if the sale fails due to inability to troubleshoot/close the sale!

 Average amount of time for average results: 10 hours
Average amount of time sellers estimated this component would take: 6 hours

---

What the Numbers and Ratings Mean for Sellers

As the facts and figures reflect in the synopsis found in Figure 3.4, real estate consultants polled felt it would take approximately 83 hours to sell a house. As previously mentioned, this reflects the fact that the consultant or other real estate service provider often orchestrates the behind-the-scenes puzzle pieces while the seller's focus is on getting the house sold. If you're the least bit concerned that you cannot tackle one or more of the selling components, it may be wise to enlist the assistance of a real estate consultant for that task prior to leaping headlong into the sale.

Figure 3.4   Homeseller's Road Map Synopsis

Six Seller Checkpoints:	Average Time*	Importance Rating**
1. Prepare the property for sale	20 hrs.	6
2. Gather property information/ price the property	20 hrs.	9
3. Market the property	15 hrs.	5
4. Locate/prequalify the buyer	10 hrs.	5
5. Draft the sales agreement/ negotiate with the buyer	8 hrs.	9
6. Troubleshoot the sale/close the transaction	10 hrs.	10
	83 hrs. time	7 average importance rating

(Scale of 1 lowest, 10 highest)
*Average time per task as estimated by 100 professional real estate consultants.
**Importance rating is the impact the component has on the seller in orchestrating a timely sale, at the best price, with the fewest hassles.
What the Numbers and Ratings Mean for Sellers

As the facts and figures reflect, real estate consultants estimate that it takes an average time of 83 hours from beginning to end to sell a house. When it comes to the impact each of the six checkpoints has on obtaining the best price in a timely fashion with the least hassles, the average rating for all tasks is a 7 in importance.

When it comes to the impact each of the six checkpoints has on obtaining the best price in a timely fashion with the least hassles, the average rating for all tasks is a 7 in importance.

In Chapter 5, we'll pinpoint how you can best apply this synopsis and road map information to trim even more off the cost of selling a house on your own and/or in tandem with real estate consultants and other fee-for-services providers.

Where Do You Need Help in the Sales Process and How Do You Know?

Use the Miniquizzes to Help You Decide

Hopefully this seller's road map has given you ample insight into what it takes to be a successful seller on your own. You may find it overwhelming, or feel fairly confident that you can handle the process by yourself. But because the stakes are high and the penalties for failure expensive and time-consuming, use the miniquizzes that follow to test your ability at each checkpoint of the sale. They'll help you determine which aspects of the sale you're likely to need help with and which ones you can tackle on your own. And don't worry. Unlike school days when taking every test was essential for passing, feel free to skip any of the quizzes that don't apply to your individual situation at this time. You can think of it as the adult equivalent to cutting class!

Should you/can you go it alone to sell your own property? Take the quiz for each seller checkpoint.

Seller Checkpoint 1:
Test Your Ability to Prepare the Property for Sale

YES NO

☐ ☐   1. I am prepared to spend the time necessary to deep-clean the house prior to putting it on the market.

☐ ☐   2. I am prepared to spend the time needed making necessary repairs inside and outside the house prior to putting it on the market.

☐ ☐   3. I understand the importance of curb appeal when attracting buyers and will spend the time, money, and effort it takes to get the lawn, shrubbery, walkways, and driveway in showing condition.

☐ ☐   4. I am prepared to paint any worn or peeling areas, especially in the kitchen, bathroom, and near the front door of the house.

☐ ☐   5. I will clear all clutter in the house, boxing up unnecessary items prior to placing the house on the market.

☐ ☐   6. I will make sure flooring in the kitchen, bathroom, and living room is spotless at all times when showing the house to prospective buyers.

If you answered yes to three or more questions, you have a better-than-average chance of being able to complete this homeselling phase on your own or with only a moderate degree of help. If you answered yes to less than three questions, you may need full-menu assistance on this part of the sale.

Seller Checkpoint 2:
Test Your Ability to Gather Property Information and Price the Property

YES NO

☐ ☐ 1. I will obtain a comparative market analysis (CMA) to help confirm the market value of the property.

☐ ☐ 2. I will obtain the legal description and property tax information from either the courthouse or title company.

☐ ☐ 3. I can gather and double-check property facts and amenities and complete the property information sheet for prospective buyers.

☐ ☐ 4. I can measure and calculate the square footage of the house and dimensions of the lot.

☐ ☐ 5. I can obtain and complete the property disclosure form and present and explain it to potential buyers (if required in your state).

☐ ☐ 6. I will gather all information regarding homeowners insurance, zoning regulations, and conditions, covenants, and restrictions to present to prospective buyers.

If you answered yes to three or more questions, you have a better-than-average chance of being able to complete this homeselling phase on your own or with only a moderate degree of help. If you answered yes to less than three questions, you may need full-menu assistance on this part of the sale.

Seller Checkpoint 3:
Test Your Ability to Market the Property

YES NO

☐ ☐ 1. I am Web savvy and will place information about the property on various no-cost/low-cost Web sites in order to attract buyers.

☐ ☐ 2. I am capable of writing advertising and placing it in various print and Web media.

☐ ☐ 3. I know the profile of the buyer most likely to purchase my house and will target all advertising (including signage) to attract him or her.

☐ ☐ 4. I'm aware of the market type (seller's or buyer's) and can structure my advertising to attract the best buyer prospects at this time.

☐ ☐ 5. I can design my property information fact sheet to address the most pressing needs of my target buyer.

☐ ☐ 6. I will deliver copies of my property information fact sheet to at least 20 homeowners across from, behind, and adjacent to my home to enlist their help in finding qualified buyers.

If you answered yes to three or more questions, you have a better-than-average chance of being able to complete this homeselling phase on your own or with only a moderate degree of help. If you answered yes to less than three questions, you may need full-menu assistance on this part of the sale.

Seller Checkpoint 4:
Test Your Ability to Locate and Prequalify the Buyer

YES NO

☐ ☐   1. I know the prescreening questions I will ask of all prospects before allowing them to make an appointment to see the house.

☐ ☐   2. I will never show the house without someone else being home.

☐ ☐   3. I understand the difference between a buyer being prequalified and preapproved and will allow only preapproved buyers to view the house.

☐ ☐   4. If a motivated buyer is not preapproved, I have conduits in place to assist him in becoming preapproved.

☐ ☐   5. I know the proper closing questions to ask prospects as they tour the house.

☐ ☐   6. I will follow up within 24 hours with each prospective buyer who views the house, asking what he liked and disliked about the house.

If you answered yes to three or more questions, you have a better-than-average chance of being able to complete this homeselling phase on your own or with only a moderate degree of help. If you answered yes to less than three questions, you may need full-menu assistance on this part of the sale.

Seller Checkpoint 5:
**Test Your Ability to Draft the Sales Agreement and
Negotiate with the Buyer**

YES NO

☐ ☐ 1. I will spend time understanding the property sales purchase agreement most commonly used in my locale and will be able to complete it to serve my best interests in any offer or counteroffer I receive.

☐ ☐ 2. I will design a negotiating strategy to prioritize what I want to win while allowing the buyer to win on issues of importance to him or her.

☐ ☐ 3. I am able to determine my costs of sale (including closing costs) prior to accepting any offer from the buyer.

☐ ☐ 4. I understand the procedures and legal ramifications of offers and counteroffers in real estate negotiating.

☐ ☐ 5. I understand various contingency clauses in purchase and sale agreements, including the ramifications they have on my bargaining position as a seller.

☐ ☐ 6. I consider myself a strong yet fair negotiator when it comes to financial matters.

If you answered yes to three or more questions, you have a better-than-average chance of being able to complete this homeselling phase on your own or with only a moderate degree of help. If you answered yes to less than three questions, you may need full-menu assistance on this part of the sale.

Seller Checkpoint 6:
**Test Your Ability to Troubleshoot the Sale and
Close the Transaction**

YES NO

☐ ☐   1. I understand and can describe the sequence of events in closing a real estate transaction and can effectively navigate each one on my own.

☐ ☐   2. I will prioritize the time and effort it takes to monitor the buyer's mortgage process, keep current on the progress of the closing with service providers, and be available to answer questions and troubleshoot the sale to closing.

☐ ☐   3. I know the approach to take, what to look for, and the documentation required when the buyer makes the walk-through inspection prior to closing.

☐ ☐   4. I am capable of reviewing and interpreting all closing documents on my own.

☐ ☐   5. I can calculate the approximate amount of net proceeds I'll receive at closing.

☐ ☐   6. If need be, I am capable of renegotiating any or all terms of the sale with the buyer prior to closing.

If you answered yes to three or more questions, you have a better-than-average chance of being able to complete this homeselling phase on your own or with only a moderate degree of help. If you answered yes to less than three questions, you may need full-menu assistance on this part of the sale.

4

The Buyer's Fee-for-Services Road Map

It's more important than ever for consumers to take the time to educate themselves in the steps involved in buying and selling real estate. Then they should put together an honest, ethical real estate service team that can help them sift through the information available and select the services they feel they need. A good real estate service team can help ensure the consumer does not get ripped off by unethical people in the business.

Patricia Boyd, CFS
Certified Finance Specialist
Author, *How to Buy & Sell Your Home without Getting Ripped Off!*, Dearborn

The Buyer's Road Map: Where to Go and What to Expect

The Six Buyer Checkpoints

You're all charged up and ready to buy a house on your own. Don't you dare preview properties, visit open houses, or heaven forbid, make an offer on anything until you've thoroughly reviewed this road map! Not following the checkpoints in proper order can result in loss of your earnest money or failing to qualify for the mortgage you need. Worse yet, you might pay thousands too much for a house, which compounded by mortgage interest over the life of the loan can drain tens of thousands from your pocket!

As seen in Chapter 1, the buyer's road map contains the following six checkpoints:

1. Design a purchase strategy
2. Be preapproved for a mortgage
3. Choose the neighborhood and the property
4. Check property information and pricing
5. Draft the purchase agreement/negotiate with the seller
6. Troubleshoot the purchase/close the transaction

We'll cover each in depth to convince you that thoroughly performing each checkpoint is imperative for negotiating the best price and terms for a house. This is particularly important if you're only marginally qualified for the house you want to purchase or are in a very hot seller's market where competing buyers are more dangerous than any seller!

Use the Estimated Time Frames, Costs, Ratings, and Barometers as Guides

Using the barometers. Throughout this chapter, barometer graphics indicate the level or degree of participation. Minimum participation is shown by the 25 percent barometer, average participation by the 50 percent barometer, and above-average participation is represented by the 75 percent barometer for each phase/checkpoint in the purchase. That way, if you decide to do only the minimum amount of activities specified (and they are the bare-bones minimum), you'd have an idea of what to expect (or not expect).

Checking time estimates. It's important to note that the time estimates (symbolized by the clock face) are averages. These estimates are gathered from my experience and the experiences of 100 real estate consultants polled as part of my "Frugal HomeOwner®'s Consumer Assessment Survey." But as you'll see at the conclusion of each checkpoint, when buyers were asked to estimate the amount of time it would take for each component of the purchase, their estimates were approximately 37 percent low! This points to the fact that while the buyer's focus is on making the offer and showing up at closing, the consultant or other real estate service provider often orchestrates the behind-the-scenes puzzle pieces of which the seller is often unaware.

Using cost estimates. $ Rough cost estimates (to achieve average results) are listed for each checkpoint (with the dollar sign symbol) to help you determine the approximate cost of your time and other resources. Using $25 per hour for each hour of time you'll spend completing a task, it's two to six times less of what a professional would charge you to perform many jobs, especially those of a technical or highly specialized nature. Even though you wouldn't expect to be compensated for time spent in the process of purchasing a home, knowing these costs can help you gauge if it makes more sense to use a consultant to facilitate and expedite the purchase for you.

Pay attention to the checkpoint rating. Because each component in the sale can, to some degree, make or break it, we've assigned each checkpoint a numerical rating (10 highest, 1 lowest) to indicate the potential impact this checkpoint has on creating a successful purchase. The number represents how likely this phase of the transaction is to interfere with the typical buyer's goals of best price and timely closing with the fewest number of headaches.

Buyer Checkpoint 1: Design a Purchase Strategy

Most first-time buyers have no idea the amount of detail, paperwork, and level of commitment it takes to purchase a house. It's estimated that you'll deal with approximately 40 or more people on your trek to home ownership. Many will make demands on your time, your money, and often, your patience!

That's why if you don't have a concrete, definitive plan to assist you in evaluating everything from your level of commitment as a homeowner to whether it might make more financial sense to keep renting for now, you'll find the process long and the road very rocky.

Are you ready to commit to home ownership? In order to be a successful homeowner you must be willing to sacrifice some of those gypsy feelings of freedom you get by moving often. Instead of leisurely weekends, you'll be stuck mowing the lawn and painting the eaves. Home ownership is a bit like nurturing a child (albeit one that doesn't talk back or require college tuition).

It's important to mentally commit to owning a home, in part because of the amount of time you'll spend in it. If you live in the home you select for the average time period of seven years, you will have spent more than 2,500 days in it! That's a considerable investment in time, effort, and money.

Parting with your hard-earned savings and income (again and again!). You may not have a problem shelling out thousands of dollars of your hard-earned savings for a down payment. And it may not even bother you to pay hundreds of dollars in closing costs. But, unfortunately, those up-front purchase costs are just the beginning.

You no longer have a landlord to call when the water heater is on the fritz. You'll be alone in the dead of night when the furnace gives up the ghost. And you won't see anyone coming to the rescue with a checkbook when the plumber says, "It took a few hours more than I thought to repair that leak!" And even if nothing breaks, there are still the annual costs of homeowners insurance and property taxes.

Emotional and financial commitment aside, there are times when purchasing a home may not be in your best financial interest.

Could it pay to keep renting? If you're relocated often, staying in an area for less than three years, and/or you face circumstances that may require you to sell quickly after purchasing, buying a home may not be the best financial move for you. As you can see when accessing one of the many online rent versus buy calculators (one of my favorite is at <www.homefair.com>, a small down payment coupled with a short holding period could require you to bring a check to closing when you sell the house. Even if you're sure you won't be moving or selling early on, using an online calculator will show you approximately what you stand to gain (or lose) compared to renting. By plugging information into the calculator about your income, the estimated time you'll keep the property, current rent you're paying, and your tax bracket, you'll have your own rent versus buy analysis in less than a minute. Just one of the many ways online real estate power tools empower you as a buyer.

25%

Minimum requirements to design a purchase strategy (estimated time: 1 to 4 hours)

- Determine if you're willing to remain at one location for a time and make long-term payment commitments on a mortgage, property taxes, insurance, and other costs of home ownership

Outcome buyer can expect using minimum requirements:
- Be willing to take a loss (or even bring a check to closing for a deficit) if selling shortly after purchasing
- Failure to use an online calculator to compare renting versus buying may cause you to realize too late that it's not in your best financial interest to have purchased at this time
- End up losing the house to foreclosure or bankruptcy due to the inability to manage and prioritize housing costs

50%

Average requirements to design a purchase strategy
(estimated time: 4 to 8 hours)

- Determine if you're willing to remain at one location for a time and make long-term payment commitments on a mortgage, property taxes, insurance, and other costs of home ownership
- Determine approximately how long you will keep the property (should retain until at least breaking even on the purchase)
- Use one of the many online rent versus buy calculators (named in the Resources section at the end of this book) to determine if it makes financial sense to purchase a home at this time
- Be willing to part with your hard-earned savings for the down payment, closing costs, and repair costs that occur

Outcome buyer can expect using average requirements:
- Reaching breakeven-plus by holding the property long enough to recoup purchasing costs
- Preserve/build credit rating by making timely mortgage payments
- Equity buildup over time, allowing owner to sell/purchase another property

75%

Above-average requirements to design a purchase strategy
(estimated time: 8+ hours)

- Determine if you're willing to remain at one location for a time and make long-term payment commitments on a mortgage, property taxes, insurance, and other costs of home ownership

- Determine approximately how long you will keep the property (should retain until at least breaking even on the purchase)
- Use one of the many online rent versus buy calculators (named in the Resources section at the end of this book) to determine if it makes financial sense to purchase a home at this time
- Be willing to part with your hard-earned savings for the down payment, closing costs, and repair costs that occur
- Be willing to use savings and/or income to make repairs on the house
- Understand how real estate ownership fits in your financial and investment strategy
- Are willing to follow the homebuying steps in the proper order (e.g., be preapproved for a mortgage before house hunting)
- Are willing to be patient through the time frame of days or months it takes to close the purchase

Outcome buyer can expect using above-average requirements:

- Reach breakeven-plus by holding the property long enough to recoup purchasing costs
- Preserve/build credit rating by making timely mortgage payments
- Equity buildup over time, allowing owner to sell/purchase another property
- Best opportunity for equity to contribute to overall financial picture

Potential impact this component has on best price, timely purchase, and few hassles: 5

 Cost for average results: Between $200 and the total of your entire down payment and closing costs, loss of good credit rating, etc., should you lose the house to mortgage default due to lack of homeowner preparedness

 Average amount of time for average results: 8 hours
Average amount of time buyers estimated this component would take: 5 hours

Buyer Checkpoint 2:
Be Preapproved for a Mortgage

Unless you've got a mattress (or bank account) with enough money in it to pay cash, being preapproved for a mortgage will be vital in securing the house (and loan) you need.

Prequalify versus preapproval. Prior to 1995, lenders used the term *prequalified* to refer to buyers who had been preliminarily qualified for a mortgage. In essence, it meant that the lender had taken a cursory look at how the buyer's income compared to his debts.

But today's version of the process, preapproval, goes much deeper. Most lenders will not only compare debts to income but will pull a mortgage credit report (one merged from at least two of the three credit-reporting agencies). It's a good idea for a prospective buyer to check his own credit prior to visiting the lender in case there are errors on the report that could stand in the way. Once preapproved, the buyer can obtain a letter or certificate from the lender, stating how much he can afford and at what maximum rate of interest. He's now able to put a strong financial foot forward to a seller.

The importance of preapproval. Preapproval is vital in order for a buyer to aptly compete with other buyers. Today's competitive market penalizes a buyer who has not prearranged for financing. Savvy sellers will ask if the buyer is preapproved not only when considering an offer but also when the prospect first views the home. All other things being equal, the prospect already preapproved for a mortgage has a much stronger chance of getting the nod from the seller.

Second, it can prove disastrous if you commit to purchase a house before knowing that you can obtain financing. Dire consequences like losing the earnest money deposit or even being sued by a seller can occur if financing isn't available and the purchase agreement fails to address it as a contingency.

The bottom line is prepare in advance of need when it comes to checking your credit prior to visiting the lender and being preapproved for a mortgage before you start the househunting process.

Pull information together before visiting the lender. The more prepared you are for your first visit to the lender, the easier the process should be. In Figure 4.1 you'll find a buyer's loan application checklist of the information required by the lender. And in Figure 4.2, there's a quick qualifying worksheet to help you gauge approximately what size mortgage you'll qualify for with a corresponding loan payment table in Figure 4.3. If you don't have access to all information prior to your first interview, provide it to the lender as soon as possible. One major reason the mortgage process bogs down is a buyer's failure to promptly deliver requested information.

Don't stop loan shopping when you find the lowest interest rate. Many buyers stop shopping for the best mortgage as soon as they locate an acceptable interest rate and discount points. But there's so much more that influences the cost-effectiveness (or lack thereof) in comparing mortgage products.

Ask the lender to calculate and print detailed cost comparisons for you. This will break down each closing cost for the loan programs you're considering so you can compare apples

Figure 4.1 Buyer's Loan Application Checklist

Personal Information
❏ Social Security number(s) including coborrower
❏ Former address(es) if less than two years at present address

Employment Information
❏ W-2s; personal tax returns with all schedules, most recent two years
❏ Name, address, and phone number of employer(s); also dates of employment and gross income
❏ Previous employer(s) and/or school attended if less than two years in current position
If self-employed:
❏ Personal federal income tax returns for past two years
❏ Business returns for the past two years plus most recent year-to-date profit and loss statement

Current Housing Expense Information
❏ Amount of rent/first mortgage payment (P&I)
❏ Name, address, and phone number of landlord (if applicable)
❏ Amount of any other finance payments
❏ Hazard insurance
❏ Real estate taxes
❏ Mortgage insurance
❏ Other (including condo fees, flood insurance, etc.)

Monthly Income
❏ Pay stubs (most recent 30-day period)
❏ Other regular income
❏ Rental income
❏ Retirement/Social Security
❏ Alimony/Child support (if you want it/them considered for the purpose of loan application)
❏ Commission income
❏ Investment interest/dividends
❏ Other

Figure 4.1 Buyer's Loan Application Checklist (Continued)

Monthly Obligations
❑ Auto loans/lease payments
❑ Revolving charge accounts (include account number and balance)
❑ Real estate loans (state the outstanding balance)
❑ Alimony/Child support
❑ Other

Assets
❑ Checking, savings, and investment account statements (most recent three months)
❑ Other certificate of deposit, bonds, etc.
❑ Real estate owned
❑ Vested interest in retirement fund (most recent statement)
❑ Automobile(s) owned (makes and years)
❑ Life insurance cash value
❑ Other

For New Construction (if available)
❑ Contract to build, plans, and specifications
❑ Purchase agreement with full address, including ZIP code
❑ Real estate agent's name, address and phone number (if applicable)
❑ Property information

Other Information (if applicable)
❑ Divorce, bankruptcy papers
❑ If relocating, copy of corporate relocation agreement

---

to apples in the cost department. Pay particular attention to any junk fees that are included. These are miscellaneous extra costs that can often be negotiated with the lender. They include amortization and payment schedules for the buyer and excessive document preparation fees and can vary widely between loan programs and lenders. You'll find a loan comparison worksheet in Figure 4.4.

Figure 4.2   Quick Qualifying Worksheet

	Column A	Column B
Annual gross income:	$ _____	
Divide by number of months:	÷ 12	
Monthly gross income (Record it in both columns. Perform operations only on figures in the same vertical column.):	= _____	= _____
Lenders allow 28% of monthly gross income for housing expenses.		× .28
Maximum monthly housing expense allowance (Colulmn B):		= _____
Lenders allow 36% of monthly gross income for long-term debt:	× .36	
Monthly expense allowance for long-term debt:	= _____	

Calculate your monthly long-term
obligations below:

Child support	$ _____	
Auto loan	+ _____	
Credit cards	+ _____	
Other	+ _____	
Other	+ _____	
Total long-term obligations	= _____	

	Column A	
Subtract total from your monthly expense allowance:	− _____	
Total monthly housing expense allowance:	= _____	
Look at the last amounts in Column A and B above. Record the smaller amount.	$ _____	
About 20% of the housing expense allowance is for taxes and insurance, leaving 80% for payment of mortgage (principal and interest):	× .80	
Allowance monthly principal and interest (PI) expense:	= _____	
Divide this amount by the appropriate monthly payment from Figure 4.3:	÷ _____	
	= _____	
Multiply by 1,000:	× 1,000	
Affordable mortgage amount (what the lender will lend):	$ _____	

Figure 4.3   Loan Payment Table

Monthly payment for each $1,000 borrowed

	Term of Loan		
Interest rate	15 years	20 years	30 years
6.00%	$ 8.44	$7.16	$6.00
6.50	8.71	7.46	6.32
7.00	8.99	7.75	6.65
7.50	9.27	8.06	6.99
8.00	9.56	8.36	7.34
8.50	9.58	8.68	7.69
9.00	10.14	9.00	8.05

Note: Chart represents principal and interest only.

This table helps you calculate your monthly housing costs (not including property taxes, insurance, and any mortgage insurance premium). Each amount represents the principal and interest cost for each $1,000 borrowed.

For example, if you're considering a $100,000, 30-year mortgage at 8 percent, you would multiply 100 × $7.34 = $734 per month principal and interest payment.

25%

Minimum requirements to be preapproved for a mortgage (estimated time: 5 to 6 hours)

- Meet with the lender for prequalification to determine how much house/mortgage you can afford

Outcome buyer can expect using minimum requirements:
- Offers that are never accepted by a seller due to failure to be preapproved for a loan

Figure 4.4 Loan Comparison Worksheet

	Conventional	FHA	VA	
		Loan Type		
Sale price	$_____	_____	_____	_____
Interest rate	$_____	_____	_____	_____
Down payment	$_____	_____	_____	_____
Total loan to be amortized	$_____	_____	_____	_____

Estimated Loan Costs

MIP (unless FHA included above)	$_____	_____	_____	_____
Loan origination fee	$_____	_____	_____	_____
Assumption fee	$_____	_____	_____	_____
Credit report	$_____	_____	_____	_____
Appraisal fee	$_____	_____	_____	_____
Recording fee	$_____	_____	_____	_____
Title (ALTA) policy (use loan amount)	$_____	_____	_____	_____
Attorney fee	$_____	_____	_____	_____
Escrow closing fee	$_____	_____	_____	_____
Interest proration	$_____	_____	_____	_____
Tax proration	$_____	_____	_____	_____
Fire and hazard insurance first year	$_____	_____	_____	_____
Lender's application fee	$_____	_____	_____	_____
Purchaser's buydown points	$_____	_____	_____	_____
Long-term escrow set-up fee	$_____	_____	_____	_____
Tax service fee	$_____	_____	_____	_____
Misc., LID, city code, reserves	$_____	_____	_____	_____
Home inspection fee	$_____	_____	_____	_____
Total estimated closing costs	$_____	_____	_____	_____

Reserves and Prorates

Property taxes (minimum two months)	$_____	_____	_____	_____
Fire and hazard insurance (minimum two months)	$_____	_____	_____	_____
Mortgage insurance	$_____	_____	_____	_____
Total reserves and prorates	$_____	_____	_____	_____
Total cash outlay	$_____	_____	_____	_____

Estimated Monthly Payment

Principal and interest	$_____	_____	_____	_____
Tax reserves	$_____	_____	_____	_____
Insurance reserves	$_____	_____	_____	_____
MIP insurance (unless FHA included above)	$_____	_____	_____	_____
Total estimated monthly payment	$_____	_____	_____	_____

The undersigned hereby acknowledges receipt of a copy of this estimation.

By _____ Signed _____ Date _____

- A loan that never closes due to failure to provide lender with all required documentation
- A loan closing that takes longer than the median amount of time

    [Note: even though the time you spend being prequalified is minimal, revisiting the lender for formal application in tandem with more troubleshooting throughout the process can more than double the time required.]

50%

Average requirements to be preapproved for a mortgage (estimated time: 6 to 8 hours)

- Be preapproved for a mortgage prior to viewing any properties
- Bring many of the required financial documents to first meeting with lender
- Ask lender to provide cost comparisons between the various mortgage programs under consideration
- Be prepared to write a check to the lender at time of application for credit report and appraisal fees (approximately $400 in most cases)
- Review the good faith estimate of closing costs provided by the lender

Outcome buyer can expect using average requirements:
- A loan that closes in the median amount of time
- A few more glitches than normal because all financial information not provided to lender initially
- Paying approximately the same amount in closing costs and fees as quoted on the good faith estimate

75% ⬤▬▬▬▬▬▬▬▬▬▬

Above-average requirements to be preapproved for a mortgage
(estimated time: 8+ hours)

- Be preapproved for a mortgage prior to viewing any properties
- Bring all required financial documents to first meeting with lender
- Ask lender to provide cost comparisons between the various mortgage programs under consideration
- Be prepared to write a check to the lender at time of application for credit report and appraisal fees (approximately $400 in most cases)
- Review in detail the good faith estimate of closing costs provided by the lender; ask the lender about any cost you don't understand
- Check your credit report prior to meeting with the lender; correct all errors
- Obtain the mortgage that best suits your overall financial picture and ownership time frames (e.g., savings with an adjustable rate mortgage because keeping loan and property only a short time, etc.)
- Ask the lender to explain any special requirements of the loan (e.g., prepayment penalty, etc.) that could cost you money downstream
- Respond promptly to lender requests for additional documentation, explanations, etc.
- Ask the lender to tell you your credit score number

With the onset of technology in the real estate industry, the buyer is empowered to be much more informed and educated and allowed to choose on an à la carte basis the services needed to assure a successful closing.

Sheri Moritz, C-CREC, Broker/Owner
Concept 2000 Realty, Inc.

Outcome buyer can expect using above-average requirements:

- A smooth mortgage process with a loan closing in the minimal amount of time
- Closing costs the same amount as quoted on good faith estimate from lender
- Long-term purchasing costs minimized because the most cost-effective mortgage was chosen
- No financial surprises later with the mortgage because special requirements and clauses (like prepayment penalties) were clarified before signing the mortgage

---

 Potential impact this component has on best price, timely purchase, and few hassles: 8

 Cost for average results: $550-plus (includes credit report and appraisal fees paid at time of loan application)

 Average amount of time for average results: 8 hours

Average amount of time buyers estimated this component would take: 5 hours

---

Buyer Checkpoint 3:
Choose the Neighborhood and the Property

While searching for a neighborhood and a house may be more fun than airing your financial picture to the lender, there's a lot more to it than meets the eye. Purchasing the wrong house or one in a neighborhood that's deteriorating can be a financial nightmare in the making. You may have to take a loss when selling or spend thousands of dollars in repairs to hold the house together. That's why doing your homework is important to maximize your investment now and for the future. There are four primary ways to gather information about the neighborhood and the house:

1. Driving around
2. Walking around
3. Asking around
4. Checking around

Information by driving around. If you've ever purchased a home, you know how important it is to take a long look at surrounding neighborhoods. By accessing the property by various routes, not just the main artery for traffic, you're likely to uncover neighborhoods and/or eyesores that instantly eliminate the house you're considering.

Of equal importance is checking the traffic flow close to the house. Be sure to monitor it at certain times of the day as well as at various days of the week. What appeared to be a quick entry and exit of a subdivision during the weekend could become a bottleneck for weekday commuters.

If you're in the car a lot, it's good to take test runs from the house to various places you typically visit, like the market, the soccer field, or the drugstore. There's nothing worse than realizing after you move in that your car is your true new home and the house merely a place you'll visit occasionally!

Information by walking around. Just as you did by driving around, compile information by walking around the neighborhood. At a minimum, stroll down your side of the street for several blocks and circle back behind the property you're considering for several blocks. On your walk, notice any noxious odors or loud noises (like barking dogs) as well as pride of ownership by other homeowners. Check the condition of the streets and sidewalks as well as street lighting. Poorly lit streets could cause higher crime in the area.

Information by asking around. After walking the neighborhood, talk to two or more of the neighbors. Ask them if they like the area, if they'd purchase there again, and what they'd like to change in the neighborhood. Most people will be happy to share (often vent) their feelings, and by asking more than one neighbor, you won't be swayed by someone who has an ax to grind or is otherwise biased.

It's a good idea to call the local planning and zoning department to inquire if any zoning changes are pending for the neighborhood. What appears to be a vacant house next door, could be rezoned to become a round-the-clock day care center tomorrow.

Information by checking around. It's often the least obvious problems that can have the greatest impact on the value of the property. That's why it's imperative to check the crime information for the neighborhood. Contact the information officer for the local police department. By providing the property address and cross streets closest to the property, the officer can give you an overview of the type and frequency of crime near the property. In addition, many police departments will come to the property to perform a safety check and provide suggestions for improving the safety and security in the home.

Even if you don't have children in school, be sure to check the scholastic reports and ratings for the schools applicable to the property. In addition to safety in the neighborhood, school ratings are of paramount importance to a majority of homeowners. Even though you may not care which school district and corresponding schools the house is located in, it can make a significant impact (either pro or con) when you're ready to sell. Check the Resources section at the end of this book for online resources to assist your school report search.

25%

Minimum requirements to choose the neighborhood and the property
(estimated time: 10 to 15 hours)

- Fall in love with the first house you see and not bother to check out the physical aspects of the property and the neighborhood; type, amount, and trends in crime; school district; or traffic flow

Outcome buyer can expect using minimum requirements:
- A house that's tough to secure financing for due to deteriorating neighborhood, etc.
- So many work requirements to get the house in shape that midtransaction the seller decides not to sell
- High crime in the neighborhood makes it impossible to feel safe in the home; spend hundreds of dollars on crime-detection devices and additional deadbolts and window locks
- Weak school scores and high crime in the neighborhood make the property difficult to resell
- Having to take a loss when you sell
    [Note: Even though you fall in love with the house immediately, it takes an extraordinary amount of time to troubleshoot the work repairs, renegotiate with the seller, and find suitable financing.]

50%

Average requirements to choose the neighborhood and the property
(estimated time: 15 to 25 hours)

- Home search launched without any specific pattern or checklist for prioritizing amenities desired
- Preview all properties you're interested in

- Drive around the neighborhood
- Check out the school ratings
- Contact the local police department to obtain latest crime statistics for the cross streets closest to the property

Outcome buyer can expect using average requirements:
- Closing in the median amount of time for the market
- Much time spent previewing properties because amenity priorities were not determined up front
- Uncover unpleasantries (e.g., a noisy handyman garage or barking dogs nearby) due to failure to walk around the neighborhood and ask the neighbors questions

75%

Above-average requirements to choose the neighborhood and the property
(estimated time: 25+ hours)

- Drive around the neighborhood
- Check out the school ratings
- Contact the local police department to obtain latest crime statistics for the cross streets closest to the property
- Begin home search online with several of the property listing sites found in the Resources section at the end of this book; decide which amenities you want in a house and use them as priorities in your search
- Register with several online sites to receive e-mail updates when new properties come on the market
- Preview three to five properties you're most interested in and take notes while touring
- Walk around the neighborhood
- Ask neighbors questions about the neighborhood
- Check the traffic patterns around the house during various times of the day and various days of the week

- Contact local planning and zoning department to determine if pending zoning changes will impact the property (or neighboring areas)

Outcome buyer can expect using above-average requirements:
- Happy years of home ownership in a safe and comfortable environment
- High resale potential due to strong schools and low neighborhood crime
- Highest possible appreciation over time due to positive neighborhood factors
- Large number of mortgage programs available to finance the house
  [Note: By taking a methodical approach using online and property preview techniques to prioritize the amenities you're looking for in a house, you can obtain above-average results in a shorter period of time than those generating minimal and average results.]

 Potential impact this component has on best price, timely purchase, and few hassles: 8

 Cost for average results: $625-plus

 Average amount of time for average results: 25 hours
Average amount of time buyers estimated this component would take: 15 hours

Buyer Checkpoint 4:
Check Property Information and Pricing

The adage "all that glitters is not gold" certainly applies when it comes to checking out property information and determining a fair price for the house you're considering. If time is at premium, this is one checkpoint where a thorough job can garner huge savings. Not being thorough can cost you through overpaying for a property, or failing to uncover structural or other severe problems can cost you thousands to repair.

Information about the property. You may feel overwhelmed in checking and double-checking facts and figures about the property, but done methodically, you'll be able to breeze through in record time (even though there are more minimum requirements in this category than in any other). As a guide, it's best to obtain a copy of a real estate agent's listing agreement (if available) to gather information (or use the form provided at Figure 3.1 in Chapter 3). While you should certainly check the seller's information/fact sheet on the property, it's important to do your own information gathering. Even in the best of situations, people make mistakes in measuring and compiling data. Gathering your own set of information will help to confirm or dispute the seller's information before moving forward with your purchase.

The legal description—what you are purchasing. Besides a street address, you need the complete legal description for the property. This can be found at the county assessor's/recorder's office or by calling a title company. The seller may show you the legal description on his tax assessment notice. But be advised, county officials make mistakes as well!

Square footage of the house. A recent homebuyer survey noted that 71 percent of buyers state that receiving the most house for their money is very important when they purchase. That's why one of your first questions to the seller may be,

"What's the square footage of the house?" In most real estate markets, the square footage is calculated by measuring the outside dimensions of the house (width × length = total square feet). But be careful not to include any footage that's not actually living space (e.g., the garage, an attic too low to stand in, etc.). Take care when calculating split-level and multilevel square footage because the configuration (and size) of each floor could vary. You may want to sketch a floor plan on paper to help you visualize and calculate square footage if the house you're considering is unique in design. If the seller built the house, the construction plans/blueprints can assist you as well.

Floor plan and room configuration. Buyers always want to know the number of bedrooms and baths, whether the house has a family room/den and office room, and the type and size of garage (if any). Often, as with elderly buyers, the location of a room (like a main-floor bedroom) is important. Take a tape measure because it may be important to you to have a bedroom large enough to accommodate your four-poster bed or to make sure the baby grand piano will make it through the front door.

Evaluate improvements on the property—good news or bad? You may gravitate to a house because of the Olympic-size swimming pool. But be sure to gather facts in order to make an informed decision before taking the plunge. How much does the pool cost to heat, clean, and maintain? Is there adequate fencing to prevent children from entering unattended? Improvements are just that—extras that can be great or an added burden depending on the time, effort, and money they require.

Pricing the property. It's vital to remember that the price you pay a seller for a property has nothing to do with what he paid for the house, what he still owes the lender on the mortgage(s), or how much he's spent improving it. Market value is determined by what a ready, willing, and able buyer has paid recently (usually within the last six months) for a property with similar amenities in neighborhoods similar to the one in which this house is located.

To calculate an estimate of what the property is worth, you need to complete a comparative market analysis or CMA. (See the example in Figure 3.2 in Chapter 3.) It rates how this property stacks up against other properties similar to it. The market value of the house is determined by adding or subtracting the value of amenities from the sale prices of comparable properties. If the house you're interested in has an amenity not found in the comparable sale, you'd subtract the value of the amenity from that house's selling price (because it lacked the feature present in the house you're considering).

You can obtain a CMA in several ways. Information is available from real estate agents who take listings and participate in the local multiple listing service. The agent may or may not charge you for preparing this CMA, but his motive is to convince you to purchase the house through him. This may be okay if he represents you and works with you as a buyer's agent and/or if his percentage commission fee is being paid by the seller. Absent that, it will be more objective to hire an unbiased real estate consultant to prepare a CMA for you. (Note that in a handful of states, real estate licensing law prevents a licensee from taking a fee to prepare a comparative market analysis.) Depending on the level of computerization used, it should take most consultants between one and two hours to prepare a fairly thorough CMA (plus the time it takes in visiting the property and consulting with you on the findings).

Estimates of market value can also be obtained online. Some service providers (like <www.experian.com> and <www .cswonline.com>) charge between $15 and $30 to give you comparable sales information for your neighborhood. If going this route, be careful to note both the sales dates and the date the information was last updated online. Without the most current sales information in a volatile market, you could overpay for a property (in a buyer's market) or underbid and lose another chance to obtain the property (in a seller's market).

25% ⬤━━━━━

Minimum requirements to check property information and pricing
(estimated time: 4 to 8 hours)

- Check legal description and property tax information (from courthouse or title company)
- Review (but not confirm) property facts and amenities as shown on information sheet provided by seller
- Obtain a property disclosure statement (if your state is one of the 30 or more that requires sellers to complete and present to prospective buyers). The form can be obtained from a real estate licensee or from the real estate licensing division in your state. (A list of the states requiring the disclosure as well as locations for each state's licensing division can be found in the Resources section at the end of this book.)

Outcome buyer can expect using minimum requirements:
- In a best-case scenario, find no errors or omissions in the seller's information, or find ones that are not significant enough to sue over
- Could overpay for the property due to failure to research the CMA or hire a real estate consultant to do it
- Could be denied a mortgage or have to renegotiate with the seller if the appraised value comes in lower than the offered price

50% ⬛⬛⬛⬛⬛⬜⬜

Average requirements to check property information and pricing

(estimated time: 8 to 10 hours)

- Check legal description and property tax information (from courthouse or title company)
- Double-check/confirm property facts and amenities as shown on information sheet provided by seller
- Obtain a property disclosure statement (if your state is one of the 30 or more that requires sellers to complete and present to prospective buyers). The form can be obtained from a real estate licensee or from the real estate licensing division in your state. (A list of the states requiring the disclosure as well as locations for each state's licensing division can be found in the Resources section at the end of this book.)
- Measure the square footage of the house
- Make purchase contingent upon receiving and reviewing a satisfactory home inspection report
- Obtain information about the seller's current homeowners insurance (premium paid, exceptions to coverage, etc.). In parts of the country where insurance is tough to obtain (like Florida and California), it's often easier/more cost-effective if the buyer uses the seller's current carrier.
- Prepare or have someone else prepare a CMA, from one or more of the sources listed at the beginning of this section

Outcome buyer can expect using average requirements:
- A closing within the median period of time
- Some possible negotiation/softening on price if information gathered by seller proves to be inaccurate
- Having to search out missing or additional information after the sale is in progress which can cause roadblocks in the sale and delay closing

75% ━━━━━━━━━

Above-average requirements to check property information and pricing
(estimated time: 10+ hours)

- Check legal description and property tax information (from courthouse or title company)
- Double-check/confirm property facts and amenities as shown on information sheet provided by seller
- Obtain a property disclosure statement (if your state is one of the 30 or more that requires sellers to complete and present to prospective buyers). The form can be obtained from a real estate licensee or from the real estate licensing division in your state. (A list of the states requiring the disclosure as well as locations for each state's licensing division can be found in the Resources section at the end of this book).
- Measure the square footage of the house
- Make purchase contingent upon receiving and reviewing a satisfactory home inspection report
- Obtain information about the seller's current homeowners insurance (premium paid, exceptions to coverage, etc.). In parts of the country where insurance is tough to obtain (like Florida and California), it's often easier/more cost-effective if the buyer uses the seller's current carrier.
- Prepare a CMA or hire a real estate consultant to prepare and interpret it using one or more of the sources listed at the beginning of this section.
- Obtain a copy of the conditions, covenants, and restrictions (if applicable) for the property; a title company is a good source for this information
- Obtain a copy of the plat map or subdivision map for your property (from title company or county zoning department); boundary lines or property measurements in question may require the property to be surveyed

- Check public records to determine if any liens or other legal actions are posted against the property (such as mechanic's liens for unpaid improvements, federal tax liens, etc.). Liens (unpaid debts that can attach to real estate in order to secure their eventual payment from the proceeds of the property) could cause purchasing problems and slow or prevent your purchase. A title company is a good source for this information.
- If rural property, find information about any water rights or shares of water district stock that would transfer with the property (especially important if the property is farmed or animals are raised)

Outcome buyer can expect using above-average requirements:

- Timely closing
- Fewer costs to buyer because outside assistance with attorneys or other professionals is kept to a minimum
- Greater assurance of property value because information has been confirmed
- Pay a fair price for the house because a consultant has prepared and interpreted the CMA

Successful real estate negotiating requires knowledge of and experience in the process; an awareness of current market conditions; and the self-discipline to stay focused on the desired outcome to avoid getting caught up in the emotion of the moment. Consumers may have knowledge of the process, and occasionally they may be aware of market conditions, but they cannot avoid letting their hearts dictate the decisions that should be made by their heads. This is where consumers must call upon the assistance of a trained professional.

Roger Turcotte, DREI, C-CREC
National real estate educator and negotiations specialist

Potential impact this component has on best price, timely purchase, and few hassles: 9

 Cost for average results: between $250 and $1,000-plus, depending on activities/assistance required (e.g., property survey, real estate consultant compiling/interpreting the CMA, and/ or overpaying for the property)

 Average amount of time for average results: 10 hours
Average amount of time buyers estimated this component would take: 8 hours

Buyer Checkpoint 5: Draft the Purchase Agreement/Negotiate with the Seller

You want to make every dollar count in the purchase of your home. And one way to make it happen is to employ sound negotiating tactics that make a difference between small cents and dynamic dollars.

Let's cover steps you can take to negotiate a fair price with sellers and not leave money on the table.

It's not necessarily about price. It's perceived that price is often a major concern with sellers. In fact, a common seller's lament is "We have to get our price because . . ." (I'm sure you can fill in the blank with statements you've heard).

But it's really not the highest price sellers are after. Moreover, it's the greatest net proceeds from the sale. *Net* is determined by subtracting the seller's closing costs and any outstanding loans, liens, and other financial encumbrances from the sales price. For example, you might lower your offered price by $2,000, but show the seller that by not having to pay discount points and heavy closing costs, she's actually netting more than she would with a full-price offer! Bottom line: It's the net amount of proceeds the seller walks away from the closing table with that count to most sellers.

Make your first offer count! A second way home buyers lose out when negotiating the purchase price is to make a low, often ridiculous first offer. Yes, I know, sellers sometimes do take less (even though it's done far less often in today's strong seller's market than in a buyer's market). Put yourself in the seller's position. How happy would you be to continue negotiations with a buyer who just insulted you and your property? First offers set the stage for all other negotiations that follow. In fact, the seller may become enraged and refuse to make any counteroffer. Or, if there is a counteroffer, the seller might turn the tables and insult you by asking for a price higher than the property's list price. (Yes, this does happen in a hot seller's market!) If you do make a lesser offer, be prepared to defend it by listing repairs that need to be made or other reasons for the lower offer. Sellers will be more willing to listen to a price cut if it's rational and fair.

Earnest money talks! It's true. Earnest money talks loud and clear. When evaluating two offers side by side, the one bearing the heftiest amount of earnest money/good faith deposit gives the perception that the buyer is more serious about the property and is perhaps a better financial risk (even if it isn't true!). This is an important tactic in a seller's market where many buyers are vying for relatively few properties with multiple offers to the seller simultaneously.

Negotiating strategies to assist you. When negotiating with the seller, remember:

- It's unlikely that you'll win everything from the lowest purchase price to the antique dining room table, so decide what you really want to win and what you're willing to give up.

- Never have just one last issue to negotiate because one person will win and one will lose. You want the seller to come out with at least one strong win. Otherwise, your offer may not be accepted.
- Try to determine the seller's hot buttons and make concessions on at least some of the items. Don't forget that there may be something more important to the seller than receiving the highest price for the property (e.g., a quick closing, limiting his costs of sale, etc.).
- Place yourself emotionally in the seller's shoes especially before making an offer or a counteroffer. It can help you frame a reasonable offer that best addresses the seller's needs while winning the property for yourself.

25%

**Minimum requirements to negotiate with the seller
(estimated time: 2 to 6+ hours)**

- Make a full-price offer to the seller (with little or no negotiating)

Outcome buyer can expect using minimum requirements:
- A purchase that takes longer than normal to close (if at all)
- Higher purchasing costs than anticipated (due to lack of negotiating)
- Negative consequences, like personal property the seller was willing to leave if the buyer had only negotiated for it
- Seller could ask buyer to make additional concessions prior to closing because buyer didn't put up negotiating resistance early in the transaction

50% ━━━━━━

Average requirements to negotiate with the seller
(estimated time: 4 to 6 hours)

- Outline various approaches to make in offers, weigh the pros and cons of each
- Determine your costs of purchase prior to making any offer to the seller
- Make concessions to seller in order to finish negotiating process

Outcome buyer can expect using average requirements:
- Closing the purchase in median period of time
- Caving in to seller concessions that aren't in your best interests
- Additional costs/expenses due to concessions made to appease seller
- Average number of glitches to troubleshoot prior to closing the purchase

75% ━━━━━━

Above-average requirements to negotiate with the seller
(estimated time: 8+ hours)

- Outline various approaches to make in offers, weigh the pros and cons of each
- Determine costs of purchase prior to any offer being made to the seller
- Make concessions to seller only on items that don't impact achieving primary end result (e.g., quick closing time, lowest purchasing costs, etc.)
- Ask the lender to clarify any loan costs payable at closing
- Look for other properties on the market in case the seller fails to close the sale

Outcome buyer can expect using above-average requirements:

- Quicker than average closing
- Paying fewer-than-average closing costs
- Fewer-than-normal glitches to troubleshoot
- Safety net with potential backup properties

 Potential impact this component has on best price, timely purchase, and few hassles: 9

 Cost for average results: between $1,200 and $10,000-plus based on how much money you leave on the negotiating table

 Average amount of time for average results: 8 hours
Average amount of time buyers estimated this component would take: 4 hours

---

Buyer Checkpoint 6: Troubleshoot Your Purchase/ Close the Transaction

After all the hard work of finding a house, checking information about the property, and applying for a mortgage, you may be tempted to coast through this phase of the purchase. But don't. You could stand to lose everything you've accomplished up to this point if you fail to concentrate on keeping the purchase together until closing.

Respond quickly to remedy problems. As in many business situations, once a problem surfaces in a real estate transaction it often gets worse before it gets better. That's why it's vital to respond quickly to requests from parties to the transaction (including the inspector, the seller, and the lender). Remember that until roadblocks are removed, there won't be a closing.

Monitor the progress of the sale (especially the mortgage process)! Don't assume that the mortgage is processing smoothly just because you hear nothing from the lender. No news is not necessarily good news where the loan process is concerned. If the lender isn't communicating with you, turn the tables and call him. When you do receive progress reports, pass them on to the seller. He'll appreciate the update and it's another opportunity to check his pulse to make sure his side of the sale is progressing as planned.

Complete the property walk-through prior to closing. You may not have been back in the house because your offer was accepted; or you may have visited every day. Either way, don't sidestep your final opportunity to inspect the house before closing. You need to make sure that nothing has dramatically changed that could impact the value of the house and/or your desire to purchase it.

What should you focus on? Everything! No matter the time of year, turn on the furnace, the air conditioner, and all appliances remaining with the house. Move area rugs out of the way in order to view flooring and swing pictures back to expose any holes in the walls that should be repaired. Turn on all plumbing (including outside water spigots). This is your last chance to make sure the property you're purchasing is in the same shape it was when your offer was accepted. It's also wise to document in writing that you accept the property in its condition or list items that need to be repaired before signing the closing documents.

Review all documents prior to closing. As a buyer, you are entitled under federal law to review all closing documents at least one business day prior to signing the closing papers.

This includes mortgage documents. Be aware of this legal right afforded to buyers and don't let an eager closing agent, mortgage company, or seller push you into signing until you've reviewed the paperwork and had your questions answered.

If the closing agent or lender can't or won't answer a question about what you're signing, it's best to seek legal counsel for interpretation. As perhaps the largest purchase you'll ever make, delaying a closing is a small price to pay for getting your questions answered in advance of final commitment.

25%

Minimum requirements to troubleshoot the purchase and close the transaction
(estimated time: 4 to 5 hours)

- Respond to requests from seller and any other parties involved in the transaction (home inspector, lender, etc.)
- Show up to sign the closing documents

Outcome buyer can expect using minimum requirements:
- Taking longer than average to close the purchase
- Many more glitches to troubleshoot than normal
- More personal time than normal spent troubleshooting the purchase
- Potentially higher purchasing costs because seller could require extra concessions if sale not closed by the target date on the purchase contract

50%

Average requirements to troubleshoot your purchase and close the transaction
(estimated time: 5 to 10 hours)

- Make sure mortgage loan, title insurance, and homeowners insurance are obtained in a timely manner
- Keep in touch periodically with all parties to the transaction

- Complete the walk-through inspection prior to closing
- Obtain keys to property, garage door opener, etc., from seller after he vacates the property

Outcome buyer can expect using average requirements:
- Closing in a median period of time for the marketplace
- Potentially higher purchasing costs because seller could require extra concessions if sale not closed by the target date on the purchase contract

75%

Above-average requirements to troubleshoot your purchase and close the transaction
(estimated time: 10+ hours)

- Make sure mortgage loan, title insurance, and homeowners insurance are obtained in a timely manner
- Keep in touch on a weekly basis with all parties to the transaction (especially seller and lender)
- Complete the walk-through inspection prior to closing, writing down any unusual findings and rectifying them prior to closing
- Obtain keys to property, garage door opener, warranties, etc., from seller at closing (or arrange to obtain them later)
- Ask to review your closing documents (including mortgage paperwork) one day prior to closing; take extra time to ask all questions and obtain answers
- Show up to sign closing documents; use this as your last opportunity to ask questions before signing documents

Outcome buyer can expect using above-average requirements:
- Closing in shorter time than market median
- Cash outlay for closing at or near initial amount quoted by lender in the good faith estimate

- Able to follow through on your plans to occupy the house in a timely fashion with least headaches

---

 Potential impact this component has on best price, timely purchase, and few hassles: 10

 Cost for average results: between $250 and the total of your earnest money and/or other nonrefundable down payments and time involved if the purchase fails due to inability to troubleshoot/close the purchase!

 Average amount of time for average results: 10 hours
Average amount of time buyers estimated this component would take: 6 hours

---

What the Numbers and Ratings Mean for Buyers

As the facts and figures reflect in the synopsis in Figure 4.5, real estate consultants polled felt it would take approximately 69 hours to purchase a house. This is 37 percent longer than buyers estimated it would take on average. As previously mentioned, this reflects the fact that while the buyer's focus is on making the offer and closing the sale, the consultant or other real estate service provider often orchestrates the behind-the-scenes puzzle pieces of which the seller is often unaware. If you're the least bit concerned if you can tackle one or more of the homebuying components, it may be worth your time and money to enlist the assistance of a real estate consultant for that task prior to leaping headlong into the purchase.

When it comes to the impact each of the six checkpoints has on obtaining the best price in a timely fashion with the least hassles, the average rating for all tasks is an 8 in importance.

Figure 4.5   Homebuyer Road Map Synopsis

Six Buyer Checkpoints:	Average Time*	Importance Rating**
1. Design a purchase strategy	8 hrs.	5
2. Be preapproved for a mortgage	8 hrs.	8
3. Choose the neighborhood and the property	25 hrs.	8
4. Check property information and pricing	10 hrs.	9
5. Draft the purchase agreement/ negotiate with seller	8 hrs.	9
6. Troubleshoot the purchase/close the transaction	10 hrs.	10
	69 hrs. time	7 average importance rating

(Scale: 1 lowest, 10 highest)
*Average time per task as estimated by 100 professional real estate consultants.
**Importance rating is the impact the component has on the buyer orchestrating a timely purchase, at the best price, with the fewest hassles.
What the Numbers and Ratings Mean for Buyers

As the figures show, real estate consultants estimate that it takes an average time of 69 hours from beginning to end to purchase a house. When it comes to the impact each of the six checkpoints has on obtaining the best price in a timely fashion with the least hassles, the average rating for all tasks is an 8 in importance. When comparing the overall importance ratings and complexities of the buying process to those of the selling process, the statistics indicate that buyers have a tougher time overall (an importance rating of 8) compared to sellers (an importance rating of 7).

When comparing the overall importance ratings and complexities of the buying process to those of the selling process, the statistics indicate that buyers have a tougher time overall (an average importance rating of 8) compared to sellers (an average importance rating of 7).

How Can You Apply these Facts and Figures?

Now that you know how long it could take you to go it alone as a buyer as well as the costs and tasks involved, you can decide which phases of the transaction (if any) you feel comfortable executing without assistance. Conversely, it may be apparent to you that certain tasks in buying a home are beyond your capability and you'll require a real estate consultant or other professional on your purchasing team. Last, but certainly not least, is the element of time. The average time of 69 hours worth of effort spread over a 30-day period of time (the average time it takes most motivated buyers to get to the final purchase agreement phase) is astounding. In essence, you'll have a new part-time job four days per workweek for a minimum of four hours per day! But that's only part of it. With this new buying job, you can expect high stress coupled with pressure to make a quick decision. And then there's the money. Instead of making money as you would with part-time work, you'll be unloading thousands of dollars in hard-earned cash from your bank account!

If the facts and figures haven't scared you into hiring the first real estate consultant you can find, I commend you.

In Chapter 6, we'll pinpoint how you can best apply this synopsis and road map information to trim even more off the cost of purchasing on your own and/or in tandem with real estate consultants and other fee-for-services providers.

Just to be sure that you've given this buying journey thorough consideration, you may want to take the miniquizzes to test your ability in each of the six checkpoint areas.

Where Do You Need Help in the Sales Process and How Do You Know?

Use the Miniquizzes to Help You Decide

Now that you've viewed the various phases of the path you'll take as a real estate purchaser, it's time to take the miniquizzes that follow. They'll help you determine which aspects of the purchase you're likely to need help with and which ones you can tackle on your own. And don't worry. If one of the tests doesn't apply to your situation, feel free to skip over it. After all, unlike school days, the quizzes provided are totally optional.

☑ Buyer Checkpoint 1:
Test Your Ability to Design a Purchase Strategy

YES   NO

☐ ☐   1. I have access to an online rent versus buy calculator to determine whether purchasing a home at this time makes financial sense.

☐ ☐   2. I won't move from the house I purchase for at least a minimum of three years.

☐ ☐   3. I have paid my rent on time for three or more years.

☐ ☐   4. I have savings that could help cover most major repairs in a home.

☐ ☐   5. I have enough patience to follow through the purchase step-by-step and not jump ahead or eliminate any of the six major checkpoints.

☐ ☐   6. I believe it's a good investment in my future to purchase real estate at this time and it doesn't bother me to use my savings to do so.

If you answered yes to three or more of these questions, you have a better-than-average chance of being able to complete this homebuying phase on your own or with only a moderate degree of assistance. If you answered yes to fewer than three questions, it may be advisable to obtain full-menu assistance with this task.

☑ Buyer Checkpoint 2:
Test Your Ability to Be Preapproved for a Mortgage

YES NO

☐ ☐ 1. I'll wait to begin viewing prospective properties to purchase until I've been preapproved for a mortgage.

☐ ☐ 2. I have accessed a copy of my credit report, have repaired errors found on it (if applicable), and believe I have average or above-average credit.

☐ ☐ 3. I have all of my financial information assembled and will make sure the lender receives it during our first appointment.

☐ ☐ 4. I will select a mortgage only after reviewing cost comparisons between various programs for which I qualify.

☐ ☐ 5. I'm prepared to write a check for several hundred dollars at the time of loan application to cover items like the credit report and appraisal.

☐ ☐ 6. I am not afraid to ask questions about any information and costs I find on the good faith estimate provided to me after loan application.

If you answered yes to three or more of these questions, you have a better-than-average chance of being able to complete this homebuying phase on your own or with only a moderate degree of assistance. If you answered yes to fewer than three questions, it may be advisable to obtain full-menu assistance with this task.

Buyer Checkpoint 3:
Test Your Ability to Choose the Best Neighborhood and Property

YES   NO

☐ ☐   1. I have made a list of priorities/amenities I desire in a home and will eliminate properties without these features.

☐ ☐   2. I will begin my home search online to get an idea of locations and neighborhoods I would consider.

☐ ☐   3. Before making an offer on a house, I will spend time driving around the neighborhood, talking to several neighbors, and visiting the property during various times of the day and various days of the week.

☐ ☐   4. I will check with the police department to determine the type and amount of crime in the neighborhood before making an offer on any property.

☐ ☐   5. I will check with the school district regarding ratings for all schools within the district for the house I'm considering.

☐ ☐   6. Before making an offer, I'll confirm the type of zoning for the area as well as check any pending zoning changes anticipated for the area.

If you answered yes to three or more of these questions, you have a better-than-average chance of being able to complete this homebuying phase on your own or with only a moderate degree of assistance. If you answered yes to fewer than three questions, it may be advisable to obtain full-menu assistance with this task.

Buyer Checkpoint 4:
Test Your Ability to Check Property Information
and Pricing

YES NO

Prior to making an offer, I will:

☐ ☐ 1. Obtain a comparative market analysis (CMA) to help confirm the market value of the property.

☐ ☐ 2. Check the legal description and property tax information with either the courthouse or title company.

☐ ☐ 3. Double-check/confirm property facts and amenities as shown on the information sheet provided by the seller.

☐ ☐ 4. Measure the square footage of the house.

☐ ☐ 5. Obtain a property disclosure statement from the seller (if your state requires it).

In the purchase agreement, I will:

☐ ☐ 6. Make the purchase contingent upon receiving and reviewing a satisfactory home inspection report.

If you answered yes to three or more of these questions, you have a better-than-average chance of being able to complete this homebuying phase on your own or with only a moderate degree of assistance. If you answered yes to fewer than three questions, it may be advisable to obtain full-menu assistance with this task.

Buyer Checkpoint 5:
Test Your Ability to Draft the Purchase Agreement and Negotiate with the Seller

YES NO

☐ ☐   1. I will spend time understanding the property purchase agreement most commonly used in my locale and will be able to complete it and present it to the seller.

☐ ☐   2. I'll design a negotiating strategy to prioritize what I want to win while allowing the seller to win on issues of importance to him or her.

☐ ☐   3. I'm able to determine my costs of purchase (including closing costs) prior to making an offer to the seller.

☐ ☐   4. I understand the procedures and legal ramifications of offers and counteroffers in real estate negotiating.

☐ ☐   5. I am able to draft an offer that includes contingencies for financing, home inspection, and walkthrough inspections in order not to lose my earnest money and/or down payment if roadblocks occur in the purchase.

☐ ☐   6. I consider myself a strong yet fair negotiator when it comes to financial matters.

If you answered yes to three or more of these questions, you have a better-than-average chance of being able to complete this homebuying phase on your own or with only a moderate degree of assistance. If you answered yes to fewer than three questions, it may be advisable to obtain full-menu assistance with this task.

Buyer Checkpoint 6:
Test Your Ability to Troubleshoot Your Purchase and Close the Transaction

YES NO

☐ ☐ 1. I understand the sequence of events in closing a real estate transaction and can describe each.

☐ ☐ 2. I will prioritize the time and effort it takes to monitor the mortgage process, review the title insurance policy, and obtain cost-effective homeowners insurance in a timely manner.

☐ ☐ 3. I'll keep in touch on at least a weekly basis with the seller and other service providers in the transaction.

☐ ☐ 4. I know the approach to take and what to look for when completing the walk-through inspection prior to closing and can adequately document my findings with the seller.

☐ ☐ 5. I am capable of reviewing and interpreting all closing documents at least one day prior to closing the transaction.

☐ ☐ 6. I understand my legal rights in signing mortgage documents and agreeing to their terms.

If you answered yes to three or more of these questions, you have a better-than-average chance of being able to complete this homebuying phase on your own or with only a moderate degree of assistance. If you answered yes to fewer than three questions, it may be advisable to obtain full-menu assistance with this task.

Seller's Applications for Fee-for-Services Real Estate

Technology has created efficiencies to the benefit of the consumer when selling a home. Choices have been created that bridge the gap between the For-Sale-by-Owner and traditional percentage based real estate commissions.

Ruth Hopke, Public Relations Manager
Homebytes.com.

Are You Really Prepared to Handle the Sale of Your Own Home?

Lights, Camera, Sell Your Own Home!

Several years ago, I taped a television show for Lifetime Television's *New Attitudes* show. They wondered if I could apply the information from my books and my syndicated newspaper column, "The Frugal HomeOwner,® " to the for-sale-by-owner market. Could I find a FSBO in the Los Angeles area where they could shoot footage for one-half day? Not one to miss a challenge, I accepted.

I found a willing seller at owners.com (the Web's largest FSBO resource at the time). While I consider myself somewhat savvy about the myriad online homeselling resources available, I was totally amazed how this FSBO husband and wife team navigated the Web to empower themselves! It wasn't that they didn't want to use a real estate professional. It was financially prohibitive. They had purchased their home for $260,000 during the California upturn, and in the current market it was currently in the $235,000 range. Even with prepayments against their loan (which was another story, turned error) they were almost upside down in their equity. Paying a commission meant bringing a hefty check to closing, which was impossible.

They designed a game plan to maximize their time frame and their resources. Because they were moving overseas, the husband decided to leave his full-time job six weeks early to sell the house. Being very computer literate, they:

1. Listed with all of the free online FSBO sites
2. Purchased professional-looking signage and a flier information box from the Web
3. Used software to create a snappy-looking brochure
4. Obtained prequalifying and preapproval information from <www.countrywide.com> and <www.e-loan.com>
5. Obtained market valuations (for less than $30 each) from both <www.experian.com> and <www.cswonline.com>

Two kind real estate agents they knew personally volunteered that the market range shown from the Web site resources was on target. Lastly, they purchased two consumer real estate books (neither were mine!) and were following the flow of the transaction chapter by chapter. The husband commented "We don't want things to occur too quickly. We've been working 16-hour days getting the house in shape and we're exhausted at night. I can only stay awake long enough each night to read one chapter!"

The television camera crew arrived at the house for the shoot. The Chans' house couldn't have shown better. They spent more than 40 hours cleaning, painting, and sprucing up. The curb appeal was incredible, complemented by an equally well-kept neighborhood.

The testament to this fact was that within a period of one week, they had four offers in a pile on their kitchen table. Motioning to the offers the wife said, "We won't get to the offer chapter in the book for two more nights!" After I picked up my jaw off the floor, we discussed how they needed to act promptly on the offers. While I'm licensed in three states, California isn't one of them. They needed local professional help. The cameraman commented, "The market's so hot here for these cheap houses, they might have another four offers overnight."

The sellers then admitted that they had no clue what the forms meant; and more importantly, they knew negotiating was not their forte. I asked if they knew of a real estate consultant who could assist them on an hourly basis to sort things out and negotiate on their behalf. They said they knew real estate salesmen (were those the same?) but weren't aware that anyone could work that way. While they couldn't afford to pay tens of thousands from their sales price for an agent's help, they could afford hourly assistance.

Everything worked out fine. We completed the shoot. It was fun and we even included a segment about how to access property information online. The Chans contacted the real estate professional they knew and he charged them for five hours' worth of work at $100 per hour to negotiate with the buyers. The sale closed quickly and they were happily moved within one month.

Even though I'd been asked to assess what they'd done to prepare their home to show, to criticize their shortcomings, and basically be the expert from afar, I went away humble. I realized that consumers have a right to do what they can to financially maximize the American Dream experience. And that real estate professionals need to do a better job of providing unbundled services to consumers. This book should give you a strong start.

Analyze the Results from Your Seller Miniquizzes

Glance back at the answers to the miniquizzes you took in Chapter 3 to gauge your strength as a prospective seller on your own. What did they reflect about your desire and ability to sell your home? Did you rate average or above-average in every quiz, or were there some where you didn't rate as high as you'd like? Or perhaps you scored fairly well, but realize that you have better things to do than take on the part-time job (all 83 hours of it) of selling your home. The quiz results can be an indication that unbundled, fee-for-services assistance can aid you in various steps of the selling process.

The Assistance You Need Is Either Level One or Level Two

Determine What Type of à la Carte Assistance You Need

As covered in Chapter 2, there are two primary categories or levels of help you need. Level one skills focus on information gathering, administration, and interpretation of the information. Once you have the information you need from a level one service provider, you can often make your own choices on what to do and how to do it. Level one real estate services would include gathering information on recent listings and sales in your neighborhood, deciding what to replace and repair in your home prior to listing, and prescreening buyers before showing the house. At level one, a service provider or consultant gives you the information you need, but does not make decisions for you or represent your interests with third parties (like buyers). Think of it much like purchasing a new car from a dealer. The salesman shows you brochures about the vehicle and tells you the important facts about warranties, but it's up to you to make up your mind about whether or not to purchase the car. While you know the salesman works for the auto dealer, he's giving you information you need. The salesman and dealership have a customer relationship with you, a prospective buyer. In most cases, level one skills will be compensated at a lower rate than skills performed for level two services.

Level two skills are those tasks that require the consultant or service provider to negotiate on your behalf, advocate for you, and represent your interests with third parties (like buyers). Because it is a higher skill level, it requires the completion of more difficult and personal tasks employing one-on-one skills like negotiating and representation. For example, a level two skill could require a consultant to negotiate with one or more buyers simultaneously on your behalf to determine the best purchaser capable of the quickest closing on your house. Think of level two services like those of an attorney. You employ an attorney to negotiate with others on your behalf. The attorney must keep your best interests in mind at all times. This type of business relationship is very different from the customer relationship formed with the car dealer and salesman. Level two services and relationships (like those with an attorney) form a client relationship providing negotiating, advocacy, and representation on your behalf.

Not only will most level two skills be compensated at a higher rate than those of level one, you may find consultants working in level two more likely to participate in risk/reward fee-sharing programs. For example, let's say you have several different real estate needs but are short on cash to cover all of the level two services required. You might negotiate with the consultant to receive an hourly fee on one project, a flat fee on another, and be compensated by a percentage of the price savings on yet another. As with most professionals, real estate consultants desire to build long-lasting, ongoing relationships with as many quality clients as possible in order to limit the amount of new business they have to seek. Repeat and referral business is the lifeline for the successful consultant.

It's Important to Understand the Difference between Level One and Level Two Skills

Understanding the difference between level one and level two skills is vital as a for-sale-by-owner. Level one skills are those that you're more likely to feel confident tackling and are apt to sail through without much help, if any. These include preparing the house for the market, prescreening buyers, and writing and placing advertisements. Level one skills are also the skills you're most likely to find no-cost or low-cost assistance with through print or online mediums. You only have to glance at the Resources section at the end of this book to see the vast array of online service providers touting free information for homesellers and buyers alike.

Level two skills often require more expertise in real estate (like knowing which clauses and contingencies in the purchase agreement to eliminate). And many level two skills contain an element of negotiating that some sellers (and buyers) are not comfortable with on their own behalf. Many of us admit that when it comes to negotiating for ourselves, we often have a fool for a client, especially on emotionally charged issues like selling our own home. The more personal the service and the higher the expertise required (like level two negotiating), the more likely that task is to play a pivotal role in the sale and require another party to provide it. As covered in Chapter 2, level two skills will often be more expensive than those offered in level one assistance.

The Meat in the Middle May Be Your Greatest Hurdle

What Is It and How Can You Best Tackle It?

When selling your home, you're likely to find more vital, level two tasks facing you in the middle of the process. So much so that I term them the meat in the middle! As in a sandwich, the meat in the middle is often the most important, substantive part of the whole. If the meat is lacking in quantity or quality, it's likely to be an unsatisfying or even a distasteful experience. If a FSBO pays inadequate attention to the meat in the middle, she could find herself back at square one—no buyer, no sale, left only with wasted time and expenses to show for her effort.

Six Major Components Comprise the Meat in the Middle for Sellers

In the real estate transaction, the meat in the middle for a seller comes when you've advertised for a buyer, a serious one is found, and you must then put the sale together and bring it to a successful close (the most important part!). The meat of the sale includes vital components like making property disclosures to the buyer, writing up and negotiating the sales agreement, and troubleshooting the sale to a successful close. The majority of real estate transactions that fall apart do so as a consequence of inadequate preparation midstream in the sale. In other words, there's not enough attention paid to the quantity and quality of the meat.

The six greatest hurdles in navigating this critical middle portion of the transaction are to:

1. Ensure buyer preapproval and monitor the loan process
2. Draft or assist in drafting the purchase and sales agreement
3. Negotiate with the buyer
4. Complete and check the due diligence information and paperwork.
5. Orchestrate the puzzle pieces (e.g., the appraisal, the home inspection, the termite inspection [if applicable], the buyer's final walk-through inspection, etc.)
6. Renegotiate with the buyer (if necessary) in order to close the sale

To make sure you don't overlook or discount any of the components of the meat in the middle, we'll outline each one in detail.

Tips for Navigating the Meat in the Middle

Ensure buyer preapproval and monitor the loan process. The first component is to make sure the buyer is preapproved for financing and stay apprised of loan processing (and subsequently, the closing). Hopefully, you're working with a savvy buyer who is preapproved with a lender for the loan he needs. But if the topic hasn't yet come up, you need to bring it up before entering into a sales agreement. Why waste precious time negotiating with a buyer who doesn't yet have financing nailed down? Once you know that the buyer is preapproved for a mortgage (with documentation from the lender), you'll need to stay abreast of the loan processing, either through the buyer or by interfacing with the lender. This is critical especially for orchestrating the closing and timing the move for both parties.

Draft or assist in drafting the purchase and sales agreement. This meat can be some of the most difficult to navigate without professional assistance. It requires you to understand the components of the sales agreement and interpret how various clauses and contingencies can impact your position in the sale. Drafted improperly, the purchase agreement may have too few teeth to bind the buyer or too many hooks to prevent your escape if need be. One of the greatest missteps is not understanding which contingencies are commonplace in contracts and which should be avoided. A contingency is an event that must take place before the transaction can progress. Some of the most common contingencies/clauses include:

- *Financing contingency.* Even though the buyer is preapproved for a loan, most agreements give the buyer a window of time in which to be formally approved for a mortgage before removing this contingency. This contingency might also state the approximate amount of the mortgage, a maximum interest rate, and the maximum number of discount points (if any) the buyer agrees to pay. This serves as an escape clause if financing becomes too cost-prohibitive and/or the buyer wouldn't have sufficient funds to close the size loan he needs. In most cases, this contingency won't negatively impact you because you wouldn't want a buyer tied to you in a purchase agreement if there was no possibility of arranging financing. You may want to check with the buyer's lender to make sure that the length of time anticipated to remove the contingency is not unduly restrictive to your efforts, especially if the buyer washes out and you need to keep marketing the property. You might want to negotiate with the borrower that until the contingency is removed, you are allowed to keep the property on the market and accept backup offers.

- *Home inspection contingency.* This makes the buyer's purchase contingent upon receiving an acceptable home inspection report. While this is a prudent move for both buyer and seller, unfortunately many purchase agreements must be renegotiated after home inspection reports are received. This can result from minor work repairs or more severe and expensive needs like a cracked foundation. If you feel the home inspection may reveal major problems and/or repairs that you could more cost-effectively tackle, it may be wise to pay for and obtain your own home inspection prior to putting the house on the market. Although the buyer may still choose to request and pay for his own home inspection, you'll know up front what to expect and can use your report as a benchmark.

- *Work repair maximum clause.* Hand in hand with the home inspection contingency comes the work repair clause. Most are written "that should the home inspection require repairs to be made, the seller agrees to make repairs up to a maximum amount equal to ___" which can be stated as a flat amount or a percentage of the sales price. Any amount over and above that ceiling is optional for negotiation between seller and buyer.

- *Insurance contingency.* The impact of natural disasters on real estate makes it almost necessary for buyers to secure homeowners insurance before finding the house to purchase! And because some states (like Florida and California) cap the number of policies that can be written, a buyer might place the insurance contingency in the purchase agreement pending an okay from an insurance company. This is another reason why you may want to provide potential buyers with information about the insurance company you're using because it may be less tedious to rewrite the policy for them than to write a policy with a new carrier.

- *Backup offer clause.* Just as some contingencies and clauses are standard to allow the buyer time to secure financing and complete a home inspection, you can add clauses to the sales contract that provide you with control and expand your marketing options (such as a financing contingency). Allowing you to take backup offers means that you'll keep the property on the active market and accept offers for second, third, or fourth position should the current offer wash out. Additionally, the clause that follows can serve as ammunition if you're forced to accept an offer that includes contingencies of a more indefinite nature (like the required sale of a buyer's home before purchasing yours).

- *Right of first refusal clause.* Placing this clause in the purchase agreement allows you to accept an offer with one or more contingencies yet keep the property on the active market and consider other offers. Here's how it works. The right of first refusal clause states that should another acceptable offer be received, the current buyer shall be notified (typically in writing) and have X amount of time (often several days up to a week or more) to remove the contingency and purchase the property. If the buyer can't/won't remove the contingency, the buyer's earnest money is returned and the second buyer becomes the one in the primary position. This allows you the flexibility to take a less-than-perfect offer while marketing to attract additional buyers.

If you are the least bit uncomfortable in your ability to navigate drafting or interpreting the sales agreement, it's wise to spend money to hire either a real estate consultant or a real estate attorney to assist you. The few hundred dollars it might cost you are a small investment in designing a sales agreement that addresses your needs and protects your interests.

*C*onsumers *often get caught in the middle. They can do some of the work themselves like attract buyers and show their home probably better than anyone else. But they usually need a real estate professional to negotiate the best deal with potential buyers, control the process until closing, and properly close the sale.*

> Rick O'Neil, President
> Help-U-Sell Real Estate Corporation

Negotiate with the buyer. This is one of the most overlooked areas where hard-earned equity can slip from your fingers. Often we realize too late that negotiating on our own behalf can be much more difficult than it sounds. This is one part of the sale where you stand to lose the most by going it alone if you're not a confident negotiator.

Successful negotiating and contract strategies for sellers include:

- *Obtaining as much earnest money as possible.* All things considered, the more earnest money the buyer puts down initially, the more committed he will be to follow through with the purchase. If it's impossible to receive an ample deposit up front, request that the buyer make one or more additional earnest money deposits in a short period of time. If he fails to do so, you've probably scrapped a buyer that would have otherwise fallen through later.
- *Understanding how counteroffers work.* If you understand the principles behind counteroffers, you'll be much more likely to negotiate exactly what you want in an offer while structuring a win-win agreement for you and the buyer. The first premise of the counteroffer is that it con-

stitutes an entirely new offer, one that the party you're presenting it to doesn't have to accept. Let's say that everything is fine with the first offer the buyer made you except he asked for the side-by-side refrigerator which you weren't including in the sale. So you mark through the words on the contract "including side-by-side refrigerator," initial the change, and deliver the paperwork back to the buyer. He's insulted that you'd lose a sale over a refrigerator and declines to make another offer to you. In essence, you have just bought back your house for the measly price of the refrigerator! The second premise of the counteroffer is that it's not solely the changes that are impacted. Other elements of the contract could change as well. What if, after excluding the refrigerator from the sales agreement, the buyer made his own counter to your counter, lowering the purchase price by $10,000! That and more can happen with counteroffers. The bottom line is to make sure that what you stand to win by the counter is worth the effort—and the risk!

Complete and check the due diligence information and paperwork. This includes double-checking information on the property (square footage, property tax amounts, etc.) as well as preparing and presenting the property disclosure form to the buyer (if it's required by law in your state; check the Resources section at the end of this book to access particulars for your state). Just because you're a for-sale-by-owner doesn't mean that you're exempt under state disclosure laws. A term often used in the legal profession, *due diligence* means that the FSBO must make sure that pertinent information about the property and the circumstances of the sale are shared with the buyer. For FSBOs, this may more accurately be termed *do* diligence because many of these activities require the seller to do something. In addition to the property disclosure form and facts about the property, the seller must also include any CCRs (conditions, covenants, and restrictions) affecting the property as well as documenting information about any local improvement district (LID) liens. These are financial obligations for sidewalk, lighting, or other improvements that, if still outstanding after the sale, transfer with the property at closing and become the responsibility of the buyer. Unless all of the *i*'s are dotted and the *t*'s crossed, the buyer might have recourse to back out of the sale, or worse yet, sue you for nondisclosure. That's why skimming over the due diligence can create more seller liability than any other checkpoint in the transaction.

Orchestrate the puzzle pieces. Out of all of the meat, you may find this the easiest as a for-sale-by-owner because many of the appointments are done by various professionals and service providers calling you with requests. But if problems should result from these puzzle pieces (like work repairs requested by the buyer or a lower appraisal price than agreed to on the purchase and sales agreement), you may need to renegotiate with the buyer.

Renegotiate with the buyer (if necessary) in order to close the sale. It may be something minor like adjusting the sales price downward by $500, or something major like a disintegrating roof, a lot line in question, or even a title dispute. But hang in there. If you can leap over this last hurdle and (finally) close the sale, you've done it. You've sold on your own, with just a little help from your fee-for-services friends!

The Meat in the Middle Is the Most Emotionally Charged Aspect for Seller and Buyer

We've covered the various ways the meat in the middle focuses on property facts and disclosure, but it's also prime time for flaring emotions and major cases of cold feet on both sides of the buyer-seller fence. It may have just hit the buyer that he's taking on $200,000 worth of house debt for the next 30 years. Or perhaps it hits you as the seller that you're leaving the home where your kids grew up and got married and where you accumulated thousands of fond memories. When it comes to housebuying/selling, runaway emotions can cause a buyer to back out at the 11th hour or a seller to break off negotiations midstream. It has nothing to do with rational thought. It's emotions run amok. Fortunately, sometimes emotions cool and the sale closes without another hitch. Unfortunately, some sales never cement after emotional outbursts during this phase of the sale.

How to Determine If Your Greatest Hurdle Is the Meat in the Middle

Refer back to the seller checkpoint quizzes you took in Chapter 3. In which parts of the selling puzzle did you score lowest? If your lowest scores were in checkpoints 2 (gathering property information and pricing the property), 5 (negotiating with the buyer), and/or 6 (troubleshooting and closing the sale), it could signal you need help with the meat in the middle. As we cover practical applications for each checkpoint in the seller's road map, give particular attention to meat in the middle components that might be problematic.

The Help You Need at Each Seller Checkpoint

Real-World Scenarios

We previously discussed the mountain of time required for FSBOs to successfully navigate the sale. But let's assume that you do have the time (or will find it) and the determination to do what it takes to get the sale closed.

You'll remember from Chapter 3, the six checkpoints in the seller's road map include:

1. Prepare the property for sale
2. Gather property information/price the property
3. Market the property
4. Locate/prequalify the buyer

5. Draft the sales agreement/negotiate with the buyer
6. Troubleshoot the sale/close the transaction

As indicated by the miniquizzes, some of the tasks required in each of the six checkpoints may require little time and effort from you, while others may not be worth tackling on your own.

The following scenarios will provide you with ideas on how each checkpoint can be orchestrated using unbundled fee-for-services (including online resources where appropriate) and how to design and negotiate compensation for each. As we progress through the six seller checkpoints, noting when and where it's common for sellers to need assistance, pay particular attention to the checkpoints you felt could be most problematic.

Prepare the property for sale.
Preparing the property for sale (scenario one). Karen and Ron Jones are a professional couple with two small children. Based on the thousands of dollars they can save by selling the house themselves, they decide to find and prioritize the time it will take. Their greatest concern is what to spruce up and repair because their home is in an area of more expensive homes, several of which are for sale. They decide to hire a real estate consultant to advise them because they want to maximize attracting buyers without overimproving using money that won't be recouped in the sales price. The real estate consultant's fee is $125 per hour with a minimum of two hours billed time. She estimates that the project can be completed in three hours or less.

The consultant previews the property and researches information on the other properties for sale in the neighborhood including homes that have recently sold. The consultant determines that while the Jones's home has approximately the same square footage, one-third of the house (an attic area) is unfinished. The unfinished space will allow the price to be a bit softer than for other homes in competition. And because it

makes economic sense for buyers to purchase the house on
the lower end of the market (in order to maximize improving
it and equity buildup) the house will require less spruce-up
and fix-up costs.

The consultant recommends that they prioritize their time
and money on minor repairs at the exterior of the house near
the front door including repairing the front steps, replacing a
screen door, and repainting fascia trim. In order for the house
to have the highest curb appeal, she also suggests that they
hire a professional tree trimming company to cut back foliage
from near the walkway and the front of the house.

They are so impressed with the consultant's expertise that
they hire her for up to an additional three hours of time to help
them set a competitive price for the house. During this phase
of the consulting, she outlines several ways they could structure a sale in order to generate the greatest net proceeds at
closing.

The consultant presents the Joneses a bill for $625.

As this scenario points out, an ethical and scrupulous consultant will never purposely add hours onto the consulting
project by baiting the client into unnecessary research and services. In this case, the satisfaction of the clients led to inviting
the consultant to assist them in determining the market value
for the house. While it's normal that working with a consultant
can lead you to realize other assistance you need, there's no
reason why you can't take it step-by-step if you feel comfortable doing so.

Preparing the property for sale (scenario two). Martha Rob-
erts is a spry, 85-year-old woman who will be selling her house
to move to a retirement village. She knows there's lots of deferred maintenance to be tackled because she's been unable to
keep up with repairs and yard work since her husband died several years ago. Once the house is in showing shape, her son will
handle the formal sale and closing for her.

Martha is referred to a real estate consultant who specializes
in preparing homes for the market. The consultant states that

her initial consultation fee is $250 which includes not only a thorough review of the work to be done, but provides a complete information packet showing which improvements could add to market value and which will not. Additionally, the consultant's fee includes a booklet on how to evaluate and choose contractors and workmen for the repairs. There are even several pages of names and addresses of repair companies, complete with licensing, bonding, and workmen's compensation coverage information. Martha feels the consultant's value is more than justified because she can now determine what to repair as well as access ready sources of repair people to perform the work.

The consultant in this scenario was offering much more than advice on what to fix up prior to putting the home on the market. Sellers, especially the elderly, don't want to be bothered with the tedium of searching for and interviewing myriad potential workmen. And there's often the risk of being taken by an unscrupulous contractor who's only out for a quick buck. However, no matter who supplies the referral information, it's always in the consumer's best interest to verify references and insurance information prior to contracting with anyone. Although unlikely, the real estate consultant could be serving merely as a front person for the contractor to help legitimatize his value or services.

Gather property information/price the property.

Gathering property information. The Carmichaels have purchased and sold several homes and are fairly confident they can pull together the necessary information to start the marketing process to sell their current home. They use their tax assessment notice to obtain the current amount of their property taxes and a copy of their previous title insurance policy helps them double-check the legal description of the property. Mary Carmichael is adept at online searches so she logs into the general database for the local title insurance company and prints out a copy of the plat map as well as a copy of the conditions, covenants, and restrictions (CCRs) for their subdivision.

It sounds like the Carmichaels are well on their way to navigating the sale of their own property, but what they'll later uncover (unfortunately not before losing a potential buyer) is that both the lot size (as represented by the county) and the home's square footage (as mismeasured by Mr. Carmichael) are incorrect. Even though sellers have had experience purchasing and selling on their own, it's always a good idea to hire an objective third party (like a real estate consultant) to double-check facts and figures before they damage a sale.

Pricing the property. Marion O'Keefe is a first-time homeseller who is trying desperately to squeeze every cent she can out of the sale. She's savvy enough to know that pricing the property can make the difference between a house that sells and one that doesn't. She hires Ben Benjamin, a real estate consultant specializing in pricing and marketing property, to prepare a comparative market analysis for her and interpret approximately where the market value should be set to affect a quick sale with maximum net proceeds in her pocket.

Market the property.
Renting signage; placing ads. If you're Web savvy, this is a great place to save money in the sale. There are a number of sites online where you can rent everything from signs and lockboxes to talking ad boxes for your front yard! While online, sign up with several of the no-cost/low-cost for-sale-by-owner sites, or use one or more software programs to draft an ad in a matter of seconds. When it comes to FSBO marketing, the Web makes it as easy as point, click, deliver!

Locate/prequalify the buyer.
Prescreening/preapproving buyer prospects. Jeremy Johnson has carefully drafted five prescreening questions he'll ask buyers prior to allowing them to view his home. In addition, he's accessed several mortgage sites online and printed out prequalifying information to hand to prospective buyers.

Obtaining the information is one thing, but properly applying it is another! With the first prospect's visit, Jeremy confuses prequalifying with preapproval, which further confuses the buyer. In order not to alienate the buyer, both agree that it's in their best interests to visit over the phone with a real estate consultant the buyer has talked to previously. The buyer is able to be preapproved in a matter of minutes, and she ends up purchasing Jeremy's home.

Draft the purchase agreement/negotiate with the buyer.

Negotiating with the buyer. Ken Carpathian has three buyer/prospects interested in purchasing his house. He's a bit unsure about the negotiating process and is reluctant to begin negotiations on his own for fear of losing one or more of the buyers. He contacts Frank Ferne, a real estate consultant specializing in negotiations. Frank quotes Ken a flat fee of $1,000 which includes monitoring and troubleshooting the sale until it closes. Frank drafts their working agreement and receives a $300 retainer from Ken. The consultant then begins negotiations with all three parties which results in securing a full-price offer from one buyer.

Compared to many of the real estate listing agreements used by real estate salespeople, the agreement to provide consulting services form used by consultants is very simplistic. As we'll cover in Chapter 8, it's rare for the form to exceed two pages. And often, it's contained in only a paragraph or two. The consultant in this scenario is wise to include monitoring and troubleshooting the sale in his bundle of services. There's nothing more frustrating for a seller to have secured a buyer only to have him wash out as the end of the sale nears. If, like Ken, you have apprehension about troubleshooting the sale on your own, this package of bundled services could be best for you.

Drafting the purchase agreement. Colleen Garrison locates a buyer to purchase her six-plex. They negotiate a price and terms Colleen is willing to accept. But because the buyer wants to review Colleen's rent rolls as a contingency of the purchase agreement, she is unsure how to draft that language properly into the purchase agreement. She contacts Joyce

Jones, a real estate attorney, to draft it for her. Joyce's fee is $200 per hour for a total of $400.

You'll notice that Colleen hired a real estate attorney. Just as consultants have various niches and specialties, so too do members of the legal profession. Although similar to general-practice attorneys in the fees they charge, a real estate attorney is adept at not only completing forms but making sure that the transaction is structured to the benefit of her client.

Troubleshoot the sale/close the transaction.

Renegotiating with the buyer. Sally Smithton is a for-sale-by-owner who's having trouble communicating with her buyer. When she calls to ask him how his financing is progressing, he responds by saying, "I'm not happy with the rates I'm finding, but I'll keep looking." Because it's less than six weeks from the closing date, Sally decides to hire a real estate consultant to try to communicate with the buyer.

As a one-person for-sale-by-owner, you may find it impossible to be all things to all people, especially to a buyer who's being evasive! That's why hiring a "new face" to contact the buyer on your behalf may get to the root of solving communication and closing problems. Often for an investment of several hundred dollars, you'll be able to save thousands of dollars that may result from losing a sale.

Orchestrating and documenting the walk-through inspection. It's only two days until Paul Blount's home sale closes, but tomorrow is the buyer's final walk-through inspection of the home, and Paul is dreading it! Not only has the buyer become argumentative about everything, but now he's threatening to refuse to close if the bathroom flooring is not completely replaced. A friend at Paul's office suggests he hire a real estate consultant to interface with the buyer on his behalf to help sidestep a last-minute explosion that could blow the already fragile sale apart. A consultant is hired for $200 to accompany the buyer through the property and document the walk-through. And because the buyer knows his claim for new flooring is bogus and one that the consultant could easily see through, he drops the request and signs off on the walk-through inspection.

*B*ased on surveyed consumer demand and industry feedback, the nontraditional segment of the online homebuying and selling markets (e.g., FSBO, fee-for-services related transactions) could represent as much as 75 percent of total sales by 2005.

gomez.com

Five Rules of Thumb for Seller Fee-for-Services

Make Sure You Don't Overlook Any!

Now that we've reviewed how à la carte real estate services can assist your efforts in selling your own home, let's cover the five major rules of thumb when working with fee-for-services professionals.

1. The tougher the task or service is to duplicate, the more value it commands. This is especially true with level two services requiring negotiating and advocacy skills.
2. The more a task or skill requires personal strengths (like negotiating or troubleshooting), the more likely the seller is to require that a professional provide it.
3. The more personal strengths a task or skill requires, the higher the price the consumer should be willing to pay to obtain it.
4. The closer you are to closing a sale, the more important it is to secure the professional services you need in order to bring it to a close.
5. Don't forget that time is money. While scrimping on the professional services you need seems like a cost-saving measure, meeting deadlines and saving time could prove more cost-effective in the long run.

What to Do If You're Short on Time

Guideline to Streamline the Process

Pay for all of the level two skills you'll need and/or strongly consider having the entire sale orchestrated by a real estate consultant.

What to Do If You're Short on Money

Guidelines to Cut Costs

Prioritize paying for the level two skills you know you need and try to accomplish all the level one tasks you can on your own. Your money could potentially go further by paying an attorney to draft the purchase agreement and/or hiring a real estate consultant to negotiate with the buyer. Conversely, look to the Internet or other free service providers to accomplish the level one tasks you can't perform. These could include placing a property listing on no-cost/low-cost Web sites for exposure, using software to draft an ad, and/or accessing checklists online to keep you informed of what to do first, second, and third.

What to Do If You're Short on Patience and/or Know-How

Guidelines to Cut Down on Stress

Prioritize hiring a real estate consultant to provide level two skills as well as double-check all facts and figures regarding the property. When we're under stress, we're more apt to make critical errors in calculating square footage, lot size, and other figures. You'll want to ensure that careless errors and omissions don't end up costing you money or, worse yet, a lawsuit from a disgruntled buyer.

The same is true in the know-how category. When you've captured a hot buyer, it's no time to speculate on what forms to fill in or make missteps improperly interpreting a contingency clause. Even if you scored well on the seller miniquizzes, if your gut tells you you're treading on thin ice, pay attention and hire a professional.

Obtaining Fee-for-Services as a Risk Reduction Tool

Additional Help for Sellers

Is it possible that using fee-for-services assistance can reduce the risk of the for-sale-by-owner? Depending on the type and degree of risk you're trying to shed, the answer is possibly yes. Particularly for troubleshooting the meat in the middle, it's wise to hire one or more professionals to double-check the paperwork at various phases of the transaction. This would include a real estate consultant to check property information before presenting it to buyers, a real estate attorney to review the purchase and sales agreement before your final signature is obtained, and perhaps a home inspector to do a prelisting inspection. The latter is a great way to know the condition of the property before putting it on the market and help prevent a buyer from later uncovering problems (often when they obtain their own inspection) that might cause the transaction to fall apart. In many real estate markets today, home inspectors will give an all-inclusive fee that covers the prelisting inspection plus another inspection once the buyer is found.

Reducing risk is much different than covering up potentially damaging information or problems about the property. Contrary to popular belief, just because you're selling your own home, you are still responsible for the following (based on the real estate laws and disclosure regulations in your state):

- Preparing and presenting the property disclosure statement to buyers
- Disclosing all material facts about the property that are within your knowledge (for example, the buyer has a right to know that two years ago you added a room and failed to obtain a building permit)

Fee-for-Services Can Serve as the FSBO Lifeline

Grab it!

While saving the commission is the primary motivator in going it alone as a seller, you can see it's a time-consuming, laborious, even emotional process. Here's hoping that making it through the process finds you pleasantly on the uphill side of the sale. If you stumble somewhere in between, know that there's help from unbundled, fee-for-services professionals, in a variety of specialties and fee structures, prepared to throw you a FSBO lifeline.

Buyer's Applications of Fee-for-Services Real Estate

There is no doubt in my mind that the fee-for-services sector of the real estate industry will grow. I believe that within the next few years, a vast majority of all properties offered for sale will be offered through this method. Consumers are becoming very aware that the real value for services in the transaction is located almost exclusively on the buyer side of the transaction. I foresee the industry splitting the two functions, selling and buying, with the selling side featuring fee-for-services pricing and the buying side featuring bundling of services under the heading of one-stop shopping.

> Tom Hathaway, President
> The Buyer's Agent, Inc.
> National Franchise Company

How Consultants Can Assist Even the Most Savvy Buyer

Don't Cut Corners—Especially in a Seller's Market

I've long maintained that the real estate purchase process is so fraught with emotion that we're likely to buy with our gut and then justify the purchase with our wallet! This is never more dangerous than when a low housing supply is pressured by high demand, coupled with a buoyant economy and high employment. Anxious to be the lucky party in the bidding for a house, an overzealous buyer is likely to cut corners by eliminating contingencies in his offer, waiving the home inspection, or taking other precarious and potentially costly shortcuts.

That's why it's vital to employ professional help when you need it in order to come out on the other side of the purchase in strong financial shape and with few (if any) regrets.

The Assistance You Need Falls into Two Major Categories

When reading Chapter 4, you may have noticed that the help you need falls into two primary categories or levels. Level one skills focus on information gathering and administration of the information (informative in nature). Once you have the information you need from a level one service provider, you can often make your own choices on what to do and how to do it. Level one real estate services would include being preapproved for a mortgage, checking information regarding school ratings and districts, and checking out the crime statistics for the neighborhood in which you're interested. At level one, a service provider or consultant gives you the information you need, but does not make decisions for you or represent your interests with third parties (like sellers). Think of it much like grocery shopping. The store posts information on caloric, protein, and carbohydrate content for the fresh foods you purchase, but it's up to you to decide if you want to purchase anything at all! You know that the store is promoting the wares of its suppliers, and that it only makes money when it sells something to you. In the purest sense, you're a customer of the grocery store.

Level two skills are those tasks that require the consultant or service provider to negotiate on your behalf, advocate for you, represent your interests with third parties (like sellers), and interpret information for you (interpretive in nature). Because it is a higher skill level, it requires the completion of more difficult and personal tasks employing one-on-one skills, like negotiating and representation. For example, a level two skill could require a consultant to negotiate with several sellers simultaneously on your behalf in order to secure the best house for the least price and the quickest closing. Think of level two services like those of an attorney. You employ an attorney to negotiate with others on your behalf. The attorney must keep your best interests in mind at all times. This type of business relationship is very different from the customer relationship formed with the grocery store. Level two services and relationships (like those with an attorney) form a client relationship providing negotiation, advocacy, and representation on your behalf.

To Be a Savvy Buyer, You Must Understand the Difference between Level One and Level Two Skills

If you really want to stretch your buying power and navigate smoothly through the real estate purchase, it's vital to understand the difference between level one and level two skills. Level one skills are those that you're more likely to feel confident tackling and are apt to sail through without much help, if any. These include checking out the neighborhood you're considering by driving around and posing questions to the neighbors. Level one skills are also the skills you're most likely to find no-cost or low-cost assistance with through print or online mediums. You only have to glance at the Resources section at the end of this book to see the vast array of online service providers touting free information for homebuyers and sellers alike.

Level two skills often require more expertise in real estate (like being able to accurately fill in all of the lines of the purchase agreement), and many level two skills contain an element of negotiating that some buyers are not comfortable traversing on their own behalf. Many of us admit that when it comes to negotiating for ourselves, we often have a fool for a client, especially on emotionally charged issues like purchasing a home. The more personal the service, and the higher the expertise required (like level two negotiating), the more likely that task is to play a pivotal role in your purchase and possibly require another party to provide it.

Buyers Must Be Aware of the Meat in the Middle

What Is It and How Can You Best Tackle It?

In purchasing a home, you're likely to find more level two tasks facing you in the middle of the process. So much so that I term them the meat in the middle. As in a sandwich, the meat in the middle is often the most important, substantive part of the whole. If the meat is lacking in quantity or quality, it's likely to be an unsatisfying or even a distasteful experience. If you fail to pay adequate attention as a buyer to navigating the meat in the middle, you could find yourself back at square one—without a house and only wasted time and expenses to show for your efforts.

Six Major Components Comprise the Meat in the Middle for Buyers

You may be tempted as an unassisted buyer to jump into the market in search of an unsuspecting for-sale-by-owner that will trim his price to offset the fact that he isn't paying a professional to locate you. If only it were that easy. In fact, as a buyer, you have to negotiate more meat in the middle than the seller. And not only do you have more potential landmines to side-step, they carry a higher importance rating than do the seller's meat in the middle tasks (an overall average rating of 8 for buyers compared to only 7 for sellers).

As you navigate this often problematic portion of the purchase, keep in mind the real estate adage "you don't make money when you sell it, you make money when you purchase it." Money lost by overpaying and other purchasing errors can snatch profit from your hands when you sell.

The six greatest hurdles in navigating the critical middle portion of the transaction for buyers are to:

1. Make sure you're preapproved for the mortgage
2. Check the property information
3. Determine the market value for the property
4. Properly draft the purchase agreement
5. Negotiate with the seller
6. Troubleshoot the purchase and close the transaction

Because these six components are critical to your success as a buyer, we'll cover them in detail.

Make sure you're preapproved for the mortgage. After you complete the loan application, stay apprised of the loan processing and promptly answer all requests from service providers (like the lender, title company, etc.). This becomes even more critical as the closing approaches in order to close on time and orchestrate moving for you and the seller. Make sure you contact the lender at least once a week to check on the status of the loan. When it comes to real estate lending, no news isn't necessarily good news!

Check the property information. Even if the seller has completed all forms with facts and figures, it's part of your job as a savvy buyer to check and double-check the information. This means measuring the square footage of the house, checking that all appliances are in working order, and even reviewing the plat map, the property boundaries, and the county assessor's records. It may seem like wasted time now, but it's your last chance prior to making an offer to uncover an inaccuracy that could end up costing you thousands!

Determine the market value for the property. The price may seem reasonable, but you need to obtain your own information (including information on comparable sales in the area) to determine if the market value is justified. Even if other eager buyers are breathing down your neck for the property, you could stand to lose thousands overpaying for the house. If you aren't comfortable enough performing this segment of the transaction, hire a real estate consultant to do it for you or access at least one of the online sites that perform market valuations and pay to receive the information. It typically costs less than $30 to obtain an evaluation online. The Resources section at the end of this book can guide you to several sites.

Properly draft the purchase agreement. If you're going it alone as a buyer, this can be one of the most difficult parts of the purchasing puzzle. As the buyer, you're typically the one making/drafting the initial offer to the seller. Besides being fully apprised of what to put in each blank and what to check in each box, you need to know how to protect yourself using contingencies and contract clauses. Several of the more prevalent ones are:

- *Financing contingency.* This contingency clause allows you valuable time to receive mortgage loan approval before being bound to complete the purchase of the property. Even though you've been preapproved for a loan, this contingency specifies that unless you can obtain a mortgage of the size, type, and approximate maximum interest rate you desire, you can be released from the purchase. Be sure to contact the lender you're working with to obtain an estimate of approximately how long the approval process will take. While you want to give yourself ample time to finalize the financing, you don't want the seller objecting to a time frame too broad that could make your offer less attractive than another buyer's.
- *Appraisal contingency.* Used in tandem with the financing contingency, this clause states that should the property appraisal come in at a figure different than the price offered in the purchase agreement, you don't have to buy the property and the seller doesn't have to sell. In practical terms, should the appraised price be lower than the

negotiated one, most sellers wouldn't expect a buyer to pay more, especially when it would mean coming up with the difference in cash.

- *Home inspection contingency.* Even if it's a hot seller's market with more buyers than available properties, don't waive the home inspection in order to make your offer more attractive to the seller. This contingency gives you the ability to withdraw your offer with your earnest money deposit being refunded should the home inspection report show repairs necessary that can't be negotiated between you and the seller. Most home inspectors welcome a prospective buyer to accompany him or her on the inspection. Not only will you learn a lot about the construction of the home you're purchasing, the inspector may point out ideas for making the home more cost-effective (like adding extra insulation, replacing window caulking, etc.). A recent trend is for the seller to obtain a prelisting home inspection on his own. This allows the seller to troubleshoot any problems and make repairs prior to launching the home on the market. It's up to you whether or not you want to accept the home inspection he's purchased or pay for and conduct your own. While your inspection might result in the same findings, it's not out of the realm of possibility that the seller "bought" a satisfactory home inspection from an unethical, unscrupulous home inspector.

- *Insurance contingency.* Depending in which part of the country you live, obtaining homeowners insurance can be a tedious and costly process. That's why removing this contingency is perhaps one of the first ones on which to work. If insurance is tough or virtually impossible to find at an affordable price (as in the states of California and Florida), it may not be cost-effective for you to purchase the type or location of home you're considering. It's advisable to initially ask the seller which company she's currently insured with because rewriting an existing policy is often much easier and more cost-effective than seeking a new insurer.

- *Backup offers clause.* This is a clause that the seller may insist upon until all contingencies are removed in your offer. It allows the seller to keep the property on the active market and take other contracts in second, third, or fourth positions behind yours. The clause won't impact your contract with the seller. But knowing that it's there is certainly an incentive for you to remove contingencies in a timely fashion.

- *Right of first refusal clause.* This is another type of seller-placed clause, but one that can be helpful to you in getting a less-than-perfect offer accepted by the seller. Let's say that you must first sell your current home before closing on the purchase of the seller's. The right of first refusal clause would protect both you and the seller by stating that: "the seller's property will be kept on the market and should another acceptable offer be received, the seller will notify the buyer in writing, and the buyer will then have X amount of days to remove the contingency and perform on the contract. Failure to do so will declare this purchase agreement null and void with return of buyer's earnest money." If you do use the right of first refusal clause, make sure that the time frame specified for removing the contingency is realistic. In most cases, seven to ten days is a normal period that is fair to both parties.

Negotiate with the seller. The market climate might make it seem like you can't do much to whittle down the price. But don't overlook the fact that successful negotiations are about much more than price. Much of what occurs in real estate negotiating is actually about perception. It's up to you to convince the seller that you're not only the best buyer for the property, but that he can actually win more by accepting your offer. Here are some negotiating tips to give you leverage over the competition.

- *Thoroughly understand how counteroffers work.* If you understand nothing else about negotiating, make sure you grasp the principle behind counteroffers. A counteroffer is an entirely new offer that the other party is under no obligation to accept. You may have decided on every other aspect of the purchase agreement, except one. But you stand to throw it all away by asking for that final, single change. This often occurs over the most innocent, least important aspects. For example, let's say that in the last round of offers and counteroffers, the seller agreed to take $2,000 less on his sales price if you would agree to close your purchase ten days early on the 20th of the month. Because you don't want to lose ten days' worth of interest ($200) by taking your down payment money out of savings earlier, you cross out the closing date and reinstate the previous date of the 30th. This constitutes a counteroffer that the seller is under no obligation to accept! In other words, you stand to not only lose the $2,000 savings on the lower purchase price to which the seller agreed, but you could lose the entire purchase over a mere $200!

- *Don't scrimp on the earnest money.* Like it or not, money talks. All things considered, if two offers appear equal in almost every respect, the one offering the largest amount of earnest money is most likely to attract the seller (especially in a seller's market). A large earnest money deposit intimates (erroneously or not) that the buyer is financially capable and motivated to purchase. And because the earnest money is credited towards your down payment at closing, there's no reason not to use this ace as initial leverage to cinch the purchase.
- *Your initial offer sets the stage for future negotiations.* This is one of the primary tenets of negotiating. If you offer far less than the listed price, expect the seller to counter back to you at full price (or even above!) or be so insulted that he ignores your offer completely. Your initial offer to the seller speaks volumes about your willingness to negotiate a win-win contract. If you ask for additional personal property to be included in the purchase price, expect that the seller will return the request with an equally, if not

more costly, counterproposal to you. By putting yourself mentally in the seller's position, you're more likely to achieve a quicker and more equitable win-win contract.

- *Never have just one issue left to negotiate.* If it's down to only one issue, one party will win and one will lose. Make sure that you keep at least two issues in negotiation to the end.

Troubleshoot the purchase and close the transaction. The closer you get to closing the purchase, the more emergencies you may encounter. And while you may be inclined to brush them off and let someone else jump in and accomplish them, it's up to you to take care of them if you want things to close. Going it alone requires that you interface with the seller, the lender, the title company, and other service providers involved on at least a weekly basis as the closing nears. And don't forget that under federal law, you have the right to review all closing documents for at least 24 hours prior to closing. If you've been on your own up to this point, this is a prime time to have your closing documents reviewed by a real estate attorney prior to signing them. For the several hundred dollars it may cost you, it's more than worth the peace of mind and potential cost savings should an error be found.

If Your Greatest Hurdle Is the Meat in the Middle

Refer back to the buyer checkpoint miniquizzes you took in Chapter 4. In which parts of the buying puzzle did you score lowest? If your lowest scores were at Checkpoints 4 (checking property information and pricing the property), 5 (drafting the purchase agreement and negotiating with the seller), and/ or 6 (troubleshooting the sale), it could signal you need help with the meat in the middle.

Using a real estate consultant, especially one who's a certified buyer's agent, will result in a safe and sound purchase agreement and a negotiated settlement that's clearly to the buyer's benefit.

> Gail Lyons, DREI, CRB, C-CREC
> Don Harlan, DREI, CRE, C-CREC
> Authors of *The Future of Real Estate:*
> *Profiting from the Revolution,* published by Dearborn

Myriad Ways You Can Use Fee-for-Services Assistance as a Buyer

Real-World Scenarios

You'll remember that the buyer checkpoints found in Chapter 4 were:

1. Design a purchase strategy
2. Be preapproved for a mortgage
3. Choose the neighborhood and the property
4. Check property information and pricing
5. Draft the purchase agreement/negotiate with the seller
6. Troubleshoot the purchase/close the transaction

You'll see by the following examples that your ability to match fee-for-services options with the help you need is limited only to your imagination!

Deciding whether to rent or buy. Marcia McGee is a 30-something career woman. Because her job requires her to relocate every several years, she has never purchased a house. Being Web adept, she finds an online calculator at <www .homefair.com> to determine if it would be more cost-effective to purchase now or continue renting. She enters the information requested at the site, including the amount of rent she's currently paying and how long she anticipates keeping the house. In less than a minute, out comes the results. The response "too close to call" has Marcia puzzled. It seems that because she may sell in less than three years, she may not have time to build enough equity to pay closing costs on the resale. This is particularly true given the small down payment she was considering.

Marcia contacts Suzanne Shelton, a real estate consultant that does business with her company. Suzanne assures her that if she really wants to purchase a home at this time, there are various ways to structure financing to help her build equity quicker and not have to bring a check to closing. This includes using an adjustable rate mortgage with a lower introductory interest rate, making a 20 percent down payment instead of 10 percent, and obtaining a mortgage that has no penalty for early prepayment within the first five years of the loan. Marcia is pleased because she can now purchase a home without worrying if it was a bad economic move. Suzanne charged a consulting fee of $175 for one hour of her time which included a synopsis of the type of mortgage Marcia should shop for.

Seeking a real estate consultant not only made Marcia feel comfortable taking the homebuying plunge, it made her realize that professional help for various types of real estate information and services is just a phone call or e-mail away. While counsel from other real estate professionals, like lenders in Marcia's case, may provide number-crunching assistance to help reach conclusions, all consumers should seek more than one opinion when the professional has something to gain from the solution suggested. If Marcia's path had initially crossed with an unscrupulous lender who only wanted to make her a loan, she could find herself bringing a check to the closing table when she later sold the house.

Getting preapproved for a mortgage. The Boylans are interested in moving up to a larger home that better suits their growing family. They've called several local lenders but are not impressed with the interest rates or points quoted for loans especially given the fact that they'll be making a 50 percent down payment from the sale of their current home.

A neighbor suggests they go online to check out rates. They do and are pleasantly surprised at what they find. There are several sites, like <www.lendingtree.com> and <www.e-loan.com>, that shop with more than a hundred lenders for borrowers, eliminating the hassle of applying at every mortgage site. Others like <www.onloan.com> and <www.countrywide.com> use internal resources to match those best suited for borrowers' needs. These sites find a variety of possible matches and within 30 minutes, have the consumer preapproved for the size loan they'll need at the interest rate they're willing to pay.

The Boylans decide not to apply online. Instead, they take the competitive rates and points quoted on the Web and use them as ammunition with the local lender who has their banking business. By noon the next day, the Boylans have the competitively priced loan they want with the points and closing costs they're willing to pay.

As we noted in Chapter 1, online aggregators and information providers will provide 20 percent of the real estate solutions in this decade. This means that not only will consumers use the Web to motivate local lenders into being competitive, many more borrowers will obtain loans online and close at the local title company, never meeting the lender who has advanced tens of thousands of dollars.

Analyzing the neighborhood and property you're considering. You'll be pleasantly surprised to find that this checkpoint is one that often you'll have no trouble at all navigating on your own. But it does take time to structure your investigative work and legwork. Additionally, there are a wealth of sites online to assist you in information gathering. For checking the crime rate in the neighborhood, visit <www.crimewatch.com>. For gathering information about environmental impact in an area, go to <www.epa.gov>, and for information on schools and their ratings, you'll find <www.schoolreport.com> invaluable. Using online resources for a majority of fact-finding homework could significantly trim the prep time into quick, point-and-click "mouse work"!

For example, Joe Suarez was born in South America and has lived in the United States for three years. He works as a Webmaster for a large Chicago firm and is excited about purchasing a home in one of the city's Latin communities. Being Web-savvy, he successfully uses online information providers like <www.cswonline.com> to gather information, including U.S. Census Bureau facts, about neighborhoods in which he's interested.

Checking the property information and the property disclosure statement. Pete Viola wants to make an offer on a house he's found listed by a for-sale-by-owner. Pete's biggest concern is not what the seller has disclosed in the property disclosure statement, but information that might be overlooked or concealed by the seller. He takes a copy of the property disclosure statement to a real estate consultant who specializes in marketing and development. The consultant agrees to visit the property and compare the statement with his findings. He quotes his fee as $100 per hour, capped at a maximum of $500. Upon visiting the property, he determines that two rooms, a bedroom and a bath, have been recently added to the house. Yet in checking at the building department, he finds no record of a building permit issued or applied for at that address. The seller admits that he did not apply for the permit and that, in fact, the addition encroaches upon the neighbor's lot line. Pete is relieved that the information was uncovered prior to making his offer and that it only cost him $200 to determine, not potentially tens of thousands if the truth had been uncovered at a later stage.

Negotiate with the seller. Crystal Cochrane is a first-time buyer who knows she needs help holding her own against the three other potential buyers for the house she wants to purchase. She hires Mac Martin, a real estate consultant specializing in buyer representation and negotiation. He advises her that given the circumstances and competition, her best advantage is to offer market value, close in one month (which is one of the seller's hot buttons), and not take occupancy until the seller's children are out of school in May, which is two months from now. It looks like the seller might agree to compensate the buyer for waiting by making the buyer's new mortgage payment for that period of time. Crystal makes her offer, matching all of the terms suggested by the consultant. However, a competing buyer agrees to waive the home inspection as suggested by the seller to speed up the sales process. The other three competing buyers are encouraged to meet or beat those terms. After consulting with Mac, Crystal weighs the pros and cons and declines to make a counteroffer to the seller. Mac informs her that if she should find a defect in the house, there would be little or no recourse having waived the home inspection. Mac is successful in helping Crystal purchase another property in the same neighborhood and a thorough home inspection is conducted without incidence. Two months after closing, the buyer of the first house Crystal made an offer on files a lawsuit against the sellers for nondisclosure of a major crack in the foundation.

The lesson here is that a truly knowledgeable and professional real estate consultant would inform a consumer about the good, the bad, and the potentially ugly, not focusing on the real estate commission in limbo. Because the consultant had the ability to be unbiased, he provided Crystal with a most valuable service—the ability to advise her when the stakes of the homebuying game were too high and too risky for her to chance.

Troubleshoot the purchase and close the transaction. Robin Myer is purchasing her fifth house in ten years. As a seasoned buyer, she's learned there are places to cut costs. However, working without the aid of a real estate attorney is not one of them! She delivers a copy of her purchase agreement, closing papers, and mortgage documents to her attorney for review one day prior to the formal closing. In comparing the purchase agreement with the closing statement, the attorney finds that the cost of discount points has not been appropriately divided between the buyer and seller, resulting in a $950 overcharge on Robin's closing statement. Once again, buying one hour of a professional's time has resulted in net savings to her.

Five Rules of Thumb for Buyer Fee-for-Services

Make Sure You Don't Overlook Any!

When considering what type of fee-for-services assistance you need and why, it's important to keep the following five rules of thumb in mind:

1. The tougher the task or service is to duplicate, the more value it commands
2. The more a task or service requires personal application and skill (like negotiating or troubleshooting the purchase), the more likely you are to have someone else provide it
3. The more personalized and skill-related the task, the higher the price you should be willing to pay for it
4. The closer you are to closing a purchase, the more important it is to secure the professional service you need
5. Time is money; while scrimping on professional services might appear to be a cost-saving measure, meeting deadlines and closing the purchase in a more timely fashion could prove more cost-effective in the long run

What to Do If You're Short on Time

Guidelines to Streamline the Process

- Pay for all or as many of the level two skills you can afford in order to expedite the transaction. In general, those will be the skills that occur once you find the property, while negotiations are under way, and up until the time the purchase is closed. Delegate (or drop) as many of the level

one tasks as possible unless doing so could have a negative
impact on the purchase.

- If the seller is paying the agent's fee, consider working
  with a full-service real estate broker/licensee. In most
  states, you can obtain the assistance of an exclusive buyer's
  agent. This real estate licensee would represent your interests (not the seller's) and provide you with valuable negotiating and troubleshooting assistance.

What to Do If You're Short on Money

Guideline to Cut Costs

Prioritize paying for all of the level two services you need
and locate no-cost/low-cost ways to obtain the level one help
you need (including information and assistance from online
resources). Make sure the services you access are unbiased
and have nothing to benefit by sharing useful information
with you.

What to Do If You're Short on Patience and/or Know-How

Guidelines to Cut Down on Stress

- Pay a real estate consultant for the assistance you need.
- Work with a full-service real estate agent to represent your
  interests in a buyer's agent capacity. As mentioned in
  Chapter 2, buyer's agents are often compensated from the
  proceeds of the sale. This means that unless you require
  services outside of the normal scope of representing a
  buyer, you'd pay nothing additional to the agent representing you. Even if the seller hasn't agreed to pay a buyer's
  agent's fee, the following clause can become part of the
  purchase agreement with the seller to provide compensation to the buyer's agent: "All parties agree that included

in the price being offered shall be a fee equal to X dollars (could be a percentage of the sales price) paid to the buyer's agent (brokerage name) at time of closing from the proceeds of the transaction provided by the buyer and/or lender; and that the buyer's agent is receiving no compensation whatsoever from the listing brokerage."

- Make sure a real estate attorney reviews all documents, including, but not limited to, the purchase agreement, the closing statement, and any mortgage documents you'll be signing.

As noted in this chapter, when it comes to needing assistance, buyers have a greater potential need than sellers. Make sure that in your rush to purchase and minimize costs, you don't scrimp on obtaining critical professional assistance and services that could eventually make a difference between profit and loss when you sell.

Unique Real Estate
à la Carte Applications
to Save You Money

Since our society is consumer driven, we must put our comfortable way of doing business as a traditional real estate professional on the shelf, look at it once in a while, and allow nostalgic thoughts about how things used to be. Then we must turn from the shelf to what the consumer demands and embrace the industry that lies before us, fulfilling the specialized needs of those who come to us for service they can't or prefer not to do for themselves.

Bonnie Sparks, CRB, CRS, DREI, C-CREC
National real estate educator
Author of *Client Advocacy in the New Marketplace* (Real Estate Education Company, 2001) and *If You're Clueless about Selling Your House and Want to Know More* (Dearborn Trade, 1999)

Where to Go, How to Know, and
What to Expect on Your Side Trips

A Wide Variety of Possible Locations—Some by Accident

While using unbundled, fee-for-services consulting as a seller or buyer may be the first application that comes to mind, it is far from being the only way you'll use à la carte real estate services. In fact, because most of us only purchase and sell an average of four homes during our lifetime, yet own real estate for approximately 60 years on the average, chances are we'll need other types of real estate problem solving just as much, if not more. This is especially true when we stand to risk a lot financially by not seeking the help needed when a real estate calamity strikes. Various types of specialty or niche real estate consulting is cost-effective when the economy is booming, and vital in times of economic downturn as shown by my first consulting experience in 1980.

The Accidental Real Estate Consultant

My initial (accidental) experience as a real estate consultant occurred just as mortgage interest rates were topping 18 percent in 1980. Mr. Cantrell was a frustrated contractor referred to me by a longtime client. While he was under contract with a large national corporation to construct an 8,000 square foot building to serve as a western distribution center, the project stalled. He had completed 40 percent of the structure when the precarious economy made the corporation rethink their expansion strategies. They decided to scrap the project until the economy improved, and wanted Mr. Cantrell to take the building and land for what they still owed him in labor and materials.

That's why he came to see me. He needed to know how he could best complete the building to attract tenants (not an easy task during a recession). He also needed information on what he could expect to collect in rents and how to structure a win-win lease agreement as well as mount an effective marketing campaign to attract tenants.

He said he'd heard that I was good at fixing real estate problems which was true. Owning a real estate brokerage in the early 1980s required the ultimate in problem fixing! He stated that he wanted to hire me as his real estate consultant, and then asked, "What will you charge me?"

I was stunned. I'd never had anyone ask me what I'd charge for something as insignificant as information. Being a typical real estate broker of the time, I only got paid when I sold something or someone else (another real estate agent) sold one of my listings. More times than not, I'd give hours', days', weeks' worth of information away for free before I'd see any compensation. Being a supersleuth by nature, wading through layers of information and analyzing it was fun. In fact, I thought of it as my stock in trade. Now this man wanted to pay me for finding information. Was it even legal?

But I knew that not responding to his question would blatantly show my ignorance. Grasping for a number, I knew that other professionals, like my real estate attorney, charged by the hour. In fact, he charged $150 per hour (the upper end of professional fees at the time). I knew I couldn't charge that; after all, I had never gathered information for money before. But I took a deep breath, cut the attorney's fee in half, and in a barely audible voice volunteered, "$75 per hour."

"How much?" he questioned.

Sinking deeper into my chair, I repeated a bit more coherently, "$75 per hour."

"That's fair," he said.

"How many hours will it take you to complete the job?" he asked.

The only thing I could think of was, beats me, I'm new to this approach! But that wasn't true. I'd been in the real estate business for nearly ten years. I did this type of work all day long. I'd just never been paid for it like this. So, I mentally tallied up approximately how long it would take me to complete the various tasks, and resolutely answered, "Ten hours at the most."

"Great," he replied. Here's a retainer for $200 and I'll pay you the balance when you report your findings."

I thanked him, stood up, shook his hand, and walked him to the door. Noticing the deer-in-the-headlights expression on my face, my secretary asked, "What was that all about?"

"I have no earthly idea, but I think I like it."

And I did like it, especially when the client was so pleased with the results. He completed the building for one of the target tenant groups I suggested (a trucking firm) and, even in a roller coaster economy, had it rented in no time. He also became a great marketing tool to build my business, telling anyone who would listen that hiring me as a real estate consultant saved him tens of thousands of dollars. Hearing that additional confirmation, I promptly raised my fee!

In retrospect, real estate consulting has been one of the most satisfying aspects of my nearly 30 years in real estate. The process of teaming with a consumer or a company to map out the objectives to reach, how to reach them, and what it will take in time, effort, and money is exhilarating. Each situation is different and no two days the same. There's nothing more satisfying than helping make the American Dream better.

Real Estate Problems a Consultant Can Help You Solve

A Real Estate Consultant Can Smooth Out Your Toughest Problems

If you've got a real estate challenge, the best thing to do is consider using a real estate consultant right from the beginning because many problems don't occur in real estate situations until they're too late to repair (or at least do cost-effectively).

While it's fun to take an occasional impromptu trip without the proper map, compass, and other valuable tools, it can be a recipe for disaster in real estate–related situations. You can find yourself knee-deep in what you thought would be an exciting adventure, only to realize that your dream has become a haunting, ever-present nightmare in boring black and white! Perhaps that's why many applications and descriptions of real estate consulting projects remind us of movie titles, some new, some decades old. See if you can guess which ones are depicted in the scenarios that follow.

When Remodeling—You've Got Nail(s)!

You inherit a house from your great aunt's estate. It's in shambles, but because you know a little bit about remodeling, you take it on as a weekend project to fix up and sell.

Two years, $40,000 and ten migraine headaches later, you're still ripping and tearing out walls, have no running water, and you just want to unload the sucker! Remember the movie *The Money Pit?* A real estate consultant could help you prioritize what to finish (plumbing would be nice), how to price it to effect a quick sale, and even help you obtain a small bridge loan to float you financially until the sale closes. Much like Tom Hanks and Meg Ryan in *You've Got Mail,* your outcome using a real estate consultant should be just as sunny.

For Planning and Zoning Problems—
Who's Afraid of Virginia's Wolf?

You receive a letter from the city planning and zoning department informing you that your neighbor has applied for a conditional use permit that would allow her to have a small, commercial kennel on her property. This is the last straw because her three pitbull/wolf-breed dogs already howl at the moon, keeping you awake at night.

You hire a real estate consultant. He does research about the property and discovers that her request will be impossible because there's inadequate lot line set back to build the dog runs required to meet city code. Additionally, he learns that the conditions, covenants, and restrictions for your subdivision don't allow homeowners to keep any type of nondomestic-breed dog on a property. Even Liz Taylor in *Who's Afraid of Virginia Woolf?* would love the retribution!

Now only the neighbors' poodles keep you awake at night. There are just some things even a consultant can't solve!

For Improve versus Move—
Guess Who's Coming to Hammer?

It's official. You've decided that you and your family are either going to make improvements to your cracker-box small house or you're going to buy another one.

You call your brother-in-law, Louie (who moonlights doing carpentry work), to ask for his estimate to add on a master bedroom suite plus a playroom for the kids. Meanwhile, you hit the street, viewing several open houses in a neighborhood close to where you work.

Timing in the land of improve versus move is (almost) everything! Within several hours, Louie hustles over with his estimate (scribbled down on a cocktail napkin). It's so incredibly low that you say, "Go for it, Louie," and you seal the deal over a tall cool one (discovered to be Louie's tenth for the day).

Several hundred nails and two weeks later, a spot check by a county building inspector reveals that not only has Louie failed to obtain the proper permits (costing you a $500 fine), but the monstrosity he's constructing encroaches on the neighbor's property and must be torn down.

Besides the obvious lesson to never hire a relative, there's much more involved than merely selecting the lowest bid. Without a thorough evaluation by a specialist, launching a project improperly can erode the property's equity and/or mount your debt. Just as cantankerous Spencer Tracy took his time sizing up his dinner guests in *Guess Who's Coming to Dinner,* employing caution when deciding to improve or move is wise.

To Troubleshoot a Sale Midstream— Journey to the End of the Sale

Patterned after the movie epic *Journey to the Center of the Earth,* this trip is one you didn't want to take in the first place and, now, it seems it will never end.

Your elderly mother calls to tell you she's going to sell her house. You suggest that because you don't have the time to assist her, she list the property with a full-service brokerage company to do it for her.

She responds that she may already have a buyer, the young woman who rents the house next door, whose father agreed to give her the down payment she needs to get a loan. He'll make sure the paperwork gets done, too.

You sigh with relief, hang up, and resume your life.

As you might expect, that was the only good news heard during the entire six months of this epic transaction. The buyer's credit report is a mess, requiring months to untangle before she can be approved for the loan. The purchase agreement drafted by the buyer's dad (with snippets of advice from his golfing buddy) strongly favored the buyer, containing enough contingencies to tie up the property for six months without a closing in sight.

In total desperation (after learning that your mother has been paying rent for six months on the apartment she was hoping to move in to, funded by taking in laundry), you contact a real estate consultant. In a matter of hours, he negotiates with the buyer's father to cosign for his daughter's loan, and she's approved. Simultaneously, he insists that, for the hardship caused the seller, that the buyer reimburse her for 50 percent of the apartment rent paid. Finally, he suggests that because moving will be a physical strain on the seller (compounded by the emotional strain she's sustained during the past six months), it would be appropriate for the buyer to help the seller move. The buyer's brother (enlisted to help) brings five college buddies, and by noon, your mom is happily settled, enjoying lunch in her new apartment. Just another ordinary day in the life of a real estate consultant!

To Interface with an Ex on a Property Sale— The Agony of the Ex to See

So far, the scenarios have dealt primarily with the physical aspects of real estate or its improvements. But how about using a fee-for-services professional to do the people-rated job(s) you dread doing? Like convince a former spouse to sell a house and reach a consensus about price and terms. Sure. The last time you agreed on anything, Eisenhower was president.

When you divorced Roger five years ago, the real estate market was flat, so you decided to find a renter until the house could garner a higher sales price. And because you would like the equity to help finance a new car and take a trip to the Bahamas, you bite the bullet and call your ex.

The reception is anything but cordial. He thinks it's a stupid idea, especially because his new wife doesn't want him within two counties of you. Immediately, you have those déjà vu feelings of squabbling and never reaching a midground solution to your problems.

And then it hits you. What about the real estate consultant who prepared the comparative market analysis on the house for you? Would he be willing to intercede between you and Roger? It's worth a try. And it's undoubtedly worth the money to shed the aggravation.

The real estate consultant agrees to tackle "Roger the Terrible" and spends an hour gathering information from you about the situation. The consultant works out a strategy to offset Roger's concerns about selling, while focusing on his greatest fatal flaw—greed.

Roger sees the error of his ways (not in the divorce, but in selling the house), and due in large part to the consultant, you have a meeting of the minds on price, terms, and that you'll split the costs of the sale. Miracles do happen.

Even the new Mrs. Roger is happy because all communication is handled via the real estate consultant and you never darken their door. And contrary to how she feels about you, she thinks the consultant is kind of cute!

And the name of the movie in the scenario title is? (Say the title out loud very quickly and you'll have it.)

To Troubleshoot an Erroneous Property Tax Assessment—South Specific

"It can't be that time of year already," you moan. "Another property tax assessment notice and you can bet that the property tax gouging continues." You open the notice to find that instead of the customary 5 percent to 10 percent annual increase, the assessed value of your property has jumped a whopping 40 percent!

"This is outrageous!" you scream. "There's got to be something wrong. This property wouldn't be worth this much even in California!"

After listening to elevator music for 30 minutes while on hold with the assessor's office, you storm downtown for a personal visit. The assessor checks the computer printout and his field/log book of the notes he took when last evaluating the property, but nothing appears to be in error. Bewildered, you drag home.

At church on Sunday, you mention your plight to a woman you know is a real estate consultant. Although she specializes solely in commercial real estate, she says she knows someone who could check into it for you.

Monday afternoon, you meet with the real estate consultant who specializes in land development and tax issues. He says he can't believe that the assessor couldn't find an error because a 40 percent increase is virtually unheard of, unless a radical event impacts a property, like rezoning. He takes a photocopy of your information and has you read and sign a contract stating the work to be done. You agree to pay him by the hour, up to a maximum of five hours (with a minimum guarantee of $300). He also has you sign a release of information form in case he needs to access information only available to you as the property owner.

In less than two hours, he's uncovered the problem—it's an error in the legal description on the assessment notice that was printed out by the county's computer system. In order to link into a statewide computer system earlier in the year, legal descriptions had to be entered manually into the database. Instead of inputting the legal description to reflect the true .30 acre of land, the property dimensions equaled 30 acres—all zoned for single-family residences (accounting for the high property taxes). In specific, the south boundary dimensions in error stretched well across the bare acres of county land to the south of the property. (As in the movie *South Pacific,* Bali Hai was more plausible than this flawed legal description!)

The consultant brings the legal description error to the assessor's attention. He compares it to the recorded deed as well as to the files at the title insurance company. Yes, the legal description entered into the computer was in error, and the proper corrections are made.

The consultant drops by your home to present you with a corrected, freshly printed property assessment notice. You thank him profusely as you hand him a check for $300 because he's just saved you nearly $1,000 in property taxes!

*T*oday *a consumer interested in any aspect of a real estate transaction can hire a real estate consultant who can provide answers and advice covering a wide variety of topics. Not all questions posed by a consumer lead to a real estate transaction. For example, let's say you owned a home and wanted to compare the benefits of staying in that home and remodeling versus purchasing another home. A real estate consultant will provide you with the pros and cons along with specific costs you might incur. With this information you could make a more informed decision whether to refinance and remodel or purchase a new home.*

Doug Schmitt, DREI, ABR, C-CREC

The Top Ten Most Common Ways a Real Estate Consultant Can Assist You

Residential Real Estate Needs Are the Most Common

Even if it's unlikely that you'll ever have to squabble with your former spouse over selling a piece of property, there are a handful of common real estate situations in which you may find yourself needing help. The following is the top ten list of most common real estate problems (exclusive of purchasing and selling) with ideas for working with a real estate consultant to save you time, money, and aggravation in solving them.

1. Improve versus move. The homeowner's $64,000 (or more) question today is, "Would it make more sense to improve our existing home or move to another?" Unfortunately, there are many layers of information you need to gather and analyze.

If you started out working with a consultant to solve the improve versus move question, he would first ask, "Are you pleased with the neighborhood and schools here?" The primary reasons owners decide to improve rather than move is their satisfaction level with the quality of life in a certain neighborhood, low crime rates, and above-average schools (all factors that greatly improve the resale value of the home).

Next, he would ask, "How long do you plan to stay in this house?" The answer has a direct bearing on whether you'll be able to recoup the costs by the time you sell the house as well as justify the mental anguish that accompanies remodeling a home!

If you will live in the property long enough to recoup the costs of improvement (or be willing to sacrifice the cost if you don't), he would pencil out a price for what an improved version of your house would sell. By preparing a comparative market analysis showing what homes with similar improvements have sold for in neighborhoods like yours, you can gauge the impact the improvement will have on the home's resale. An overimproved home, especially in an area of more modest ones, can be incredibly difficult to sell and virtually impossible on which to recoup costs.

If you're not happy with your neighborhood and/or schools, it could make more sense to sell the current house and purchase another one. The real estate consultant can pencil out your costs of sale, the amount you would net, and the amount needed for down payment and closing costs on the new purchase.

As seen in the disastrous improve versus move scenario with brother-in-law Louie, a real estate consultant specializing in construction would have:

- Taken longer than a few hours to prepare estimates, sketches, and a complete proposal
- Secured the proper permits before hammering the first nail
- Insisted that the building inspector do a thorough site visit prior to construction

Additionally, he would have the inspector sign off on a form stating that the additions proposed are not in violation of any current building codes. This practice is standard procedure in many county and city building and planning departments across the country.

In summary, here are the most important questions to ask when determining improve versus move:

- *How long do we intend to keep the house?*
- *Will we be able to recoup the cost of improvements when selling?*
- *Are the improvements we're considering logical, given the age, size, and location of the house?* Just as you wouldn't install a new sunroof on a dilapidated car, making expensive additions to a house that's full of functional obsolescence (like the tiny bathrooms circa 1940) may not make financial sense. Appraisers agree that it's much tougher to recoup the investment from home improvements if they aren't similar in style and design/era to the existing home.
- *Could additions/changes overimprove the house?* A house at the top of the market for the neighborhood can take longer to sell because buyers often purchase on the low side, hoping to maximize equity and improvements made over time.

These primary questions can serve as tethers and talking points to help you find answers for the improve versus move question. Check out these additional resources online:

- <www.nahb.com>, Web site of the National Association of Homebuilders; a good source for weighing the cost of improvements to the corresponding value you could recoup at time of resale
- <www.buildscape.com>, a great source for construction ideas and answers to construction questions

2. Remodel the house. In the fourth quarter of 1999, remodeling outlays totaled a record seasonally adjusted rate of $165.2 billion, a figure that is expected to increase annually in the current decade.

But similar to improve versus move, costs expended in remodeling may not be recouped when you sell. And there are some changes and additions that aren't welcomed by certain buyer demographic segments.

For example, families with young children might shy away from owning a swimming pool because drowning is the number one cause of death for children under age five. A remodeled master suite in a third-floor loft could be undesirable if the prospective buyer/targets were retirees. Even though you may want to make additions/changes based on your immediate needs and desires, it never hurts to look downstream at who a potential future buyer might be in order to avoid overimprovements you can't recoup.

One of the most valuable ways a real estate consultant can contribute to your remodeling decisions is by analyzing which financing options are most cost-effective.

Let's say you need approximately $70,000 to add on a master bedroom, bath, and expand your garage. You currently owe $55,000 on your mortgage, and the property should be worth approximately $150,000 after the improvements are complete.

You've checked mortgage rates online at sites like <www.on loan.com>, <www.lendingtree.com>, and <www.country

wide.com> but the options are overwhelming. After strategizing how long it will take you to complete the remodeling job as well as how long you'll keep the property, the consultant makes the following suggestion: Obtain a line of credit now with a low introductory rate of interest. When the remodeling is complete, refinance into a zero-closing-cost adjustable rate mortgage.

But you're confused. Wouldn't you merely be duplicating loan costs? Probably not, depending on the costs to set up the equity line of credit.

Here's why. The consultant explains that making improvements funded by an equity line allows you to pay less interest initially and requires you to only make payments on the outstanding balance. For example, if your total equity line is $70,000 but the contractor bills you $15,000 for improvements the first month, your payments would be based only on the $15,000. Unlike a second mortgage where you receive loan proceeds for the entire amount at closing and repay in equal payments, a line of credit gives you the flexibility to borrow only what you need, when you need it.

If you initially obtained funds by refinancing into one new, larger loan, what you could borrow would be based on the property's current value, not the improved value. That could mean you'd be short of the total funds needed. Even if you were to obtain all you needed by refinancing, your payments would be higher than the equity line because you'd be borrowing more, probably at a higher interest rate. And with the anticipated amount you'll need for improvements (plus being able to pay off your current loan of $55,000) the refinanced loan could require private mortgage insurance because you'd need a loan that exceeded 80 percent of the property's value. This, too, would increase your monthly payment.

The consultant advises you to obtain a firm commitment on the future refinance barring anything changing in your financial picture. One of the downsides of most equity lines is that it must be paid off when the property is sold, lenders usually won't allow other loans to be placed while outstanding lines exist, and the low introductory rate of interest will typically expire in less than one year. Once the low interest rate expires, the new rate is often based on the prime rate plus 2 percent. If you later found you couldn't qualify for refinancing, you'd be saddled with higher payments on a large balance, realizing no savings, only more costs, by taking the equity line of credit route.

You may be wondering why you'd access a real estate consultant for comparing financing options instead of going directly to a lender? The rationale is similar to not consulting a real estate sales agent to help make the decision to improve or move. Someone being compensated based on selling you something (a mortgage or a new house) may not be unbiased in her approach. A real estate consultant who specializes in weighing the pros and cons of various financing programs will help you analyze information from sites like <www.mortgage marvel.com> and <www.gomez.com>, two excellent sites that compare and rate online mortgage companies and the loans they offer.

3. Refinance your mortgage(s). I once had a consumer volunteer that she wouldn't trust any lender who told her not to refinance her mortgage because lenders are in the business of making loans. And today, with all of the new mortgage products available, including subprime loans, even borrowers with incredibly blemished credit can refinance their property. It's done to pay off credit card debt, fund a child's college tuition, or finance a trip around the world.

With refinancing programs and money so readily available, the potential for choosing the wrong loan product, the wrong lender, or both is extremely high.

John and Sue Bolling want to tap into their home's equity to retire credit card debt, pay off a loan on their boat, and take a nice vacation. They have received mortgage loan program quotes from three lenders, one online company and two companies locally. The interest rates are the same for two of the three companies with the third one-quarter percent lower.

In order to sort out the information, they contact a real estate consultant who specializes in equity management issues to assist them. She helps them complete a Consumer Needs Assessment and learns that they may be selling the house in four years or less. By comparing closing costs between each of the loan program quotes, she discovers that one of the companies is charging substantially higher closing costs. And the company offering the lowest interest rate has a hefty prepayment penalty that will apply to the loan during the first five years. By process of elimination, she suggests the Bollings return to the third remaining lender to negotiate a lower interest rate (comparable to the one offered by the other company) on a mortgage with no prepayment penalty and no junk (miscellaneous) closing costs. The real estate consultant also suggests that the couple have the lender pay off the credit cards and the boat directly at closing. That way they won't be tempted to spend the money elsewhere, on a much longer vacation, for example.

A real estate consultant is an excellent resource to show you how to maximize your equity buildup when you refinance by using a shorter-term mortgage. More and more buyers realize that it makes little sense, especially in the era of affordable interest rates, to take on another 30-year mortgage. With a long-term loan, you're postponing whittling down that principal balance. And in some cases, it's time and money lost forever.

Here's an example of the equity building power of a shorter-term, 20-year loan. Let's assume we're comparing two $100,000 mortgages at 8 percent—one for 30 years and the other for 20. Although we don't know exactly how long we'll stay in this house, let's assume that we know we'll be there for two years.

In the payment department, we'd pay $733.77 principal and interest for the 30-year loan, compared to $836.45 for the 20-year loan. That's a monthly difference of $102.68. For many buyers, this is where the comparison ends because they may not be able to qualify for the higher payment and/or the larger monthly payment scares them. The rationalization (the one often touted by lenders) is that the buyer could always make prepayments on the lower-payment loan, while the higher payment would be tougher to make, especially if there's a job loss or other financial downturn.

But when we look at the rest of the story, we see just how much more we're paying for the longer-term loan. In two years' time, the 20-year loan is paid down to 95.6 percent of its original balance, or to $95,600. But the 30-year loan is reduced to only 98.3 percent of its original balance, or $98,300. That's a difference of $2,700. So the $2,464.32 we thought we were spared by taking the lower monthly payments (with the longer-term loan) is more than offset with the loss in equity buildup; and the longer we make payments, the greater that savings gap becomes. Five years into both loans, the 20-year loan balance will be at $87,500 while the 30-year loan will still be at a whopping $95,100—roughly an 8 percent difference in equity buildup in just five years!

But there's even more to consider. We compared two loans with the same interest rate. In the mortgage world, there's no reason why you should pay the same rate of interest for a 20-year loan that you would for a 30-year loan. Even if a lender doesn't quote you much of an interest spread between the two loan terms, always bargain. After all, if you qualify for a higher monthly payment, it can indicate that you're a stronger borrower; thus, the lender's risk is potentially less.

After weighing the payment difference and the rate of equity buildup in tandem with your financial goals for owning the property, the dollars and sense of a shorter-term mortgage may be just the boost your equity needs. A real estate consultant can pencil out the savings as well as the potential risks of the higher payment for your individual situation.

Some excellent Web sites where you can obtain information on refinancing include <www.championmortgage.com>, <www.homeshark.com>, and <www.quickenmortgage.com>.

4. Prepay your mortgage. If you haven't received a letter from your lender, requesting that you consider swapping to their biweekly payment program to cut years of payments off your mortgage, you will soon. It's part of the I-want-my-mortgage-paid-off trend sweeping the nation (especially for baby boomers who know their retirement income won't be nearly enough to fund their current sizable mortgage payments).

Is it always wise to pay off your mortgage when there are other places you can put the cash to allow it to grow? No. That's why before falling prey to any lender's often expensive solutions to accelerate your mortgage payments, visit with a real estate consultant.

Similar to an evaluation by a financial planner, the consultant will determine what your long-term goals are for owning the home, whether another mortgage would be in your future, and where you could invest the money to obtain a greater return on your money. With the affordable interest rates of today's market, it may not pay to retire a low-interest-rate debt when the prepayment money could be invested to compound to many times its value over time.

Most consultants would advise you to pitch the lender's biweekly mortgage solicitation flier in the trash. Converting your current mortgage to make one-half of the payment twice a month is nothing that you can't do yourself, without wasting the $300 or more setup payment required by the lender. Some owners apply their annual income tax refund to reduce their mortgage debt. Others make one extra payment annually to trim years off the loan. Still others make an extra principal prepayment equal to the next month's principal reduction when they pay the current month's payment. A real estate consultant can help you decide if, how, and when prepaying your mortgage should be part of your overall financial picture.

Online financial calculators like the ones found at <www.homefair.com> and <www.homepath.com> can give you an indication if prepaying your mortgage makes sense.

5. Evaluate your real estate holdings. Many owners of real estate mistakenly consult with a CPA about how to financially maximize their real estate holdings. This is great if all you need is tax advice or depreciation information. But when it's important to whittle down costs or increase cash flow, the definitive expert is the real estate consultant.

I am acquainted with consultants who are experts at showing owners how to leverage and free up equity from one property in order to purchase three more. There are real estate consultants who specialize in tax-free exchanges, resulting in deferred taxes and fewer costs of sale. Still other consultants assist estates and estate planners in evaluating and marketing properties to disperse cash to heirs in a timely fashion.

There's a growing need for additional real estate consultants in the area of evaluating senior housing alternatives. These consultants assist homeowners in deciding whether it's best to remodel a person's home to suit handicap accessibility standards or to relocate to a more modern, perhaps shared living, arrangement. Because so few homes in the nation are handicap accessible (and we're living longer), this problem will compound in the next few years as baby boomers approach their golden years.

6. Protest the assessed value of your home/protest your property taxes. We've all had the inclination to protest the assessed value placed on a piece of real estate we owned (unless we were preparing to sell it), but having the inclination is much different than possessing the expertise to not only fight, but win the war with the assessor.

The most cost-effective way to mount your case is by using a real estate consultant to do the research and present the information. Often requiring less than two hours of her time, it's possible to show cause to trim thousands of dollars off the property's assessed value, resulting in hundreds of dollars less in property tax payments!

One example was a man who hired a consultant to research why the assessed value failed to decrease even after the property suffered a fire destroying a three-car garage, barn, and several storage sheds. In another instance, a real estate consultant reviewing the closing papers for a couple selling a duplex realized that the county had two tax roll numbers for the same property and had been double-assessing and double–tax billing the owners for more than three years. Based on the laws governing property taxation in their area, they received a refund of more than $3,500 due to the consultant's knowledge and sharp eye.

As Americans age, the toughest aspect of home ownership is paying the cost of rising property taxes. It's thought to be the number one reason that the elderly lose their homes to foreclosure and will continue to be for decades to come. That's why trimming even a few dollars off a property's assessed value, and subsequently off corresponding property taxes, can go a long way in making home ownership more affordable.

7. Tracking trends to maximize profit. While recently providing a seminar on equity management to a group of consumers, I realized that the type of questions most homeowners and real estate investors often ask have changed. Instead of many questions about refinancing their home or prepaying their mortgage, the focus was much more on how to time their sale in order to maximize profit. Several people in the audience said that because they had decided to take early retirement, they wanted to make sure they sold their 4,000-square-foot home properly at the top of the market cycle in order to reap the highest net proceeds. Yet others said they wondered if now would be a good time to purchase a home for retirement because they were concerned that supplies of vacation property could be depleting, with the price of remaining properties skyrocketing. I find it refreshing to see that those of us who have managed our dot-com stocks more efficiently than we've managed our real estate equity are starting to come around!

A real estate consultant would use several resources to find the information needed to expertly time a sale at the top or a purchase at the low side of the market. The first source would be to check out the supply of property available and find the volume selling, the time it took to sell, and how prices have increased or decreased during the past three to four years.

Because trends play a big part in determining the value of real estate, it would also be important to consider if the market for the property will be expanding or receding, who's most likely to purchase this kind of property, and the overall economic conditions (present and projected) in the area.

The investment of a few hours of a real estate consultant's time can make the difference between receiving the greatest return on your investment or having to discount the sales price just to unload it.

8. Seek solutions for sidestepping foreclosure. Even though you were financially qualified by the lender prior to taking out a mortgage, financial strength can weaken, making it tougher for you to meet monthly mortgage payments on time. Trouble signs that indicate that the mortgage is financially stifling include making payments later each month, paying less on credit card debt in order to scrape the mortgage payment together, or perhaps even borrowing money from credit cards to help fund a payment shortfall. Once these red flags appear, it's time to turn the mortgage monster around before it's too late.

Besides contacting the lender to review the alternatives available to losing the house in foreclosure, a real estate consultant can provide an unbiased, objective view of available options. He can also act as a liaison to the lender to help you negotiate a fair yet realistic settlement.

First, the real estate consultant would help you determine if it's financially feasible to commit to this size mortgage payment for the long haul as well as whether the present financial crunch is short term or long term. For example, is it likely that previous overtime could be reinstated in a few months, making the payment easier to make? Can you and/or do you want to take on a part-time job, obtain new full-time employment to substantially increase your income (without creating new debt), or make family budget cuts to stretch money further each month?

Second, you'd discuss if you're mentally committed to handle a monthly mortgage payment of this size for the long haul.

It's much easier for buyers to be motivated to make large mortgage payments during the homebuyer honeymoon phase of ownership when the blush is on the new paint and the ceramic tile still gleams. After a while, you may reorder your priorities and realize that a large, strapping house payment is not for you. If this is the case, the consultant might investigate if recasting the loan into a longer term and/or lower interest rate might help.

The real estate consultant could make the case for selling this house and purchasing a more cost-effective one. And because most mortgage payments are comprised of principal, interest, property taxes and insurance, whittling down any of these components can save money monthly as well.

Falling behind in mortgage payments and/or being at foreclosure's door is never fun, but by using the consultant to help interface with the lender, it's likely that this team of resources will uncover satisfactory results to solve the problem.

9. Income and commercial property consultants. You may have used property managers in the past to collect rents and complete light repairs on the income and commercial property you own. But have you ever thought of seeking their professional counsel on other types of questions you may have?

Real estate consultants specializing in income and commercial property are a savvy, financially adept group, who can assist you in everything from how to increase the net rents on your duplex to completing a highest-and-best-use evaluation on a commercial site you own.

Considered the top in their field, Counselors of Real Estate (CRE) are designees from the National Association of REALTORS® who specialize in the most complex of commercial property transactions. Often found at the corporate level, they acquire, manage, and sell land on behalf of some of America's largest companies.

One site that can link you to many of the largest commercial real estate companies in the nation is <www.ired.com>, the

International Real Estate Directory site. In addition, check out the CRE designation site at <www.cre.org>.

10. Other consultant specialty niches. It's estimated that there are nearly 200 smaller, yet vital subcategories of real estate consultants, many who serve their own particular specialty or niche market in solving real estate–related problems. Some of these professionals include real estate attorneys, appraisers, developers, home inspectors, and energy efficiency experts. I once asked a consultant who provided energy audits for homeowners and businesses how he explained what he did to the consumers he served. He explained by saying that if the homeowner called a window company to perform an energy audit, nine times out of ten they would end up purchasing expensive new windows (even if they didn't need them). By using his consultancy service, homeowners could review the evaluation and, without pressure to buy a thing, make their own decisions. Yet another example of the power of unbiased, disinterested, third-party information!

Intricate Real Estate Problems You May Encounter

Negotiate an eminent domain settlement. Eminent domain is the process by which the government (city, county, or state) seizes a piece of property for public use. It often occurs to widen roads, develop a green belt, or design a park. Even though just compensation is supposed to go to the property owner for the loss, what the government wants to give the owner and what the property is really worth can be as different as night and day.

That's why a real estate consultant (often an appraiser with a background in government/assessment work) can strongarm for the owner and typically double (or better) the amount they would receive.

Because the process of eminent domain can take months, if not years, to finalize, a consultant might be willing to work on a combination of lower hourly fees plus a percentage of any extra sales price gained from that of the initial price offered from the government.

Real estate consultants as expert witnesses. Many real estate educators and seasoned real estate agents often find themselves at some time in their career in the role of expert witness. I've had the opportunity to assist in several lawsuits where my role was to interpret a real estate situation or relate what constituted ethical practice in the practice of real estate.

Several of my real estate educator friends in large cities are inundated with the number of requests they receive for testimony—in person in the courtroom or taped in advance of the trial. In addition, often an attorney from a distance will require preliminary information about a local real estate market and will compensate the consultant for time spent in phone conversations and gathering information.

In today's world of ecologically based lawsuits dealing with water, mineral, and land rights, it's expected that this real estate consulting specialty will continue to grow.

Cautions in Finding Answers to Special Real Estate Problems

It's Wise to Seek Information from More than One Source

As seen in the previous overviews on how real estate consultants can address and solve your needs, you'll notice that they provide the personal skill application (the people) coupled with Web-based references (the written). Most problems are best handled by first researching a topic (via the Web) then locating and applying the people skills to create a solution. While this is the approach most real estate consultants use, many specialty real estate problems require greater expertise in both the people (consultant) and information (written) categories. If a problem is extensive, it may require more than one consultant to help untangle it, or other print resources, like a law library, to gather information. The bottom line is that your best chance for cost- and time-effective solutions is to interview more than one specialist before deciding in which to invest your time and money to help solve your problem.

Be Aware of Conflicts of Interest

Be aware that conflicts of interest (even innocent ones) can exist. For example, if the well-meaning appraiser also holds a contractor's license, a conflict could exist. The same is true for a home inspector who just happens to be a real estate broker who agrees to do the repairs and sell the property for a reduced flat fee. Most ethical real estate consultants will do all they can to sidestep conflicts and put your best interest first and foremost. At the very least, an aboveboard consultant would notify you that a potential conflict exists and he'll either let you decide or remove himself from your team.

The Need for Real Estate Consulting Help Is Everywhere!

Think about your life and the lives of your friends. How many real estate situations like the ones we've covered can you name that could have been solved or at least helped by using an impartial, fee-for-services professional? Plenty, I would guess. The next time someone relates a real estate horror story to you, offer a suggestion—that they next time consider using a real estate consultant. It could make all the difference.

Test Your Ability with a Miniquiz

Determine with What You Need Help

Now that you've seen applications of how real estate consulting can be applied to solve a variety of problems, you're ready to test your ability (and tolerance) by taking the mini-quiz that follows. It will help you determine your tolerance and comfort level for seeking professional counsel when it comes to troubleshooting your real estate needs.

Test Your Ability

YES NO

☐ ☐ 1. It's easy for me to ask for help when I need it, especially in money-related issues.

☐ ☐ 2. I don't mind paying a fair price for information and/or assistance if I know I can benefit by it.

☐ ☐ 3. Owning real estate is an important part of my long-term financial picture.

☐ ☐ 4. I pride myself on making good real estate decisions that financially pay off.

☐ ☐ 5. I manage my real estate holdings (and their related equity) well.

☐ ☐ 6. Owning real estate is more about creating wealth than it is about owning possessions.

If you answered yes to questions 1 to 3, you're an excellent candidate for working with real estate consultants and service providers to solve your real estate problems. If you answered yes to questions 4 to 6, you may feel most comfortable going it alone to solve your real estate problems.

Locating and Contracting with Real Estate Fee-for-Services Providers

The Web is a terrific place to communicate, find information, look at listings, locate professionals, and compare loans, but such informational functions cannot replace the process of physically visiting a home or seeing a neighborhood. Web or no Web, in the future buyers and sellers will still have competing interests, transactions will be complex, and all homes will remain unique and distinctive. Such realities mean there will be an ongoing need for brokerage services in the future, including traditional services, consulting programs, buyer brokerage, menu-of-service plans, and such other formats as the public demands.

Peter G. Miller
Columnist
Author of *The Common-Sense Mortgage*, Contemporary Books

Congratulations. You've analyzed your real estate needs well enough to know that fee-for-services assistance may help you reach your real estate goals cost-effectively and in a timely manner. As discovered from the results of the Frugal Home-Owner®'s Consumer Study in Chapter 1, you don't mind paying for what you need, but you want to pay only what it's worth and be able to obtain the help when you need it.

In this chapter, we'll help you locate and contract with various fee-for-services professionals and service providers. We'll also continue to provide assessment tools to help you pinpoint exactly what you need and why you need it. The Consumer Needs Assessment™ form is one such tool.

The Consultant Begins with Assessing Your Real Estate Needs

Meet the CNA—The Consumer Needs Assessment Tool

In unbundling the real estate transaction, there are some components that defy automation and application to technology. One vital component, assessing and strategizing your individual needs as a real estate consumer, is a prime example. Using in-depth analysis to pinpoint your unique needs in buying, selling, or managing real estate requires the human touch, as does applying solutions to problems. Any time human nature is involved, expecting answers from technology is of little use. Enter the level two skills of empathy, rapport, and troubleshooting in a one-on-one consulting model, the Consumer Needs Assessment (CNA). You'll find a copy in Figure 8.1.

A trademarked term and form of the National Association of Real Estate Consultants, the CNA is a systematic process in a simple format of only two pages in length. Small yet powerful, it poses questions, gathers answers, and helps clarify your needs. Additionally, it helps you isolate realistic objectives, determine logical time frames for completion, and pinpoint any roadblocks that could be encountered along the way.

As a motivated buyer or seller eager to find a real estate solution, you may be inclined to sidestep gathering even two pages of road map information for your journey. But that's all the more reason to complete the CNA. It makes little sense to rush headlong into a process fraught with competition without first having a game plan on how to work smarter and with less expense than your competitors. Whether it's designing a strategy to have the seller jump on your less-than-full-price offer or understanding the steps it will take to fight the increase in your property taxes, the CNA can be your real estate power tool. It's important to note that although a real estate consultant or licensee can legally use the CNA form only if they are a member in good standing of the National Association of Real Estate Consultants, I have acquired permission from NAREC for purchasers of this book to have limited, nonprofessional, noncommercial use of the form solely for the purpose of assessing his or her individual real estate needs.

The Rationale behind the CNA

The rationale behind the design and application of the CNA by the National Association of Real Estate Consultants is that a majority of the roadblocks in the real estate process come when your individual needs, past experiences (good or bad), and financial expectations are undetected and therefore not addressed. By committing these needs, experiences, and expectations to writing prior to beginning the real estate process, they serve as a template to attract positive outcome as well as troubleshoot problems that occur.

Here's an example. Ben and Belinda Isaac have purchased various pieces of property for their investment portfolio over the past two decades. When Jan Smith, C-CREC, a real estate consultant, meets with the Isaacs, she presents them with the CNA form and asks that they complete it together. Jan explains that even though they're seasoned real estate investors, she'd like to know a little bit about what they currently own, what they've owned in the past, and why they sold, as well as how they'd see subsequent purchases addressing their goals and rounding out their investment portfolio.

After the form is completed, they discuss the findings. Because the Isaacs's last purchase occurred in 1982 in a very sluggish buyer's market, Jan wants them to be aware of the very different rules for winning in the current seller's market. She shares experiences about how amazed other buyers have been at the fever-pitch bidding wars they've encountered when making offers (very polar to the lackluster market of the

Figure 8.1   Consumer Needs Assessment

Consumer Needs Assessment™

Prepared for _____

Date: _____

     by _____ , C-CREC™
             Consumer-Certified Real Estate Consultant™

Complete only those questions that apply to your specific need(s)

1. What do you perceive as your most important real estate objec-
   tive/s at this time? (if more than one, list in order of declining
   importance)

   My/Our Real Estate Objectives are to:
   a. _____
   b. _____
   c. _____

2. An ideal outcome for each of the previous objectives would be:
   a. _____
   b. _____
   c. _____

3. An acceptable outcome for each of the previous objectives would
   be:
   a. _____
   b. _____
   c. _____

4. Reasonable time frames for each objective are:
   a. _____
   b. _____
   c. _____

5. List any potential roadblocks in achieving each objective:
   a. _____
   b. _____
   c. _____

Figure 8.1   Consumer Needs Assessment (Continued)

6. Real estate owner/client's background in buying/selling properties, etc.:

_____

_____

7. Other pertinent real estate/financial information:

_____

_____

8. Have you had any adverse experiences purchasing/owning real estate?

_____

_____

9. Feasibility analysis for each objective (completed by consultant):
   a. _____
   b. _____
   c. _____

Recommendations: _____

_____

_____

Resources Required: _____

_____

_____

Proposed Outcome: _____

_____

_____

Time Frame(s) for Completion: _____

_____

_____

Potential Costs Involved: _____

_____

_____

_____

Figure 8.1 Consumer Needs Assessment (Continued)

Compiled, updated this _____ day of _____ , _____ ,
by _____ , Real Estate Consultant; for
proposed client(s) _____ .

_____
_____ CREC™

_____
Client

_____
Client

CC: Client's file
Referral Permitted (if applicable) to: _____
Client's nitials _____ _____

1980s). Additionally, she needs to make them aware that any
properties they purchase now (post–Tax Reform of 1987) will
employ less favorable depreciation schedules and myriad differ-
ing rules regarding the way profits are taxed when the property is sold. Jan also learns from the discussion that although
they've purchased several multifamily complexes in the past,
they've found them cumbersome and expensive to manage.
Due to this negative experience, they want to focus their purchases on office complexes and warehouses.

Jan assists the Isaacs in purchasing several properties for
their portfolio. They later remark to her and to other friends
(while singing her praise) that although they'd purchased
property for many years, she was the first consultant to ask
about the type of investments with which they'd had adverse
experiences. She took the time to listen to what had worked in
the past, and what hadn't. They also admitted that venting their
anxieties over the negative aspects helped them gravitate to
what worked and not focus on what they considered to be their
past failings as property managers.

The Isaacs understood what Jan already knew about people and their experiences owning real estate—their biography becomes their biology. In other words, the real estate experiences they have (good and bad) become a part of how they respond and react to future real estate purchasing and ownership. This is not to suggest that a real estate consultant should hold seances to get every down-and-dirty bit about consumers' past lives in real estate; but if realizing and addressing these experiences up front can help the consumer formulate the best tack to take, the amount of risk he's comfortable with, and obstacles to avoid, it's a waste not to learn from them.

Working with Real Estate Consultants with Advanced Designations

The C-CREC—The Mark of Excellence in Real Estate Consulting

You may have noticed the acronym C-CREC, the professional designation behind Jan Smith's name. Consumer-Certified Real Estate Consultant is a designation awarded by the National Association of Real Estate Consultants in recognition of exemplary consumer care and quality in the real estate consulting field. To obtain the designation, the designee candidate must have had five years' continuous experience in the real estate industry or a real estate–related field, or a combination of three years' experience and at least one nationally recognized professional designation. The candidate also must have attended the required consulting/designation courses, designed a business model for his or her consulting business, and must verify (from consumers) that he or she has had quantifiable experience as a real estate consultant. Renewed on an annual basis, the C-CREC designation requires proof of significant consumer satisfaction from the consumers served as well as compliance with the NAREC code of ethics. Additional information on NAREC and the C-CREC designation CNA can be found in the Resources section of this book. You can locate a C-CREC designee in your area via the Web at <www.ccrec.com> or at <www.narec .com>.

How Real Estate Consulting Differs from Real Estate Selling

Knowing the Difference Is Vital!

A woman recently called to inquire about the best questions to ask when interviewing a real estate consultant to potentially hire. She said that one consultant she spoke to claimed to be a multimillion-dollar real estate salesman, had a full-page ad in the yellow pages, and was running ads on TV, about which she added, "Just like those ambulance-chasing attorneys do!"

Unscrupulous attorneys aside, what the woman was describing is the poignant difference between someone who sells and someone who consults. The traditional real estate salesperson was focused on selling something to the consumer. They sold the seller on listing a house with them and then sold the house to a buyer. If they didn't sell something, they usually didn't receive compensation. And they viewed their first and foremost mission as selling themselves. This mantra evolved because of the overcrowded marketplace where real estate agents found it next to impossible to look, act, and sound different from the competition. They provided the same services (listing and selling) to the same target market (sellers and buyers). In order to differentiate, many resorted to gimmicky, eye-catching marketing tools in an effort to grab the consumer's attention and be the first one the consumer contacted. Marketing ploys range from the semiuseful like magnets and kitchen potholders to the bizarre. The most unbelievable approach I've seen was an agent's marketing logo picturing him dressed in an expensive suit with a very large fish sticking out of the jacket front. Underneath was the phrase, "I'll work for you hook, line, and sinker!" I showed the picture to my husband whose tongue-in-cheek comment was, "What a bunch of carp that is!"

Perhaps that man was the most successful real estate salesperson on the planet. Perhaps he was empathetic, intelligent, and trustworthy. I only know that if I saw a picture of my internist marketing her practice dressed up in a fish suit, I'd change doctors!

While most real estate consultants are actually licensed real estate professionals (depending on the requirements of their specialty), they approach their craft much differently than the traditional real estate salesperson. As stated in the code of ethics of the National Association of Real Estate Consultants, real estate consultants first "tell, not sell" and "guide, not decide." Because real estate consultants generate income from information sharing and performing other results-oriented tasks (often unrelated to any type of listing or selling process), they employ no high-pressure sales tactics. While the salesperson's creed is "ABC," which stands for always be closing the prospect, the consultant's focus (and the slogan of the National Association of Real Estate Consultants) is "consumer-centered; results-focused." Specific services backed by information gathering and analytical support create skill capabilities for the consultant that win out over personalities.

Consulting Assumes that Several Alternatives Exist; Selling Focuses on Only One Solution—a Sale!

As shown by the following comparisons, the methods used to approach a consumer as well as the problem-solving models employed are vastly different between the tasks of selling and consulting.

Scenario: Monica is a newly divorced mother of two who needs to find a place to live. This is the first time she's done anything of a financial nature because her husband handled all of the money matters and her parents signed her lease and paid her rent when she attended college.

Solution 1: Monica meets a real estate salesperson and buys a house. A friend recommends a real estate office that also has an inventory of properties for rent. Monica visits the office for her appointment, but is met not by the leasing agent but by Sam, a real estate salesman. He assures her that it's the company's policy to first prescreen consumers to make sure they shouldn't be investing in a home instead of paying useless rent.

Sam gathers Monica's information and announces that he thinks he just may be able to squeeze her into a house after all. It's an older house in need of some repair, but if she can come up with the $5,000 required to cover his commission and closing costs, he thinks he can make it work for her. He'll try to convince the seller to carry the balance of the purchase price in a seller-financed contract for 15 years. While her monthly payment will be considerably more than the rent she wanted to pay, he reminds Monica, "It will be your own house, not some landlord's."

Two hours and two aspirin later, Monica signs on the dotted line of the purchase agreement, gives the agent a promissory note for the $5,000 in earnest money she's pledged to pay at closing, and leaves the real estate office in a state of total shock.

It might appear that everything turned out great. Monica gets to purchase a home instead of pay rent and the equity she'll build can serve as the first puzzle piece in building her financial future. What could possibly be wrong?

Plenty. Fancy footwork might have squeezed her into a house, but she was in no way prepared (financially or emotionally) to commit to the mountain of obligations of owning a home. First, to obtain the down payment she borrowed against the only real asset she had, a car that was free and clear. After closing, she had both a mortgage payment and a car payment. Then it was the furnace. Murphy's Law of Home Warranty states that if you buy an older house that's not warranted, an expensive, major homeowner catastrophe will occur in the first 30 days. The furnace failed the first time the temperature dropped. And while her parents loaned her the $2,500 it took to replace the furnace, Monica (being a proud, self-sufficient adult on her own for the first time) insisted on paying them back at $250 per month, which pushed her into taking a part-time job.

Six months later under the weight of the hefty monthly obligations coupled with the stress of two jobs and trying to manage upside down cash flow while raising two children on her own, Monica mailed the house keys back to the seller. What started out to be a learning curve took a nosedive into a painful crash of blemished credit, a seller threatening to sue her, and being left without even enough money for a cleaning deposit let alone first and last month's rent for an apartment. The lesson is that not everyone's situation is conducive to purchasing a house. Unfortunately, when that's the only result a service provider is focused on delivering, the salesperson may find his success at the expense of the consumer.

Solution 2: Monica meets a real estate consultant and builds a financial future! Monica knows she's naive when it comes to managing money and that she needs to walk before she runs. She obtains a copy of her credit report and repairs several errors she finds on it. This allows her to rent a meager two-bedroom apartment with rent low enough that she can save $100 per month in a savings account. After more than a year building an on-time rental payment history, she contacts a real estate consultant to evaluate the steps she could take to work toward buying a home.

Martha Mayne, C-CREC, first crunches the numbers to determine whether it would pay for Monica to rent versus buy. Based on the low rent Monica's paying, she'd need a hefty down payment on a purchase in order to make the monthly payment comfortable for her budget. Because she's only saved half the amount needed to date, a purchase may be financially out of the question unless she could obtain a gifted down payment from her parents. Before that's explored, Martha crunches one more set of numbers. She determines that based on the appreciation for the type of property Monica could afford and the down payment and closing costs she would part with, Monica would need to hold the property for a minimum of five years in order to reach the breakeven point in owning the house. Because Monica wants to return to grad school in three years and will need to relocate, she makes the decision to remain a renter and begins investing her extra $100 per month as an additional contribution to her retirement fund through her employer.

P.S.: Monica is now vice president of a large midwestern bank where she orchestrates the sale of millions of dollars in real estate portfolio income into large, secondary-market investment conduits. By the way, she does own her own home—three of them, in fact!

We are in a new age of technology and e-commerce, and evaluating all your options and doing business the best way isn't getting any easier. In this confusing and changing environment it's important to remember that seeking advice from an expert or reading up from a good book can never be underestimated. It will almost always save you time, money, and a potential headache.

> Stefan Swanepoel, Author
> Chairman, iProperty and 9keys
> Author of *Real Estate Confronts the E-consumer*

Consultants First "Tell, Not Sell" and "Guide, Not Decide"

The previous scenarios were not meant to slot real estate salespeople as evil predators only out to cinch a sale, or pronounce blanket sainthood of real estate consultants. The focus was to show that just as it's in a bird dog's nature to hunt birds, it's in a salesperson's nature to sell. Once you're in the groove of what you do, it's tough to leave that focus and jump into another groove (without the necessary retraining tools and significant change of mind-set).

The biggest difference between real estate consultants and real estate salespeople is their approach to assisting the consumer. Real estate consultants gather information for consumers and first tell them what they find, not sell them on validating, accepting, or even applying the information. Similarly, real estate consultants guide consumers to alternatives, rather than decide or even imply that one alternative or answer is superior to another.

Does this mean that a real estate consultant could never assist a client in selling or listing a property, even if the client requested it? No, but ethics in professional organizations like the NAREC require that the consultant provide complete disclosure of how the business relationship will change, including how compensation will be received, the amount of that compensation, and any approach or compensation model that may not be in the consumer's best interest (even though requested by the consumer).

How to Locate and Evaluate a Real Estate Consultant

One Caveat: A Consultant Might Be a Real Estate Licensee, but a Licensee Might Not Be a Real Estate Consultant

You're convinced that seeking a real estate consultant to meet your needs is a sound move. Simultaneously, you find that the agent who sold you your last house is now marketing himself as a real estate consultant. While it's true that anyone can call himself a real estate consultant, it's up to you to determine if this consultant is capable of giving you unbiased, disinterested information and sidestepping hard-hammering you into listing or purchasing something.

Six Questions to Determine If the Consultant Is a Specialist

Here are six questions to ask to gauge the level of competence and expertise of the consultant:

1. *How long have you been in the real estate business? How many of those years did you perform fee-for-services consulting engagements for consumers or companies?* It's doubtful that someone who has had three years' or less experience in real estate has either the experience or the base of knowledge to perform in-depth consulting engagements. While they may have counseled with consumers, consulting requires a much deeper needs-based analysis often seen only in professionals with five or more years' experience.

2. *In which areas are you considered an expert?* If the person you're interviewing laughs, claiming that he's more of a jack-of-all-trades generalist, or if she holds herself out as an expert in more than half a dozen areas, it's doubtful that the person has true expertise in any area!

3. *What are the two primary specialty areas or targets you focus on in your consulting practice?* If the interviewee can't spontaneously name the specialty areas he focuses on (those which generate the majority of his work) he is not a specialist in what he does.

4. *What type of consumer profile or demographic market do you typically assist?* Anyone with a specialty can pinpoint the consumer profile of those she most often assists. This is not a marketing guru question. It's a logical business target question.

5. *May I see letters of reference from satisfied consumers? May I contact any or all of them?* Anyone who touts a history in real estate consulting will be happy (even eager) to show you his letters of reference from satisfied consumers. The only exception might be someone new to consulting, yet experienced in a specialty niche in a real

estate–related field such as appraisal or mortgage banking. At the very least, obtain personal references from the consultant and ask permission to call and talk to at least two of them.

6. *Why should I work with you over your competition? What makes your services unique?* Someone proficient in his craft won't hesitate to blow his horn about how his services exceed those of his competition. Called the uniqueness quotient, it's one of the best ways for consultants to build top-quality repeat and referral business and have you gravitating to them with in-bound requests for business.

Professional Documentation Provided by the Real Estate Consultant

Credentials Let You Evaluate Quantity, Quality, and Professionalism

Once you've found someone you deem to be a specialist in the area in which you need help, the next step is to check out professional credentials and documentation. While you may feel uncomfortable asking for information to support the consultant's background and claims, it's a small price to pay to know that the person you'll be working with has the proper sanctioning and licensing credentials, including:

- *Licenses.* Depending on the specialty and the scope of the work to be performed, the consultant may have one or more licenses with the most common being a real estate license. Many states provide pocket cards to the licensee to carry in his wallet. If a pocket card isn't available and the consultant is licensed under a brokerage firm, ask to receive confirmation from the employing broker. Additionally, you could contact the licensing division/department of your individual state. Web addresses are found in the Resources section at the end of this book. You can also ask the licensing division to inform you of any activities that threaten the status of his license. This information is kept on each licensee and can be made available to the consumer upon request.

- *Certificates and professional designations.* It's not unusual for a specialist to have one or more professional designations that shows she's spent additional time receiving education in her specialty topic. Professional designations are usually accompanied by a certificate of completion that bears the name of the sponsoring or certifying organization.

- *Bonding/errors and omissions insurance.* Depending on the type of work to be performed, the consultant may be required to be bonded and/or covered with errors and omissions insurance. If neither is required by licensing statutes in the state, most professionals carry their own professional liability policy as a rider to their homeowners insurance. It serves as a minimum requirement to protect the consultant (and the consumer) for omissions of fact or other types of oversight in the consulting engagement.

Contracting with the Real Estate Consultant for the Services You Need

Once you've narrowed down the consultants you'd feel comfortable working with, ask to view their consulting agreement before making a final decision. A detailed, well-written fee-for-services agreement will not only enumerate the services you require and what they will cost, but will pinpoint checkpoints during the process where you'll discuss the consultant's progress, pose questions, and provide feedback (if necessary) to the consultant. Checkpoints built into your fee-for-services agreement keep the consultant on track, make him responsible for communicating with you on a timely basis, and help you anticipate any additional services you may need, ideally before you need them.

You'll note in the agreement to provide consulting services provided in Figure 8.2 that the agreement excludes much of the legalese and clauses typically found in a common real estate agreement, the listing contract. Even though both are personal service contracts, the consulting agreement is more results-focused, incorporating the consumer's particular information gathered previously on the Consumer Needs Assessment form (preferably attached to the agreement for reference). Note that even though the agreement provided is for use only by members of the National Association of Real Estate Consultants, you are allowed to use the contract as a generic template for other real estate consultant agreements into which you might consider entering. But, as with any other contractual form, it's wise to make sure that your real estate attorney reviews it prior to contracting with the real estate consultant.

Minimum Contract Requirements If the Consultant Is a Real Estate Licensee

If the work to be performed requires the consultant to be a real estate licensee, most states require the agreement to have:

- Been put into writing with a copy to each party
- All parties to the agreement enumerated
- A beginning and ending date for the agreement
- The scope of work to be accomplished
- Payment of fees, how they are earned, and when payment(s) will be made
- How the agreement can be severed
- The capacity/business relationship the consultant will have with the consumer (that of client or other working relationship such as transaction broker, etc.)
- Signatures from all parties to the agreement

Besides the previous information, make sure that your agreement addresses any retainer arrangement with the consultant as well as whether expenses will be reimbursed, and if

Figure 8.2   Agreement to Provide Consulting Services
_____

Agreement to Provide Consulting Services

    This agreement made and entered into this _____
day of _____, 20____, by and between
_____, C-CREC™
(hereinafter referred to as the "consultant") and

_____

_____

(hereinafter referred to as the "consumer")
Witnesseth:
    Whereas the Consultant is experienced in the area(s) of

_____

_____

_____

and
    Whereas the Consumer is desirous of

_____

_____

_____

    Now, therefore, in consideration of the mutual benefits to be
derived herefrom, the parties agree as follows:
    I. The Consumer does hereby retain the services of the Consul-
       tant for the purposes of assisting the Consumer with

_____

_____

_____

as more specifically described in the Consumer Needs Assessment™
form attached hereto and incorporated by reference herein.
    II. The parties agree that the Consultant shall receive as compen-
       sation from the above-described services, the following under
       the time frames specified:
Retainer fee: _____ Refundable/nonrefundable: _____
Due: _____
Fees: _____
Due: _____

_____

Due: _____
_____

Figure 8.2   Agreement to Provide Consulting Services (Continued)

Further, the Consultant shall be reimbursed for expenses incurred while performing services on behalf of the Consumer. Consultant shall present the Consumer with an accounting of time and reimbursable expenses at _____ intervals. Payment to be net ten days.

III. Consultant shall at all times be considered an independent contractor of the Consumer, not an employee. If tasks requiring a real estate license are performed, the Consultant will work with the Consumer in a(n) _____ capacity.

(agency, nonagency, client, customer, transaction broker) An agency disclosure form is attached and made a part hereof.

IV. Scope of Work: The Consultant shall have only the authority specified in the Consumer Needs Assessment™ form(attached hereto) or by subsequent written instructions. The Consultant shall at all times hold all matters regarding this consulting engagement in the strictest confidence unless authorization to release such information is otherwise granted in writing by the Consumer. The Consultant shall use best efforts in all matters undertaken on behalf of this consulting engagement.

V. The parties agree that the term of this personal service agreement shall be:

_____

_____,

Unless terminated for cause or upon the mutual written agreement of the parties.

In witness whereof, the parties have set their hands the date first above written:

Consumer(s):   C-CREC™ Consultant:

_____   _____

_____   _____

Addenda attached: _____

CNA™ and C-REC™ are trademarks of the National Association of Real Estate Consultants.™ 866-260-7374 so, in what manner. While you may be inclined to ask the consultant to account for every single cent billed in expenses, it's often better to reimburse using an estimate of costs with a cap or by a flat fee determined up front. That way the consultant won't spend your billable time micromanaging his records and can often move you more quickly to the results you seek. Also, make sure that if you're sharing information of a confidential nature with the consultant, that there's a provision in the agreement to protect that information from being shared with others (unless you otherwise provide the consultant with a written release in writing).

Determine the Role the Real Estate Consultant Will Play in Helping You Reach Your Objectives

After more than a decade of fact finding and debating, all 50 states currently have what's termed *agency disclosure* laws designed to inform you up front of the various roles the real estate licensee (and thus, many consultants) play when interfacing with you.

Even though no two states refer to the roles licensees play with consumers in the same real estate "slanguage," they can be broken into two distinct types: clients and nonclients.

By definition, a client is someone with whom the licensee has a relationship of trust, honesty, and diligence, and represents the sole interest of that client in negotiating, advocating, and interpreting information.

Conversely, a nonclient relationship is one in which the licensee/consultant provides information to the consumer but does not advocate, negotiate, or interpret on the consumer's behalf. It's much like accessing an encyclopedia without having anyone to apply the information or interpret it for you.

How do you know which you need and when? It can be determined in part by the licensing laws of the state in which you reside (which govern the licensees and the majority of real estate consultants with which you'd work) and the level of service you need and are provided by the real estate licensee/consultant. For example, if you merely need information gathering (level one services), it may not be necessary for you to be in a client relationship with the consultant. Conversely, if you need the consultant to advocate or negotiate on your behalf, being in a client relationship is advised. Be sure to check with the real estate consultant for exceptions in each state. For example, in Oklahoma, the client becomes vicariously responsible for the acts of the agent when dealing with third parties which is not a role any savvy consumer would want to take. Additionally, the consultant/licensee should attach the agency disclosure form to the agreement to consult to comply with the disclosure laws in your state.

What If You Desire to Sever the Agreement with the Consultant?

Most consultants don't want to tie you to an agreement and business relationship with which you're not happy. That's why most personal service agreements, like the consulting contracts, can be severed upon the mutual agreement of the parties.

If you feel you've been damaged by a business relationship with a real estate consultant, there are several avenues available to you. First, if your complaint involves a member of the National Association of Real Estate Consultants, there are guidelines in place to suspend or revoke the designation credentials of a C-CREC for improperly addressing/handling a consumer's real estate need.

If the consultant holds a real estate license, each state has its own guidelines for filing a written complaint about the incident/licensee. Violations are punishable by fines, suspension of license, or license revocation. You'll find contact information in the Resources section at the end of this book.

If the consultant is a member of the National Association of REALTORS®, complaints about the incident and the licensee can be filed with the local board of REALTORS® in your area.

In most cases, the bottom line is to try to avoid litigation at all costs. It's not only timely and expensive, but depending on the laws in your state, may prove problematic in obtaining judgments and the restitution to which you're entitled.

What about Approaching a Real Estate Agent You've Worked with Previously to Assist You?

If you've previously worked with a real estate licensee who you feel could assist you with your current real estate needs, it makes good business sense to contact that person again. If the licensee is progressive and knowledgeable about fee-for-services real estate consulting and practices, chances are good that you can continue the business relationship where you left off. As long as the licensee evaluates your real estate needs in an unbiased manner, is willing to contract with you for only the services you need, and charge you only for what those services are worth, working again with someone you're comfortable with can be a win-win situation.

Is it possible that the licensee you worked with previously wouldn't be able to assist you in an unbundled, à la carte services capacity? Yes. In fact, it might not have anything to do with the licensee's wishes but that his principal broker won't allow consulting or à la carte services to be unbundled to consumers. Because the licensee is only permitted to contract for services permitted by his principal broker, a third party's business practices could stand in the way of returning to a licensee you successfully worked with in the past.

Red Flags When Interviewing a Real Estate Consultant

It's likely a consultant will be on his best behavior, saying all the right things during your initial interview. But as you would with any other potential business arrangement, keep your eyes and ears open for red flags that could alert you to potential roadblocks ahead:

- *The fees quoted are not only reasonable, they're markedly cheaper than other quotes you've received.* Extremely low fees can indicate a lack of business on the part of the consultant and/or that once volume picks up, your consulting engagement may lack the priority it needs for completion.

- *The consultant says that a verbal agreement and a handshake is good enough for him.* Not only does real estate licensing law require the agreement to be in writing, it's good business to do so. A written agreement should be a minimum requirement when working with a consultant.

- *The consultant asks if there is any reason you wouldn't want to work with someone on her staff to whom she would assign you?* This may indicate that once you're under contract, a junior staff member or level one assistant may actually handle your consulting assignment. Before agreeing to this, clarify why it would be done and the impact it would have on your working arrangement with the consultant.

- *You're quoted a range of fees, but no caps/maximums are provided.* If items (like caps) are missing in the agreement to consult, assume that they do not exist. Be definite in limits for fees, expenses, and time frames in each contract.

- *The consulting agreement you need to sign is not available.* In lieu, the consultant says he'll get your signature on the paperwork at a later date. Never proceed into a consulting arrangement without first reviewing and signing the entire agreement to consult form. Without it, you have few protections as a consumer.

- *The consultant asks for your consent to refer you to another service provider if the need should arise, but gives you no indication of when that might occur or why.* While it's fine for the consultant to obtain your approval to refer you to another service provider, the consultant should be able to clarify why this might happen given your individual circumstance. Just as a Web link might take you to an ancillary Web page outside of the primary site, make sure you know in advance why the outside referral could be necessary and place those conditions in the agreement to consult.

When Could Hiring a Real Estate Attorney Be Preferable over Using a Real Estate Consultant?

Depending on where you reside in the United States, real estate attorneys perform much of the same work as real estate consultants. This is especially true in states where the lobby of the American Bar Association is strong in state government and/or where real estate closings are performed under the auspice of an attorney.

In a majority of states, using an attorney versus a real estate consultant is really more a matter of preference based on what you're trying to achieve. For example, if your real estate problem is heavily laden with legal issues, like a property line dispute, an attorney could perform the majority of work for you. But if the results you're after are along the lines of negotiating and troubleshooting, many real estate consultants are superior negotiators compared to attorneys and may move you more expediently to results and end up costing less.

As seen in this chapter, the professional you use should be a competent specialist who will commit your agreement to writing, enumerate what you'll receive for the fees you pay, and be willing to communicate with you throughout the process. You're now armed to find just the right consultant for your particular real estate need.

Deciding What Help You Need If You're Stuck Midstream

If you find yourself stuck in the middle and need answers, the logical choice is to hire a real estate consultant. A consultant fee paid to an experienced, unbiased, third party offers a calm in rough seas, confidence where insecurity or inexperience prevails, and peace of mind when the pressures of a high-level decision are extreme. At that point, common sense tells you to invest in good help to save money in the long run!

Sheila Helmsley, ABR, C-CREC
Relocation specialist

If You Find You Need Help Midstream

Help! You're in the middle of the transaction all alone and need assistance. You first need to assess approximately where you are in order to determine the type of help you'll need. Are you out of control in a situation that could potentially do serious damage to the transaction and to you?

Your first step is to ask three questions:

1. *With what checkpoint or activity am I having trouble?* Refer to the three tables in Figures 9.1 to 9.3 for seller, buyer, and special real estate activities. By determining where you are, you can best gauge what has occurred and what remains to be tackled.

Figure 9.1 Determining Solutions for Sellers

Checkpoint 1: Prepare the property for sale

	In a level one activity	In a level two activity	Activity- or people-related?
Possible Solutions:	_____	_____	_____
I stand to gain/lose:	_____	_____	_____

Checkpoint 2: Gather property information/price the property

	In a level one activity	In a level two activity	Activity- or people-related?
Possible Solutions:	_____	_____	_____
I stand to gain/lose:	_____	_____	_____

Checkpoint 3: Market the property

	In a level one activity	In a level two activity	Activity- or people-related?
Possible Solutions:	_____	_____	_____
I stand to gain/lose:	_____	_____	_____

Checkpoint 4: Locate/prequalify the buyer

	In a level one activity	In a level two activity	Activity- or people-related?
Possible Solutions:	_____	_____	_____
I stand to gain/lose:	_____	_____	_____

Checkpoint 5: Draft the sales agreement/negotiate with buyer

	In a level one activity	In a level two activity	Activity- or people-related?
Possible Solutions:	_____	_____	_____
I stand to gain/lose:	_____	_____	_____

Checkpoint 6: Troubleshoot the sale/close the transaction

	In a level one activity	In a level two activity	Activity- or people-related?
Possible Solutions:	_____	_____	_____
I stand to gain/lose:	_____	_____	_____

If you can't decide at which checkpoint you're stuck, determine which checkpoint you last completed. If you're still lost, it could be an indication that you need to seek the assistance of a real estate consultant or other type of professional to get you back on course.

Figure 9.2   Determining Solutions for Buyers

Checkpoint 1: Design a purchase strategy

	In a level one activity	In a level two activity	Activity- or people-related?
Possible Solutions:	_____	_____	_____
I stand to gain/lose:	_____	_____	_____

Checkpoint 2: Be preapproved for a mortgage

	In a level one activity	In a level two activity	Activity- or people-related?
Possible Solutions:	_____	_____	_____
I stand to gain/lose:	_____	_____	_____

Checkpoint 3: Choose the neighborhood and the property

	In a level one activity	In a level two activity	Activity- or people-related?
Possible Solutions:	_____	_____	_____
I stand to gain/lose:	_____	_____	_____

Checkpoint 4: Check property information and pricing

	In a level one activity	In a level two activity	Activity- or people-related?
Possible Solutions:	_____	_____	_____
I stand to gain/lose:	_____	_____	_____

Checkpoint 5: Draft the purchase agreement/negotiate with seller

	In a level one activity	In a level two activity	Activity- or people-related?
Possible Solutions:	_____	_____	_____
I stand to gain/lose:	_____	_____	_____

Checkpoint 6: Troubleshoot the purchase/close the transaction

	In a level one activity	In a level two activity	Activity- or people-related?
Possible Solutions:	_____	_____	_____
I stand to gain/lose:	_____	_____	_____

Figure 9.3 Determining if You Need Help

Early on:

	In a level one activity	In a level two activity	Activity- or people-related?
Possible Solutions:	_____	_____	_____
I stand to gain/lose:	_____	_____	_____

Midstream:

	In a level one activity	In a level two activity	Activity- or people-related?
Possible Solutions:	_____	_____	_____
I stand to gain/lose:	_____	_____	_____

At the end:

	In a level one activity	In a level two activity	Activity- or people-related?
Possible Solutions:	_____	_____	_____
I stand to gain/lose:	_____	_____	_____

2. *What type of activity am I stuck on, level one or level two?* As a refresher, level one activities are information gathering or administrative in nature (informational) and level two activities require a higher level of skill like negotiating or advocacy (interpretative). For example, if you find you've gathered the information but now don't know how to apply it, that's a level two problem.

3. *Is the problem activity-related or people-related?* In each one of the six checkpoints for sellers and the six checkpoints for buyers, there lie potential activity-related and people-related problems. For example, you may have filled out the entire contract to purchase form and presented it to the seller, but he's failing to respond to you or make a counteroffer back. That's an example of a people-related problem.

Once you have answers to all three questions, you can fill in Figures 9.1, 9.2, or 9.3 (whichever is appropriate) to determine the solutions available and what you stand to risk by not taking them.

Steps to Take in Tackling a Real Estate Problem

You may feel like you're drowning in a sea of real estate problems swirling around you, threatening to capsize your efforts thus far, but if you tackle the problems pragmatically and systematically, you may find your own worthy, cost-effective solutions to solve them. And if not, there's usually someone else (a professional) who can assist.

When solving a real estate problem:

- Assume that there's at least one logical, workable solution and that you will find it.
- Explain the situation to yourself using only positive language (ideal for those who communicate best by talking and listening).
- Define the situation in writing, being as concise as possible (best for visual communicators who work best seeing the problem committed to writing).
- Quickly write down as many possible causes for the situation as possible (like brainstorming on a blank sheet of paper).
- Quickly list at least a dozen possible solutions for the problem.
- Evaluate the possible solutions, first choosing the top five and then narrowing them down to the best one.
- Make a plan to implement the solution by answering the questions of who, what, when, where, how, why, and how much. (This could include parceling the problem out to consultants or other professionals.)
- Set time frames to implement the various parts of the decision and a definite date for its completion.

If You're Still Stuck

What if you can't find even one possible solution for the problem and it seems to be getting worse by the minute? Here are some possible solutions:

- Turn part or all of the problem/transaction over to a real estate consultant or other professional.
- Have all parties to the transaction/situation agree that it's in their joint best interests to seek outside assistance, that they have more to gain than to lose by so doing.
- Cut your losses and try again when you feel more confident to tackle the process on your own or are ready to seek the assistance you need.
- Salvage what you can from the situation. Isolate the tasks/ activities you feel were your weak links and work towards mastering them should you decide to tackle the process at a later date or obtain help for the services you know you need.

There's no shame in not reaching the finish line alone. The shame lies in not running the race in the first place! As we've outlined all through the book, while consumers like you today have the option of navigating real estate transactions on your own, there are still a good deal of roadblocks and landmines with which even professionals have trouble. That's why it's important, especially when the finish line is in view, to obtain the assistance you need to help you complete the race. It's not about winning at all costs; it's about reaching your desired results at a fair cost! I commend your efforts for a race well run.

Frugally yours,
Julie Garton-Good
<www.juliegarton-good.com>

Print Resources

The following booklets are available free of charge from:

The Mortgage Bankers' Association
1125 15th Street, NW
Washington, DC 20005

- "A Consumer's Glossary of Mortgage Terms" Great for the first-time buyer who needs to know the language, players, and the plays.
- "Self Test" Ideal to use prior to qualifying with a lender. Will help you determine how much house you can afford and what documentation the lender may require.
- "What Happens after You Apply for a Mortgage" Walks you through the process and explains the mysteries of underwriting the mortgage loan.

The following booklets are available from:

Federal National Mortgage Association
Drawer MM
3900 Wisconsin Avenue, NW
Washington, DC 20006

- "Unraveling the Mortgage Loan Mystery" Great for information on who makes loans, types of loans available, and how to choose the best loan and lender.
- "When Your Home Is on the Line" A comprehensive booklet describing how to evaluate equity lines of credit.
- "A Home Buyer's Guide to Environmental Hazards" Alerts you to the various environmental red flags that could impact the property and its value.

When writing, ask FNMA for a list of other publications available, or request information on a certain topic.

"The Mortgage Money Guide" is available from the FTC Bureau of Consumer Protection. It gives detailed comparisons of costs borrowers can expect to pay for various types of loans. Good for loan comparison shopping. Write: Federal Trade Commission Bureau of Consumer Protection, Pennsylvania Avenue and 6th Street, NW, Washington, DC 20580.

"Home Modifications for the Elderly" is available from the National Association of Home Builders (NAHB). It is a preplanning home safety audit. For a free copy, write to NAHB Research Center, 400 Prince George's Boulevard, Upper Marlboro, MD 20772, Attn: L. Rickman.

"The Doable, Renewable Home," a home safety booklet for the elderly, is available free of charge from AARP. Write for booklet D12470, AARP Fulfillment, EE094, 1909 K Street, NW, Washington, DC 20049.

"Easy Access Housing" is a booklet regarding home accessibility, available free of charge from the National Easter Seal Society. Write to them at 70 East Lake Street, Chicago, Illinois 60601.

Federal government booklets cover homebuying, insurance, radon, and home hazards. While most of the government's booklets are free of charge, others may cost up to $1.50 to order. Write for a free catalog from: United States Federal Government, Consumer Information Center, P.O. Box 100, Pueblo, CO 81002.

Call the HUD hotline at 800-669-9777 to speak to a HUD representative, or to order a free booklet, "Fair Housing: It's Your Right" (publication #HUD-1260-FHEO/July 1990).

For a free homemade money booklet describing the reverse annuity mortgage loan and how you can turn equity into cash, contact American Association of Retired Persons (AARP), Home Equity Information Center, 601 E. Street, NW, Washington, DC 20049 (800-424-3410).

For information on real estate consultants, contact National Association of Real Estate Consultants (NAREC), sponsors of the Consumer-Certified Real Estate Consultant (C-CREC) designation, 107 Pinehurst Avenue, Fishers, Indiana 46038, (toll-free: 866-260-7374, 888-469-6892) or <www.narec.com>; <www.ccrec.com>.

Online Resources

The best comprehensive information site for real estate consumers is <www.ired.com>. As an international real estate directory, it has hundreds of links to almost every real estate topic of interest to consumers. All others are listed alphabetically by topic.

Affordable housing
<www.fanniemae.com>
<www.fanniemaefoundation.org>
<www.fha.gov>
<www.freddiemac.com>
<www.habitat.org>
<www.nehemiahprogram.org>

Attorneys
<www.abanet.org>

Auctions
<www.financenet.gov>
<www.internetauctionlist.com>
<www.sothebysrealty.com>

Buyer's agents
<www.naeba.org>
<www.rebac.com>

Calculators (real estate)
<www.homebytes.com>
<www.homefair.com>
<www.homepath.com>
<www.loanguide.com>
<www.quicken.com>
<www.ziprealty.com>

City comparisons
<www.cityguide.com>

Credit agencies/information
<www.equifax.com>
<www.experian.com>
<www.tuc.com>

Crime information
<www.crimewatch.com>

Environmental information
<www.ashi.com>
<www.epa.gov>
<www.independentinspectors.org>
<www.inspectorusa.com>
<www.nahi.org>

FHA (Federal Housing Administration)
<www.hud.gov>

Flood insurance
<www.fema.gov>

Foreclosure
<www.fanniemae.com>
<www.freddiemac.com>
<www.ginniemae.gov>
<www.hud.gov>
<www.va.gov>

For-sale-by-owners
<www.fisbo.com>
<www.fizbo.com>
<www.fsbo.com>
<www.gofsbo.com>
<www.homebytes.com>
<www.iown.com>
<www.ired.com>
<www.oldhouses.com>
<www.open-house-online.com>
<www.ziprealty.com>

Governmental sites
<www.epa.gov>
<www.ftc.gov>
<www.hud.gov>
<www.irs.gov>

Homebuilding
<www.buildingahome.net>
<www.buildscape.com>
<www.homedepot.com>
<www.nahb.com>

Homebuyer information (general)
<www.fanniemaefoundation.org>
<www.homeadvisor.com>
<www.inman.com>
<www.ired.com>
<www.juliegarton-good.com>
<www.loanshop.com>
<www.ourbroker.com>
<www.realtor.com>
<www.realtytimes.com>

Home inspections
<www.ashi.com>
<www.nahi.org>

Home repair
<www.askbuild.com>
<www.buildnet.com>
<www.misterfixit.com>

Homeseller information (general)
<www.homeadvisor.com>
<www.inman.com>
<www.ired.com>
<www.juliegarton-good.com>
<www.ourbroker.com>
<www.realtytimes.com>

Improve versus move
<www.bobvila.com>
<www.buildscape.com>
<www.homebuilder.com>
<www.homedepot.com>

Inflation statistics
<www.ofheo.gov/house>

Interest rates
<www.hsh.com>
<www.interest.com>
<www.realtytimes.com>

International real estate
<www.ired.com>
<www.sothebysrealty.com>

Insurance
<www.homefair.com>
<www.homeshark.com>
<www.insweb.com>
<www.prudential.com>
<www.safeco.com>

Listings online
<www.cyberhomes.com>
<www.erealty.com>
<www.homeadvisor.com>
<www.homehunt.com>
<www.homes.com>
<www.homeseekers.com>
<www.homestore.com>
<www.iown.com>
<www.ired.com>
<www.listinglink.com>
<www.matchpoint.com>
<www.realtor.com>

Manufactured housing
<www.mfdhousing.com>

Mortgages
<www.1stmtg.com>
<www.bankofamerica.com>
<www.championmortgage.com>
<www.countrywide.com>

<www.e-loan.com>
<www.homeadvisor.com>
<www.homefair.com>
<www.homeshark.com>
<www.lendingtree.com>
<www.loanshop.com>
<www.loanworks.com>
<www.onepipeline.com>
<www.onloan.com>
<www.quickenmortgage.com>
<www.wellsfargo.com>

Mortgage comparison shopping
<www.gomez.com>
<www.interest.com>
<www.juliegarton-good.com>
<www.loanlist.com>
<www.mortgagemarvel.com>

New homes
<www.buildingahome.net>
<www.homebuilder.com>
<www.nahb.com>
<www.newhomesearch.com>

Pricing property
<www.cswonline.com>
<www.experian.com>
<www.homebytes.com>
<www.ziprealty.com>

Private mortgage insurance
<www.mgic.com>
<www.mica.org>
<www.pmirescue.com>

Real estate consultants (unbundled fee-for-services)
<www.ccrec.com>
<www.ired.com>
<www.narec.com>
<www.onestoprealtyshop.com>

Real estate education
<www.computaught.com>
<www.dearborn.com>
<www.narec.com>
<www.reea.org>

Refinancing
<www.championmortgage.com>
<www.countrywide.com>
<www.homeshark.com>
<www.loanshop.com>
<www.onloan.com>
<www.quickenmortgage.com>

Relocation
<www.homefair.com>
<www.relo.com>

Rentals
<www.rentnet.com>

Rent versus buy
<www.gomez.com>
<www.homefair.com>
<www.interest.com>

School information
<www.homeadvisor.com>
<www.homestore.com>
<www.schoolreport.com>

Signage (home sellers)
<www.homebytes.com>
<www.ired.com>
<www.ziprealty.com>

Tax rates
<www.irs.gov>

Title and escrow companies
<www.alic.com> (American Title)
<www.cltic.com> (Commonworth Title)
<www.ctic.com> (Chicago Title)
<www.escrow.com>
<www.firstam.com> (First American Title)
<www.landam.com> (Lawyers Title)
<www.stewart.com> (Stewart Title)

Transaction platforms/closings
<www.realtor.com>
<www.iproperty.com>

Unbundled real estate services à la carte
<www.ccrec.com>
<www.fsbo.com>
<www.helpusell.net>
<www.homebytes.com>
<www.juliegarton-good.com>
<www.narec.com>
<www.owners.com>

VA (Department of Veterans Affairs)
<www.va.gov>

Real Estate Licensing Divisions/Commissions by State

Alabama	<www.arec.state.al.us>
Alaska	<www.commerce.state.ak.us>
Arizona	<www.adre.org>

Arkansas	\<www.state.ar.us/arec/arecweb.html\>
California	\<www.dre.ca.gov\>
Colorado	\<www.dora.state.co.us/Real-Estate\>
Connecticut	\<www.state.ct.us/dcp\>
Delaware	\<www.state.de.us\>
District of Columbia	\<www.dora.org/rec/rechome3.htm\>
Florida	\<www.state.fl.us/dbpr/html/re/ index.html\>
Georgia	\<www.state.ga.us/Ga.Real_Estate\>
Hawaii	\<www.hawaii.gov\>
Idaho	\<www.state.id.us/irec\>
Illinois	\<www.state.il.us/obr\>
Indiana	\<www.ai.org/pla/index.html\>
Iowa	\<www.state.ia.us/government/com/ prof/realesta.htm\>
Kansas	\<www.ink.org/public/krec\>
Kentucky	\<www.krec.net\>
Louisiana	\<www.state.la.us\>
Maine	\<www.janus.state.me.us/ homepage.asp\>
Maryland	\<www.dllr.state.md.us/occprof/ recomm.html\>
Massachusetts	\<www.state.ma.us/reg\>
Michigan	\<www.cis.state.mi.us\>
Minnesota	\<www.commerce.state.mn.us/ mainre.htm\>
Mississippi	\<www.state.ms.us\>
Missouri	\<www.ecodev.state.mo.us/pr/restate\>
Montana	\<www.com.state.mt.us\>
Nebraska	\<www.state.ne.us\>
Nevada	\<www.state.nv.us/b&i/red/ index.htm\>
New Hampshire	\<www.state.nh.us/nhrec\>
New Jersey	\<www.naic.org/nj/realcom.htm\>
New Mexico	\<www.state.nm.us/nmrec\>
New York	\<www.dos.state.ny.us/lcns/ realest.html\>

North Carolina	\<www.ncrec.state.nc.us\>
North Dakota	\<www.state.nd.us\>
Ohio	\<www.com.state.oh.us/real\>
Oklahoma	\<www.state.ok.us\>
Oregon	\<bbs.chemek.cc.or.us/public/orea/ orea.html\>
Pennsylvania	\<www.dos.state.pa.us/bpoa/ recomm.htm\>
South Carolina	\<www.llr.state.sc.us/rec.htm\>
South Dakota	\<www.state.sd.us/SDREC\>
Tennessee	\<www.state.tn.us\>
Texas	\<www.trec.state.tx.us/index.asp\>
Utah	\<www.commerce.state.ut.us/re/ udre1.htm\>
Vermont	\<www.vtprofessionals.org/ real_estate\>
Virginia	\<www.state.va.us/dpor\>
Washington	\<www.wa.gov/dol/bpd/recom.htm\>
West Virginia	\<www.wvrealtors.com/ wvcomm.htm\>
Wisconsin	\<badger.state.wi.us/agencies/drl/ index.html\>
Wyoming	\<commerce.state.wy.us/B%26C/REC\>

A

Administrative-based assistance, 40, 248
Advertising, 170
Advocacy skills, 178, 248
    fair pricing of, 37
Agency disclosure laws, 240
Agent
    see also Consultant(s)/fee-for-service providers; Real estate services provider
    advice given by, 6
    education of, 11
    time of sale and compensation, 5-6. See also Compensation
    value of services, 6-7
Aggregators, 18-19, 189
Agreement clauses, regarding fees, 55
à la carte real estate. See Consultant(s)/fee-for-service providers; Fee-for-service real estate
Appraisal contingency, 182-83
Arthur D. Little, Inc., survey, 16
Assessed home value, 202-4, 213-14
Attorney (real estate)
    vs. consultant, 244
    review of contract, 237
Auctions, online, 16

B

Baby boomers, 17
Backup offer clause, 162, 184
Bonding, 236
Boyd, Patricia, 105
Building permits, 200, 206
Buildscape.com, 207
Business model (traditional brokerage), 12-16
Buyer(s), 27-29
    checkpoints, 29, 105-42, 143
        neighborhood/property, 121-26, 148
        mortgage preapproval, 111-21, 147
        property information/pricing, 127-34, 149
        purchase agreement/negotiation, 134-38, 150
        purchase strategy, 107-11, 146
        troubleshooting sale/closing transaction, 138-42, 151
    closing and, 138-42, 151, 186
    determining solutions for, 247

fee-for-services applications, 177–94
  categories of, 178–79
  cutting costs, 193
  mid-transaction hurdles, 180–86
  rules of thumb for, 192
  scenarios, 187–92
  streamlining the process, 192–93
  locating/prequalifying, 80–85
  percentage commission rebate for, 52
  stress, 193–94
Buyers' market, 15, 76–77

C

C-CREC, 37, 39, 227–28
City codes, 199
Clark, David, 77
Cleaning house, 61–66
Client, defined, 240
Closing, 91–95, 151
  buyer and, 139–42, 186
  document review prior to, 92–93, 139–40, 141, 186
  renegotiating with buyer, 165
Code of ethics, 37, 227, 229
Commercial property, 216–17
Commissions. *See under* Compensation
Comparative market analysis (CMA), 38, 39, 69–71, 129, 130
Compensation
  clauses in agreements, 55
  consumer-designed/-driven models, 45
  consumer sharing of, 6
  ethics rules and, 233
  fair consumer pricing guidelines, 36–40
  fee for services/à la carte/ unbundling, 4, 14, 19, 24–26, 30
  fee-splitting, 10
  fixed vs. variable costs, 50

flat fee, 48–49
hourly fees, 47–48, 52
innovative models, 55–56
legal issues, 15
level of service and, 40–41, 248
negotiation of, 14, 37
paying lowest of several fee choices, 50
percentage commission, 1–3, 5, 9, 15, 46–47, 52
rebated fees, 50–51, 52–53
red flags, 242–44
retainer fees, 24, 39, 53
teamwork/shared risk (retainer, hourly, and rebate), 52
time of sale and, 5–6
tip, 56
types of, 38
Compound interest, on percentage commission, 3
Conflicts of interest, 219
Consultant(s)/fee-for-service providers
  advanced designation consultants, 227–28
  advice/services/ troubleshooting
    eminent domain settlement negotiation, 217–18
    evaluation of real estate holdings, 212–13
    expert witness, 218
    foreclosure threat, 215–16
    improve vs. move, 199–200, 205–7
    midstream sale problems, 200–201
    mortgage prepayment, 211–12
    mortgage refinancing, 209–11
    negotiations with former spouse, 201–2
    planning/zoning issues, 199
    property tax assessment errors, 202–4

protest of assessed home
value/property taxes,
213–14
remodeling, 198–99, 207–9
tracking trends, 214–15
using multiple sources,
218–19
compensation of, 21–27,
36–40
conflicts of interest, 219
consumer needs assessment,
222–26
contracting with, 236–39, 243
minimum requirements, 239
severing agreement with,
241
fee-for-services, 19
focus on customer needs, 20
hired midstream, 245, 250
income/commercial property,
216–17
locating/evaluating/
contracting with, 233–44
checking credentials,
235–36
competency level,
determining, 233–35
contract, 236–40
hiring a consultant vs.
attorney, 244
interviewing a consultant,
242–44
role of consultant,
determining, 240
severing agreement with,
241–42
miniquiz, 219–20
professional documentation
provided by, 235–36
reaching objectives with,
240–41
and real estate salespeople
compared, 228–233
specialists, 21, 217, 233–34
Consumer-Certified Real Estate
Consultant (C-CREC), 37, 39,
227–28

Consumer Needs Assessment, 210,
222–26
Consumer realities, 4–8
Contingencies, 86, 131
appraisal, 182–83
backup offers, 162, 184
financing, 160–61, 182
home inspection, 161, 183
insurance, 161–62, 183
right of first refusal clause, 162
work repair maximum clause,
161
Contingent/noncontingent fees, 39
Cook, Frank, 1
Co-op listings, 10
Counselors of Real Estate (CRE),
216
Counteroffer, 135, 136, 163–64,
184–85
Countrywide.com, 208
Covenants, 132
Credit report, 112
Crime, 122, 123, 124
Cswonline.com, 71, 129
Curb appeal, 60, 61–66

D

Disclosure form/statement, 71,
130, 164
Disclosure laws, agency, 240
Dot-com real estate companies, 18
Due diligence information/
paperwork, 164–65

E

Earnest money, 113, 135, 163, 185
Economic climate, 77
Eminent domain settlement
negotiation, 217–18
Equity, 210–11
Errors and omissions insurance,
236
Ethics, 37, 227, 229, 233
Evans, Blanche, 11
Evolution, of real estate
transactions, 8–12
Experian.com, 71, 129
Expert witness, consultant as, 218

F

Fact sheet, property, 67–68, 127
Fair consumer pricing guidelines
 (real estate services), 36–40
Fee discounting, 23–24
Fee-for-service providers. *See*
 Consultant(s)/fee-for-service
 providers
Fee-for-service real estate, 4, 14
  see also Consultant(s)/fee-for-
   service providers
  buyer's applications of. *See*
   under Buyer(s)
  consumer road maps, 27–29
  and fee discounting compared,
   23–24
  flexibility of, 26–27
  maximizing profits with, 29–30
  rebundled services, 53
  results-oriented, 24-26
  sellers and. *See under* Seller(s)
Fee-splitting, 10
Final walk-through, 92
Financing
  contingency, 160–61, 182
  neighborhood choice and, 124
  remodeling, 207–8
Fixed costs vs. variable costs, 50
Flat fee, 48–49
  plus possible hourly fees/
   rebates, 49–50
Floor plan, 69
Foreclosures, 15, 215–16
  property tax and, 214
For–sale–by–owner(s), 57–58
  see also Seller(s)
  domination of market by, 17–18
  preparation for, 153–56
  risk reduction, 175–76
  sign, 4
  Web sales, 15–16, 153–54
Franklin, Ben, 38
Frugal HomeOwner®'s Consumer
 Assessment Study, 5, 59
Frugal HomeOwner's Guide to
 Buying, Selling, and Improving
 Your Home (Garton-Good), 5

G

Gandhi, Mahatma, 57
Garton-Good, Julie, 5, 196–98
Gomez.com, 173, 209
Good faith deposit, 135

H

Harlan, Don, 187
Hathaway, Tom, 177
Helmsley, Sheila, 245
Homefair.com, 109, 212
Home improvements, 26–27
Home inspection contingency, 161
 183
Homeowner's insurance, 72, 131
Home ownership, commitment
 and, 108
Homepath.com, 212
Hopke, Ruth, 153
Hourly fees, 47–48
  with percentage commission
   rebate for seller, 52

I

Improvements
  evaluating, 128
  improve vs. move, 199–200,
   205-7
Income property, 216–17
Informational skills/assistance, 37,
 40, 156–57, 178, 248
Insurance
  contingency, 161–62, 183
  errors and omissions, 236
  homeowner's, 72, 131
Interest rates, 15
International Real Estate Directory
 Web site, 217
Internet
  dot-com real estate companies,
   18
  information, 4
  marketing property over the,
   78
  online aggregators, 18–19
  online auctions, 16
  sale information on, 14, 15, 77

Web sites. *See* Web sites
Interpretive skills, 37, 41
Ired.com, 216-17

K–L

Keys, 141
Kitchen, cleaning and painting, 61
Legal description, of property, 66, 68
Lendingtree.com, 207
Level one assistance, 40, 156, 158, 178, 248
Level two assistance, 40-41, 157, 158, 178-79, 248
Licenses, 235-36
Liens, 73, 133
Listings, 10
    Internet sites, 10
    time frame for, 11-12
Loan
    application checklist, 113, 114-15
    cost comparisons, 113, 115, 118
    payment table, 117
    preapproval for, 81, 112-21, 160
    qualifying worksheet, 116
Local improvement district liens, 164-65
Location, choosing, 121-26, 148
    obtaining information, 122-24
Lyons, Gail, 187

M

Market value, 69, 71, 128-29
Mechanic's liens, 73
Miller, Peter G., 221
MLS, 10
Moritz, Sheri, 120
Mortgage
    industry, 55
    pay-off information, obtaining, 73
    preapproval, 112-21, 147, 188-89
    prepayment, 211-12
    refinancing, 209-11

Mortgagemarvel.com, 209
Multiple listing service (MLS), 10

N

NAREC, 37, 227, 229
National Association of Homebuilders, 207
National Association of Real Estate Consultants, 37, 227, 229, 241
National Association of REALTORS®, 16, 216, 242
Natural disasters, 161-62
Negotiation, 41, 157, 178, 179, 190-91, 248
    buyer strategies, 135-38
    eminent domain settlement, 217-18
    fair pricing of negotiating skill, 37
    initial offer and, 185
    seller strategies, 87, 89, 171
    with seller, 184
Neighborhood/property, choosing, 121-26, 148, 189-90
Net sheet, 87, 88
New Attitudes, 153
Newell, Chris, 45
Nonclient relationship, 240
Noncontingent fees, 39

O

Offer, 85-87, 135, 185-86
O'Neil, Rick, 163
Online auctions, 16. *See also* Internet
Onloan.com, 207

P

Percentage commissions, 1-3, 9, 46-47
    in buyers' market, 15
Peters, Sherry, 18
Pickering, Tom, 18
Plat map, 75, 132
Pocket listings, 10

Preapproval, for mortgage loan, 81,
112-21, 160, 170-71, 188-89
   importance of, 113
   information necessary, 113,
     114-15
   shopping around, 113, 115
Preparing property for sale. *See*
Property; preparing for sale
Prepayment, of mortgage, 211-12
Prequalifying for mortgage, 80-85,
116
   obtaining information, 81-82
   vs. preapproval, 112
   showing property, 82-83
Pricing a property, 69-71, 128-30
Problems, solving, 249-50
Product-focused niches, 21
Professional designations, 235
Profits, maximizing, 29-30
Property
   choosing, 121-26, 148
   disclosure statement, 71, 130,
     190
   fact sheet, 67-68
   floor plan/room configuration,
     69, 128
   information, 127, 149, 169-70,
     190
   legal description of, 66, 68, 127
   length of time on market, 86
   marketing, 170-71
   market value, 71
   preparing for sale, 60-66, 98,
     167-69
     cleaning and painting, 61-66
     curb appeal, 60
   pricing, 69-71, 128-30, 170
   rural, 75, 133
   showing, 82-83
   square footage of house, 68,
     127-28
Property tax, 17, 213-14
   assessment errors, 202-4
Purchase agreement, 134-35, 150,
160, 171-72
Purchase strategy, 107-11, 146

Q–R
Quizzes
   buying process, 145-51
   determining need for
     consultant, 219-20
   sales process, 97-103
Real estate brokerage, 12-16
   future of, 20
Real estate holdings, evaluation of,
212-13
Real estate services provider
   See also Consultant(s)/fee-for-
     service providers
   consultants, 20-21, 29-30
   fair pricing of tasks, 36-40
   itemized breakdown of fees/
     services, 26
   value of services, 6-7
Real estate industry, evolution of,
8-12, 30
Rebated fees, 50-51
Rebundled services, 53
Refinancing, 209-11
Remodeling/renovation
   evaluating improvements, 128
   financing, 207-8
   improve vs. move, 199-200,
     205-7
Rent vs. buy, 109, 110, 187-88
Representation, fair pricing of, 37
Retainer fees, 25, 39, 53
Right of first refusal clause, 162,
184
Rogers, Jay, 31
Room configuration, 128
Rural property, 75, 133

S
Safety check, 123
Sale, monitoring progress of, 92,
139
Sales agreement, 85, 160
Schmitt, Doug, 204
Schools, 123, 189
Secondary mortgage market, 55
Seller(s)
   see also For-sale-by-owner(s)

checkpoints, 28–29, 57–58, 60, 96
  drafting sales agreement/ negotiating, 85–91, 102, 171–72
  information/pricing the property, 66–75, 99
  locating/prequalifying buyer, 80–85, 101, 170–71
  marketing the property, 76–80, 100
  preparing the property, 60–66, 98
  troubleshooting sale/closing transaction, 91–95, 103, 172–73
cost estimates, 59
determining solutions for, 246
economic climate, selling property and, 59
fee-for-services applications, 153–76
  assistance levels, 156–58
  due diligence information/ paperwork, 164–65
  mid-transaction hurdles, 158–66
  negotiating with buyer, 163–64, 172
  risk reduction and, 175–76
  rules of thumb for, 173
  scenarios, 166–73
  streamlining the process, 174
  walk-through inspection and, 172–73
percentage commission rebate to, 52
stress reduction, 174–75
time estimates, 59
Sellers' market, 14, 15, 76–77, 177–78
Senior housing, 213
Services, fair pricing guidelines, 36–40
Shinn, J. David, 18
Showing property, 82–83

Signage, 170
Sparks, Bonnie, 195
Spodek, Marie, 57
Square footage, calculating, 68
Subdivision map, 132
Swanepoel, Stefan, 232

T–U

Target market, determining, 76, 77–78
Taxes, property, 17
Team Toolbox, 18
Time frame, for listing/selling property, 11–12
Traffic flow, 122
Trends, 214–15
Turcotte, Roger, 87, 133
Unbundled real estate. *See* Fee-for-service real estate

W–Z

Walk-through inspection, 92, 139, 172–73
Water rights, 75
Web sites
  see also Internet
  commercial property links, 216–17
  financial calculators, 212
  finding a C-CREC, 227
  International Real Estate Directory, 217
  market value estimates, 129
  mortgage companies, rating, 209
  mortgage rates, 189, 207–8
  NAREC code of ethics, 227
  neighborhood information, 189–90
  refinancing information, 211
  rent vs. buy calculators, 109
  renting signage/placing ads, 170
  schools, 189
Wendel, Bill, 49
Work repair maximum clause, 161
Zoning, 123, 199